Praise for Dr. Geil Browning and Emergenetics®

"Emergenetics has given us the abili[...] [...]ver
well-roun[...]
—Donna Imperato, CEO, C[...]

"I've been using Emergenetics trai[...]
Emergenetics is effective, creative, and fun. I hope all our employees read this book."
—Luis Castillo, Vice President, Siemens Medical Solutions Health Services

"Highly readable, engaging, and practical. . . . This research can
significantly assist us both professionally and personally."
—Martin Lowery, Vice President, Education and Professional Development,
Hilton Hotels Corporation

"[Dr. Browning's] work, reinforced by science, is compelling and intuitively
easy to understand and apply."
—Robb Caseria, Chief Global Procurement and Alliance Officer,
Molson Coors Brewing Company

"A compelling analytic tool."
—Jessica M. Bibliowicz, Chairman and CEO, National Financial Partners

"We have used Emergenetics with employees and customers and it has been
an overwhelming success."
—Aaron Hilkemann, President, Duncan Aviation, Inc.

"If you want to enhance learning, sponsor effective teams, better understand your
behavior and that of others, this is a tool for you!"
—Carol A. Aschenbrener, MD, Vice President,
Association of American Medical Colleges

"Emergenetics [helped us in] creating a dynamic team that has
transformed our company into an industry leader."
—Robert Bates, President of Jefferson Pilot Benefit Partners

"Emergenetics . . . has really helped us to distinguish our scope
and depth of care in ways that are truly significant."
—E. Lee Rice, DO, FAAFP, FACSM, FAOASM,
CEO and Medical Director, Lifewellness Institute

"We continue to build on the principles we learned from Geil."
—Lee Michael Berg, President and CEO, Lee Michaels Fine Jewelry

Emergenetics®

tap into the new science of success

GEIL BROWNING, PhD

COLLINS BUSINESS

An Imprint of HarperCollins Publishers

Morgan Browning would like to acknowledge Nicole Hume Weissberg.
Her love will forever shape his life.

Emergenetics® is a federally registered trademark of Emergenetics, LLC.

FIRST EDITION

Graphics by Jane Rainwater, Rainwater Design, www.rainwaterdesign.com,
rainwaterdesign@comcast.net

Graphics Copyright © 2005 Emergenetics, LLC

Designed by Ellen Cipriano

Page 235: Reprinted with permission of Simon & Schuster adult publishing group from THINKING IN THE FUTURE TENSE: Leadership Skills for a New Age by Jennifer James. Copyright © 1996 by Jennifer James, Inc.

Printed on acid-free paper

Library of Congress Cataloging-in-Publication Data

Browning, Geil.
    Emergenetics®: tap into the new science of success /
Geil Browning.—1st ed.
        p. cm.
    Includes bibliographical references and index.
    ISBN-10: 0-06-058535-8
    ISBN-13: 978-0-06-058535-8
    1. Success—Psychological aspects. 2. Nature and nurture. 3. Neurosciences.
I. Title.

BF637.S8B734 2006
158—dc22   2005047717

09 10 DIX/RRD 10 9 8 7 6 5

To Armistead, my life partner and my biggest fan:
without you my life's work would not exist—
and, for that matter, neither would I.
To you I am forever grateful.
and
To Tyler, Ryan, and Morgan, who have given meaning to
my life and to my work.

Acknowledgments

It is October 16th and I am celebrating this day by writing the Acknowledgments for this book. The fact that I can write is miraculous, as one year ago today I experienced a "brain attack"—otherwise known as a stroke. The Broca's area and parietal lobe of my brain were affected, and thus, among other things, I lost all of my pronouns and prepositions. It is hard to read, speak, or write a book without them. Neural plasticity was the watchword that kept me moving forward (more about this in chapter 11), and today I am able to communicate again.

This book is about discovering your gifts. One of my gifts is assembling the right people to accomplish goals. This book would not have been written without the wisdom of the following people:

- Morgan Browning, an interpreter, scribe, researcher, coach, motivator, and my son, who took a semester off from law school when I most needed it,

and

- Nellie Sabin, an angel, muse, writer, editor, researcher, and psychotherapist, who took our ideas and words and turned them into a coherent and creative manuscript.

We became a united team and this book is as much theirs as it is mine.

- Wendell Williams, with whom I developed the Emergenetics Profile, and who rechecked the statistics. His intelligence, humor, flexibility, and elegant ideas are always invaluable.
- Mary Case, neuropathologist, friend, and physician, who has verified the medical aspects of this work from the beginning and who continues to teach me today.
- Carol Hunter and Tim Rouse—together we created *Influence* and *Focus*. I am grateful for their brilliance, their empathy, and their global view.
- All the *Influence* and *Focus* "launchees" whose spirits and ideas are in these pages.
- Chris Cox, Jeannine Falter, Scott Halford, Marty Lassen, Martin Lowery, Peter McLaughlin, Shirley Mitchell, and Harold Suire—my Associates who branded their creativity in many of these chapters.
- Judy Williams, Carol Kingery, Patty Greene, George Anne Hume, and Sharon Muir—readers who analyzed the copy from their unique perspectives. Together they were my Whole Emergenetics Reading Team.
- Denise Marcil, my agent, who championed this work and led me to Toni Sciarra, my editor. Denise is encouraging, committed, and practical. Toni is accessible, supportive, and creative. They are a dynamic duo.
- Jane Rainwater, graphic artist, who is imaginative, clever, funny, and flexible.
- Karen Lang, the Emergenetics quarterback, who kept the business going despite my absence, along with our other partners, Karen Hulett, Ian Habeck, and Gay Ellis. Karen Lang assembled this flawless team, and I would be lost without them. Many of their thoughts are evident here.
- The Emergenetics seminar participants whose stories are here. You are too numerous to list, but you know who you are.
- The individuals I interviewed who shared their Profiles, stories, and letters.

These Acknowledgments would not be complete without mentioning:

- Sally Crouch, my original assistant, who helped me start my business, The Browning Group International.

- PR expert Bob Schenkein, who ultimately introduced me to Frank Anfield, Jerry Fransocovitch, Andy Krupski, and Steve Parker—they were my first clients and are still good friends today.
- My Associates, who have spread the Emergenetics vision all over the world with energy and integrity.

I am also grateful to my family and to all the people who kept me inspired throughout the completion of this book:

Christy, Rebecca, John Armistead, Willis, Holden Browning, and Glenda and Len Crouch.

Carol Aschenbrener, Joanne Beach, Alan Boal, Barbara Briggs, Judith Brun, Betty Burke, Robb Caseria, Kathy Cramer, my C.P.S.W. friends, Cliff Crouch, Barbara DeGroot, Klara Deych, Marianne and Glen Furlow, Mary Gay Gordon, Connie and Andy Graham, Helen and Jim Gorman, Barbara Grogan, my LGA friends, Elizabeth and Steve Holtze, Jennifer James, John Katzer, Jim Kendrick, my Kenya friends, Sue Kirton, Bill Kingery, O. W. Kopp, Carmelita Latiolais, Kimball and Bruce Lauritzen, Jo Anne LeClair, Sherry Manning, Zhizhong Nan, Rodney Noles, Wayne Peters, Mary Jo and Tom Rodeno, Fran and Emmet Root, Dixie Rounsley, Beth and Bill Staudenmaier, Lynne Suire, Don Smith, Dave Tacha, Josh Teo, Artur Trofimov, Barbara Vierk, Nicole Weissberg, and Eng Yong.

The more I think about these Acknowledgments, the more people I wish I could mention. I feel so fortunate to have all of these wonderful brains in my life.

Ten months after having my brain attack, I sent the completed manuscript of this book to HarperCollins. In my mind, my rapid recovery was due to the thoughts and prayers of the people I have named, and have *not* named, here. Even though my pronouns and prepositions have returned, there are not enough words to adequately thank all of you. Know that you are always in my heart.

Geil Browning

Why Read This Book?

If you have an **Analytical** mind, you will enjoy learning about all of the new data about the brain that is included in this book.

If you have a **Conceptual** mind, you will discover that you aren't as weird as you thought — and you will be able to use the information in this book to make a difference in the world.

If you have a **Structural** mind, you will appreciate this book's practical applications for your professional and personal life.

If you have a **Social** mind, this book will help you better understand yourself, your colleagues, and your significant others.

EXPRESSIVENESS

FLEXIBILITY

ASSERTIVENESS

Expressiveness

If you are at the quiet end of the **Expressiveness** spectrum, this book will help you learn how to communicate effectively with all types of people.

If you are at the talkative end of the **Expressiveness** spectrum, you will learn lots of new information to share with others.

Assertiveness

If you are at the peacekeeping end of the **Assertiveness** spectrum, this book will help you learn how to implement your ideas more effectively.

If you are at the driven end of the **Assertiveness** spectrum, you will learn how to be less confrontational and more persuasive with your colleagues and significant others.

Flexibility

If you are at the focused end of the **Flexibility** spectrum, this book will help you discover what is useful about other people's ideas.

If you are at the open-minded end of the **Flexibility** spectrum, you will learn how to focus in order to make better decisions.

Contents

Introduction

I am so happy you picked up this book. I hope you enjoy reading it as much as I enjoyed writing it.

The **Analytical** part of my brain liked pulling together all the latest scientific research that applies to Emergenetics, my life's work.

The **Structural** part of my brain relished organizing the themes I have been thinking about for many years.

And the **Social** part of my brain wants to have a conversation with you sharing this information.

The **Conceptual** part of my brain derived satisfaction from considering the overview of my work and ruminating about its greater significance.

Because of my **Expressiveness**, I am eager to have this opportunity to address the widest possible audience.

Because of my **Flexibility**, I have used several formats in this book, for people who read in different ways.

And because of my **Assertiveness**, I can't wait to tell you everything!

A NOTE ABOUT THE BOOK'S FORMAT

You will see that this book has several sections. Part I discusses the science, background, and theory of Emergenetics. Part II shows you how to take the principles of Emergenetics and apply them to your work and personal life. Part III, The Emergenetics Toolbox, provides handy summaries of important information in an easy-to-read, visual format. The Appendix goes more deeply into the research that supports Emergenetics. For those who would like to pursue some topics even further, there are references to specific books and articles throughout the text, and footnotes and sources for further reading at the back of the book.

A Note about Language

Later in this book you will learn about the four Emergenetics Thinking Attributes (Analytical, Structural, Social, and Conceptual), and the three Emergenetics Behavioral Attributes (Expressiveness, Assertiveness, and Flexibility). The Behavioral Attributes are reproduced differently in the text to show different degrees of each attribute. For example, someone who is at the quiet end of the Expressiveness spectrum is described as *Expressive* (in italics), while someone who is at the talkative end of the Expressiveness spectrum is described as EXPRESSIVE. Also, the word "Profile" is capitalized when it is used to refer to the Emergenetics Profile, an instrument that illustrates an individual's unique combination of Thinking and Behavioral Attributes.

AS YOU READ, YOU ARE INVITED TO KEEP IN MIND . . .

1. Your Thinking and Behavioral preferences, which you will learn how to identify in this book, are your strengths. They make all the difference in how you think, behave, and communicate. Go with them and you'll be more satisfied and more productive.
2. This book is about your *preferences,* as opposed to your *abilities.* Some people take a Thinking Attribute and drive it around the block, while others take the same attribute to the Indy 500.
3. Being in alignment with yourself at work will make you more effective and your company more profitable. Working against your innate preferences will tire you out.
4. Change if you wish to, not because someone tells you to.
5. By using a Whole Emergenetics approach, you will improve your persuasive powers, make better presentations, improve meetings, and communicate more successfully.
6. By using a Whole Emergenetics approach, you will be more successful at bringing people together. This, in turn, will help you be a stronger leader.

Wondering what I am talking about? Let's take a look at a trip to an art exhibit and find out.

PART I

Understanding Emergenetics

What Is Emergenetics and Why Should You Care?

Knowledge Is Power—When You Know How to Use It

It's lunchtime, and four friends are going to an art exhibit featuring work by several up-and-coming artists. As they enter the room, they encounter a volunteer who gives them a sheet listing the titles and prices of all paintings.

Mr. Blue takes the sheet and quickly scans it, looking for the title of the painting that is the most expensive. He then evaluates the entire collection in the context of what makes this painting so valuable. He is at the show for one of the following reasons: (1) he wants to purchase a painting because it will be a good investment, (2) his coworker, Ms. Red, has dragged him along on this excursion, or (3) he read a review of the show in the newspaper and wanted to see if it was as excellent as the critic said it was. Mr. Blue is taking a very **Analytical** approach to the exhibit.

Ms. Green takes the sheet from the volunteer and then retires to a bench in the hallway where she carefully scrutinizes the list. She takes a high-lighter out of her bag and notes the paintings upon which she expects to concentrate. She then returns to the volunteer and asks where the restrooms are located. She does not use the restroom at this time, but she always likes to be ready for any emergencies. People are always happy to travel with Ms. Green because they can count on her good planning and readiness. Now that she is prepared, Ms. Green enters the gallery and looks at the first painting on her right. She moves deliberately along, viewing the paintings in the order in which they are placed on the wall. She spends extra time only inspecting those art works she has highlighted on her list. Ms. Green is a highly **Structural** thinker and she likes to be methodical.

Ms. Red, who is extremely **Social,** has come to this show because she knows one of the artists in the exhibit and wants to support him. Although she doesn't find the list of titles and prices particularly useful, she still accepts it to acknowledge the presence of the volunteer. Viewing an exhibit, to her, means making an emotional connection to the art. She wanders around the room until painting number 20 calls out to her. Eager to share this moment, she grabs Ms. Green, who is viewing painting number 17. Ms. Red is a little annoyed when Ms. Green says, "Just wait a minute until I get there, and then I'll look at it with you."

Mr. Yellow, the last one through the doorway, takes the sheet from the volunteer and quickly scans it. He then puts the sheet in his pocket because he plans to read and digest this information in its entirety someday. When he gets home he will put the paper on the pile on his desk. Chances are he will never see the paper again, but he will always know that it is there. Mr. Yellow then quickly tours the exhibit and is the first one finished. Mr. Yellow, who has a very **Conceptual** mind, already has grasped the importance of the exhibit and is ready to leave. However, Ms. Green is still looking at painting number 37. He wonders what is taking her so long. She wonders if he fully appreciated the artwork.

Great minds are going through this exhibit. Each thinks differently, and each is correct in its thinking. Each brain, whether highly Analytical, Structural, Social, or Conceptual, is appreciating the show in its own way.

But there's more. Ms. Red, you recall, is very excited about her favorite painting. She tried to interest Ms. Green in a conversation about it, but Ms. Green's Assertiveness is at such a level that she is unwilling to view the paintings out of order. Because Ms. Red is so Expressive, she still wants to share her feelings, so she approaches Mr. Blue. However, Mr. Blue's *Flexibility* is such that he does not want to stop his analysis of the painting he is currently viewing. Frustrated yet determined, Ms. Red grabs the nearest stranger. While the stranger doesn't really want to talk with Ms. Red, his *Assertiveness* is such that he will allow himself to be engaged in conversation.

Mr. Yellow has Flexibility and would love to talk to Ms. Red about the painting. However, he is already in the museum coffee shop speaking with other patrons about the exhibit's world significance, and how "one of these days" he plans to take up painting again.

These four friends, who have different levels of Expressiveness, Assertiveness, and Flexibility, viewed the same art exhibit in completely different ways, yet all would say they enjoyed the show and found it fascinating. It's easy to accept that there is no one "right" way to see an art exhibit.

But there's more. Now lunch is over, and Ms. Red, Ms. Green, Mr. Blue, and Mr. Yellow all return to work. They work together at a small corporation.

> Whatever any man does he first must do in his mind, whose machinery is the brain. The mind can do only what the brain is equipped to do, and so man must find out what kind of brain he has before he can understand his own behavior.
>
> Gay Gaer Luce, PhD, and Julius Segal, *Sleep*

Ms. Red immediately gets on the phone. She needs to call several friends to tell them about the show, and of course she needs to call her artist friend to let him know how much she enjoyed his painting and how excited she is for him. While she is making her calls, Ms. Red learns four interesting bits of information that could affect future sales, and one rumor about a corporate takeover that could affect her industry.

Ms. Green has to put the finishing touches on a report by 4:30. Ordinarily she would have worked through her lunch to be sure to meet her deadline, but this outing had been scheduled a month ago. Because Ms. Green's time management skills are excellent, she has allowed time to go to the exhibit and still finish her report. As she works, it seems to her that Ms. Red should have something better to do than talk on the phone.

Mr. Blue returns to his office, shuts the door, and makes two telephone calls. The first is to an art appraiser to verify the value of the expensive painting he saw in the exhibit. The next call is to his accountant to find out the tax implications of purchasing this painting for his office. When Ms. Red finds out Mr. Blue's intentions, she is upset that he is not buying her friend's work.

Mr. Yellow, inspired by the global significance of the artwork, has a brilliant idea for the company's overseas division. He interrupts Ms. Green to brainstorm about his new idea, knowing she always comes up with good ways to move his ideas forward. But to Ms. Green, Mr. Yellow's idea is coming out of nowhere and doesn't seem especially pressing. Her priority is finishing her report. She snaps tersely and says she's busy. Mr. Yellow makes a face.

Although these coworkers are doing what they do best, they have missed great opportunities to work together and to be happier people by failing to recognize one another's talents. It's not easy to accept that there is more than one "right" way to work.

This book is about using your strengths, whatever they may be, to succeed. It's also about understanding that your colleagues can use their strengths to succeed in their own way, too. You, your team, and your company will have better results.

Objectives

By reading this book, you will:

1. Identify your Thinking Attributes and learn how to increase your brain power
2. Understand how your Behavioral Attributes affect how others perceive you
3. Value your uniqueness and the uniqueness of others
4. Use this information in professional and personal settings with powerful results

WHY "EMERGENETICS"?

Who you are today is a result of certain characteristics that have *emerged* from your life experiences, plus the *genetics* with which you were born. I call this interplay between nature and nurture *Emergenetics.*

You come into the world genetically wired a certain way. Because of your environment, you may or may not grow up the way those genetics programmed you to do. While you are a child, your thinking and behaving changes dramatically. As an adult, you are who you are and only a life-altering event (marriage, divorce, children, a new job, etc.) or active, sustained efforts to change will modify this.

So to what extent is your biology your destiny? No one has yet answered this question, but it's clear that temperament and cognitive skills are partly determined at birth. Certain personality traits, such as extroversion and impulsivity, also appear to be hardwired. Studies of identical twins separated at birth and raised in different households found remarkable, even spooky similarities between them many years later. Steven Pinker's *The Blank Slate* asserts that up to 70 percent of the variation between individuals is due to genetics.

Life events can determine whether a gene is expressed or not. Every day is a new neurological dawn for your brain. Every novel sensation, feeling, thought, experience, or conversation etches fresh neural pathways through

> In my mind, genetics cuts the first path through the jungle, and environment determines whether the path becomes beaten.
>
> **Ross Judice, MD, Psychiatrist and Emergenetics Associate**

your brain. Beneficial experiences such as physical and mental activity stimulate the brain and keep it healthy, while harmful experiences such as injury, drugs, alcohol, smoking, or chronic stress have a detrimental effect on brain function.

Because the brain is ultimately responsible for how we think and behave, Emergenetics is based on the latest brain research. With the latest advances in scanning technology have come revelations about the way the brain works, from what parts of the brain solve problems to how long disturbing images resonate in the mind's eye. Throughout this book you'll find references to the studies that keep Emergenetics theory grounded in scientific fact.

SEE *THE BLANK SLATE: THE MODERN DENIAL OF HUMAN NATURE,* BY STEVEN PINKER, PhD

THE SEVEN EMERGENETICS ATTRIBUTES

As you saw with the four companions at the art exhibit, Emergenetics is a way of describing people using four Thinking Attributes and three Behavioral Attributes. Very briefly:

- **Analytical** thinking (represented by the color blue) is logical, rational, objective, factual, and skeptical.
- **Structural** thinking (represented by the color green) is practical, cautious, predictable, and methodical.
- **Social** thinking (represented by the color red) is sympathetic, connected, socially aware, and intuitive about other people.
- **Conceptual** thinking (represented by the color yellow) is imaginative, creative, innovative, visionary, and intuitive about ideas.
- **Expressiveness** is our interest in others and in the world around us. People who are *Expressive* are reserved, quiet, private, and self sufficient. People who are EXPRESSIVE like attracting attention. They are outgoing, affectionate, and easy to talk to.
- **Assertiveness** is the energy we invest in communicating our thoughts, beliefs, and feelings. People who are *Assertive* are easygoing, amiable, and even passive. People who are ASSERTIVE are driving, competitive, and even confrontational.
- **Flexibility** is our willingness to accommodate the thoughts and actions of other people and to meet their needs. People who are *Flexible* have strong opinions, prefer defined situations, and can be stubborn. FLEXIBLE people are accommodating, open to suggestions, and can be indecisive.

Each of these attributes is independent of the others and can be measured separately. An Emergenetics Profile illustrates the way an individual mixes and matches the seven attributes—that is, the unique way he or she combines preferences.

While we can watch how people behave and make some observations about their Behavioral Attributes, thought processes are hidden. One woman sat through one of my seminars with her arms folded and a scowl on her face, yet sent me a note the next day saying it was the most meaningful workshop she had ever attended. Because we are not mind readers, and because sometimes the words and pictures just don't match, knowing someone's Emergenetics Profile gives instant insight into his or her strengths, preferences, likes, and dislikes.

Whenever I give a seminar, I obtain the Profiles of the participants ahead of time so I know what kind of group I will be addressing. I know from experience that very Conceptual (yellow) minds will want an immediate overview of my work, very Analytical (blue) minds will want the scientific data that backs it up, very Structural (green) minds will want handouts to read and an agenda to follow, and very Social (red) minds will want to share stories about what they have learned. The members of the group who are *Expressive* will not speak up, while the EXPRESSIVE individuals will be excited to help me when I ask for volunteers. Those who are *Assertive* will let me do my thing, while those who are ASSERTIVE are likely to tell me how I should better prepare my graphics in the future. Members of the group who are *Flexible* will be annoyed if I don't deliver exactly what I promise, while those who are FLEXIBLE won't care if I make digressions.

Your own unique Emergenetics Profile gives you insights into how you think and behave, how you learn, how you approach new situations, how you get things done, how others see you, and how you react to others. Later in this book you will have an opportunity to estimate your own Emergenetics Profile. The importance of knowing your Profile cannot be overestimated. Over 250,000 Emergenetics Profiles have helped people to improve team effectiveness, understand their customers, increase profits, and make positive changes in their lives—to enhance their intelligence, make better decisions, access their creativity, improve their relationships, resist the effects of aging on the brain, and change how they approach their work. Emergenetics will do all this for you, and more.

WHO SAYS "NOBODY'S PERFECT"?

You can change your preferences if you really want to (more about this in chapter 7), but I'm tired of self-help books that tell people they aren't good enough. Every Emergenetics Profile is perfect as it is. You already possess everything you need to be successful. Using Emergenetics, you will discover what strengths you have and which ones are associated with the greatest energy. When you access your strengths, you can work longer without running out of gas. In addition, you will learn how to use your strengths to do things that may not come naturally to you. If you are more Analytical than Social, you can still be encouraging to your staff by making a notation in your PDA (Personal Digital Assistant) to make the rounds on Wednesday mornings. If you are more Social than Structural, you can still get to work on time if you enlist a friend to give you a wake-up call. If you are highly Conceptual, chances are you'll never read a computer manual—but you might find out what you need to know by looking at an online tutorial.

> Your brain never stops developing and changing. It's been doing it from the time you were an embryo, and will keep on doing it all your life. And this ability, perhaps, represents its greatest strength.
>
> **James Trefil, *Are We Unique?***

Unlike other books, this one is not going to tell you that you cannot change (which becomes an excuse for inexcusable behavior). On the other hand, it also is not going to tell you that you have to change (that is, you aren't good enough the way you are). My approach is:

- Here's who you are.
- Love who you are.
- If you want to consciously change, you can, but our research shows that it might be difficult. In order to do so, you will need to work through your strengths.
- If you choose not to change, don't let others dampen your self-esteem.

Today we know you have more brain power than you will possibly use in your lifetime. Wouldn't you like to harness it? Wouldn't you like to learn more easily? Remember things longer? Communicate more effectively? Make better decisions? Persuade others? Enhance your team's creativity and productivity? This book will help you understand yourself, your staff, your customers, colleagues, and employer, and even the opposite sex (always a mystery). This in turn will enable you to get the most out of your work relationships, whether you are making a sale, running a meeting, making a presentation, managing conflict, or training new hires. Using Emergenetics principles, you will be able to unlock your own personal potential as well as that of the people around you.

GETTING STARTED

Different minds will read this book in different ways. (If you're curious, turn to "How Will Different Minds Read This Book?" at the end of chapter 5.) In fact, I have written this book to appeal to all types of minds. Personally, I am so excited about this research that left to my own EXPRESSIVE devices, I would end every sentence with an exclamation point. I wish I could personally leap off the page, grab you by the collar, and shout, "Listen to this! This information can add new meaning to your life!" However, at least 33 percent of you would see this as highly offensive behavior, and any attempt at credibility after that would be destroyed.

Before you begin to read, you can boost your brain activity with two simple exercises. These will help you stay alert, understand what you are reading, and remember it longer.

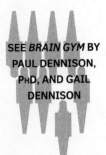

SEE *BRAIN GYM* BY PAUL DENNISON, PhD, AND GAIL DENNISON

1. *Cross-Crawls.* With your right hand, touch your left ankle. Now with your left hand, touch your right ankle. This is most effective done standing up, but it works sitting down, too. This exercise is thought to integrate the right and left hemispheres of your brain. And by clearing the potassium and sodium that builds up in your brain when you concentrate, it will help you read faster and comprehend more.
2. *Crazy Eights.* Make big "eights" horizontally in the air with your right hand. Without moving your head, follow your thumb with your eyes. Make the eights as big as your peripheral vision will allow. Now do the same thing with your left hand. This may help integrate both sides of your body.

Why does the brain respond to these exercises? You'll find out in the next chapter.

$$E = mb^2$$

Emergenetics = Merging Brains and Behavior

I started out as a teacher. My mother, grandmother, and great-grandmother were all teachers, so I believe education is my birthright. My earliest memories are of sitting around the kitchen table listening to them discuss Johnny's behavior problem or Susie's inability to do math. When I became a teacher, and after that a school administrator, I was able to join their conversations, but unfortunately we had no clear method for determining why Johnny and Susie thought and behaved as they did.

In the late 1970s, while teaching human growth and learning at a university, I began studying the "split brain" research of Dr. Roger Sperry, which was cutting edge at the time. I was mesmerized by his insights into the workings of the "left brain" and "right brain" (as the popular press labeled his research), and knew intuitively that this information could be helpful to educators as they tried to help the Johnnies and Susies of the world.

I intended to stay in education, but a funny thing happened on my way to the rest of my life. The CEO of a bank in Omaha asked me to discuss my research on leadership with his team. He also was willing to pay me almost as much money as I made teaching at the university for an entire semester. It turns out the rest of the world was as interested in understanding John and Suzanne as I was in Johnny and Susie. I took a detour from education and started doing postgraduate work with the leaders in the field of brain dominance and psychometrics. As you'll learn later in this chapter, I developed a brain-based approach to personality profiling called Emergenetics.

I started sharing my insights with others, helping them understand how people think and communicate, and teaching them how to put effective teams together. Soon I started my own business and began working with all kinds of organizations, from Fortune 100 companies to entrepreneurial startups, from government offices to nonprofit groups to educational institutions. I also started business coaching and began training others to use Emergenetics.

My detour turned into a fascinating journey. Here is a little of what I have learned.

NATURE AND NURTURE

As the saying goes, it helps to choose your parents carefully. You arrive in the world wired to think and behave in certain ways. Then as you grow and socialize with other people, your innate tendencies are tempered.

Today, most neuroscientists believe there is no simple answer to the nature-versus-nurture controversy, but it's clearly not solely nature or nurture. With this in mind, Emergenetics is based on a metaphor proposed by Harvard psychologist Jerome Kagan. He said that children are like a pale, gray fabric. The black threads of genetics are woven with the white threads of the environment to produce a material in which neither thread is obvious.

Your Genetic Inheritance

Whether you are a morning person (a "lark") or a night person (an "owl") may be largely genetically determined. Studies also show that your genes may affect your attitudes about authority, unconventional behavior, reading, television viewing, and how criminals should be treated. Genes may also be implicated in your degree of religious interest, your likelihood of getting divorced, and whether or not you throw dishes and slam doors when you are mad. Genes do *not* appear to be associated with your politics, your choice of a romantic partner, or whether or not you yell when you are angry.

Through the miracle of genetic shuffling, we are who we are, and to a large extent we stay that way. Tests show that certain traits stay stable into old age, and that identical twins tend to become more alike even if they are not together. Perhaps the winds of time wear away characteristics that are not genetically based. This could help explain why Emergenetics attributes generally stay stable over our lifetime.

A greater number of marriages cannot cause a woman's D4 gene to change from four to seven repeats. Instead, a change of repeat number must have increased the divorce/remarriage risk.

David C. Rowe, PhD,
in Robert Plomin, et al.,
Behavioral Genetics in the Postgenomic Era

Studies of Twins

If attributes are genetically based, then it stands to reason that identical twins would be very similar. However, if they were raised in the same household at the same time, the argument could be made that their shared environment caused their resemblance. So what happens when twins are raised apart? Do they still end up being similar?

Behavioral geneticist David Lykken has studied thousands of twins (and triplets) from all over the world. In one of his studies, he describes Jerry Levey and Mark Newman, identical twins who did not meet until they were thirty years old. At that point, both had similar mustaches and hairstyles. Both wore aviator glasses and belts with big buckles, and carried big key rings. Both were volunteer firefighters, and both made a living installing safety equipment. Each drank Budweiser—and crushed the can when he finished!

The story of the "twin Jims" is even more incredible. Jim Springer and Jim Lewis were identical twins who were raised separately in Ohio, eighty miles apart. By the time they met each other, both were six feet tall and around 180 pounds, with dark hair. They had the same health issues, such as migraine headaches, and their heart rate and brain waves were almost identical. Both bit their nails, chain-smoked Salem cigarettes, and drank Miller Lite. They moved and gestured in the same way, and their voices and speech patterns were indistinguishable. Both liked stock-car racing, but hated baseball. Both had been poor students, and both had worked as sheriff's

The degree of likeness [of twins] of concordance on personality tests, holds up remarkably well, even into the eighth and ninth decades of life. Some tests even suggest that identical twins grow more alike with time, whether reared apart or together.

William Clark and Michael Grunstein, *Are We Hardwired?*

deputies. Both took their families to Florida one winter and stayed along the same three-mile stretch of beach on the Gulf Coast. Both married women named Linda, got divorced, and then married women named Betty. Jim Springer named his son James Allan, and Jim Lewis named his son James Alan, just because they liked the sound of the name. Both had dogs named Toy. Both liked woodworking, and had created basement workshops with a similar layout and tools. Both made a circular white bench around a tree in their front yard, even though no one else in the neighborhood had done so. On personality tests, their scores were as close as when one person takes the same test twice.

One study of the personality traits of twins queried everything from athletic ability to attitudes about euthanasia, loud music, chess, and sweets. According to the study results, the five items with the largest genetic component (at least 50 percent heritability) were people's attitudes toward reading books, abortion on demand, playing organized sports, roller coaster rides, and the death penalty for murder. Who would have imagined that attitudes about capital punishment could be genetically influenced?

Another interesting discovery from the twin studies is that twins share a similar mood, as if they had the same set point for happiness. They also tend to experience the same level of job satisfaction. One twin who was adopted by a rather somber family laughed a great deal, even though nobody else did. When she was finally reunited with her long-lost sister, they spent a great deal of time in a state of hilarity.

When we have done Emergenetics Profiles of identical twins, their Profiles have been nearly identical. When we have profiled fraternal twins, their Profiles have resembled those of brothers and sisters. We even have a few Profiles of mirror twins—twins who are genetically identical but whose features mirror each other. For example, one is left-handed and the other is right-handed. You guessed it. Their Profiles mirror each other.

Coincidence? I don't think so.

Please know that identical twins are not identical people. They share the same *genotype* (DNA) but not necessarily the same *phenotype* (physical and behavioral characteristics). I know one set of identical twins who are nearly impossible to tell apart—except one of them has one blue eye and one green eye. Even between identical twins, there is always wiggle room for a little individuality.

Is Personality Genetically Determined?

Now that the human genome has been sequenced, behavioral geneticists are attempting to link specific parts of the human DNA code to particular tendencies. Because genes so often work together, it's unusual to find a direct link between one gene and one particular characteristic, but researchers have made some remarkable discoveries.

Behavioral geneticists have focused on two major areas of interest: dopamine receptors, and a serotonin transporter promoter region, 5-HTTLPR. Because dopamine and serotonin are so intricately involved in brain function, they have an enormous effect on personality. Our genes determine the way our brains use these chemicals, which in turn helps shape the way we think and behave.

> For the first twenty years of my career, I wrote essays critical of the role of biology and celebrating the role of the environment. I am now working in the opposite camp because I was dragged there by my data.
>
> Jerome Kagan, MD, quoted in *Born That Way* by William Wright

Introversion and extroversion are probably among the most highly heritable traits. In a study by Debra Johnson, PhD, and her colleagues, eighteen adults were tested using a questionnaire to discover their introversion/extroversion scores. Then the participants' brains were scanned while they were free to think about whatever they liked. The introverts showed increased blood flow in the anterior thalamus and in the frontal lobes of the brain, which is thought to be involved in tasks such as mediating memory, retrieval, and making plans for the future. This reflected the "inward focus of cognitive processes in introverts." Interestingly, the scan also showed increased blood flow in Broca's area, a part of the brain that processes language. The authors speculated that "introverts might engage in a running monologue in the absence of external stimulation," and they called it "self-talk." In the extroverts, the frontal lobes were not active and, different areas, including the temporal lobes, the cingulate gyrus, and the posterior thalamus, were. The authors believe that this may underlie a high drive for sensory and emotional stimulation.

It is important to understand that most of us fall on a spectrum between the two extremes of introversion and extroversion. Some researchers believe our brains are wired for introversion or extroversion when we are born. Others point out that these differences could be the result of the environment. It's the old chicken/egg conundrum.

Researchers Jerome Kagan, MD, and Carl Schwartz, MD, at Harvard note that some kids are bold, while others are shy or vigilant about things that are new. As they grow up, the shy children may become more sensitive and develop an anxiety disorder, or they may learn to manage and cover up their shyness so it is not readily apparent. However, a study shows that even when the children appear calm, a scan of their brains reveals increased activity in their amygdala (a part of the brain associated with emotional memory). This telltale activity is regulated by serotonin.

After serotonin is released and has done its job, the neurotransmitter is reabsorbed. The gene that affects serotonin reuptake comes in two variations, or alleles. People with the short variation of the allele are more likely to show signs of fearfulness or anxiety on clinical personality tests. To corroborate this, researchers showed volunteers pictures of faces with an angry or frightened expression while scans were taken of their brains. Sure enough, people with the short allele showed more activity in their amygdala.

And what happens to the bold babies when they grow up? People who love novelty may participate in dangerous sports, enjoy changing jobs, or use recreational drugs for the fun of it. It appears these individuals may have a genetically influenced craving for new experiences. Dopamine mediates pleasure in the brain, and a specific variation in a gene that affects the brain's use of dopamine is associated with thrill-seeking behavior and impulsivity.

Your Life Experiences

Every cell in your body has the same genes. What matters is how each cell expresses the genes it contains. As it turns out, biology is not destiny. Genes work by interacting with the environment—that is, through your life experiences.

Genes are constantly switching on and off. Some swing into action before we are born, due to the cosmic unfolding of our genetic plan. Others are dormant until they are triggered by life experiences. The relationship between genes and life experiences is so tightly woven that considering them separately misses the point.

A "genetic tendency" is like a bomb that may or may not go off, depending on what occurs. If you are at risk for alcoholism, but you never drink, you will not become an alcoholic. On the other hand, if you start drinking, you could take the pin out of the genetic grenade and develop a serious problem. Same genes. Different life experience. Different outcome.

Your Changing Brain

Your brain changes with each movement, thought, experience, or conversation you have. It will be different by the time you finish reading this paragraph. New experiences cause new neural connections to be made in the brain, and repeated experiences reinforce existing neural pathways. Sometimes you cause this to happen deliberately, such as when you study for an exam, and other times this process takes place unconsciously. In my seminars I sometimes joke, "Does the name Pavlov ring a bell?" Pavlov showed that dogs will salivate in response to a bell before dinner—a classic example of environmental conditioning.

> The brains of domestic rabbits are considerably reduced in bulk, in comparison with those of the wild rabbit or hare; and this may be attributed to their having been closely confined during many generations, so that they have exerted their intellect, instincts, senses and voluntary movements but little.
>
> **Charles Darwin,**
> *The Descent of Man*

Back in 1874, Charles Darwin observed that the brains of domesticated rabbits are smaller than those of wild rabbits. I have never spoken to a domesticated bunny, but my guess is they don't have too much on their minds. Wild rabbits, on the other hand, probably would make better conversationalists. They have to find food, outwit foxes, survive the winter, and so on. They have bigger brains because over the years, nature selected wild rabbits that were more capable. In addition, the life experiences of each individual rabbit affect the size and complexity of its brain.

To measure the effects of life experiences on the brain, scientists have conducted many animal experiments. In a classic study, neurobiologist Marian Diamond divided rats into three different environments: a group of twelve rats in a large cage with a variety of rat toys, a group of three rats (a "standard colony") in a small cage with no toys, and a lone rat in a small cage with no toys. Her study showed that the more playmates and toys a rat had, the larger its brain structures grew, and the better it performed in tasks like maze challenges. At the time Dr. Diamond did these experiments, these results were startling. No one knew just how much the brain responded to the environment. Dr. Diamond found that placing a rat in an enriched environment caused changes to occur in its brain on a microscopic level within thirty seconds, with measurable changes occuring in just four days.

Later studies compared solitary rats with those that had lots of friends, rats that got exercise with those that didn't, and rats that ran on wheels with rats that had to find their way through mazes. The parameters of each study varied, but the results all indicated that the more interaction, enrichment, and challenges the rats had, the larger and more complex their brains became. How was this possible? Because the brain is always a work in progress.

BRAIN FUNCTION 101

The human brain is estimated to have about one hundred billion nerve cells, two million miles of axons, and a million billion synapses, making it the most complex structure, natural or artificial, on earth.

Tim Green, Stephen Heinemann, and Jim Gusella, "Molecular Neurobiology and Genetics: Investigation of Neural Function and Dysfunction"

The adult brain is about three pounds of soft, gray, wrinkled matter divided down the middle into two hemispheres. It is a made up of 80 percent water. It accounts for 2 percent of the body's weight, yet consumes 20 percent of the body's energy, about twenty-five watts. Billions of neurons communicate across tiny spaces called synapses, allowing every thought, sensation, and event to trace or retrace neural pathways. There are more synapses in the brain than there are stars in the universe, so if you imagine what it would be like to play connect-the-dots in the night sky, you have a small idea of the brain's capabilities.

Probably because our ability to respond to experiences is linked to survival, the human brain records minute changes in the environment. On a clear, dark night we can detect a light twenty miles away. In a quiet place, we can hear a watch ticking twenty feet from us. We can feel the wing of a bee falling one centimeter onto our cheek. We can taste a teaspoon of sugar in two gallons of water and smell a drop of perfume in a three-room apartment.

All these impressions are recorded in different locations in the brain. Separate parts of the brain, and different layers within each part, are associated with different kinds of information. But language, for example, does not reside in just one place. Different parts of the brain are used for speaking, seeing, or hearing words. And it turns out that nouns, verbs, adjectives, adverbs, prepositions, and so on are all stored in different areas. One stroke patient had no trouble reading "there is a *crack* in the mirror," yet she stumbled when trying to read "don't *crack* the nuts in here."

Experience Alters the Brain

At birth, the brain is only a quarter of its adult size. While genes help determine what kind of brain you are born with, your early life experiences determine how your brain will work throughout your life. Early experiences link neurons to each other and build the neural circuitry in your brain. Cells that are not used are simply pruned away.

Synaptogenesis (Synapse Formation)

Synapses are the tiny gaps between neurons across which information flows. Each time we have a new experience, the brain creates (or reuses) a synaptic connection. Rats living in an interesting environment have denser, more complex brains with more synapses. Whether you are a rat or a human being, a range of experiences constantly strengthens existing connections in the brain and forms new ones.

> **Cells that fire together wire together.**
>
> **Called "the Hebb Rule," based on the writing of neuroscientist Donald Hebb, PhD**

Dendritic Branching

A neuron's synapses are located at the end of its dendrites, which are the branches extending from the nerve's end. Life experiences and increased stimulation cause increased branching of the neurons in the brain. New branches means more synapses as nerves reach out to each other. The opposite is also true: a lack of stimulation decreases the branching of the dendrites.

> **Axons are promiscuous little things.**
>
> **Douglas Smith, "Scientists Foresee Bridging Nerve Damage with Grafts"**

Myelination

Myelin is a sheet of protein and fat wrapped tightly around axons, like insulation around a wire. It helps to speed nerve impulses on their way. When myelin breaks down, nerves do not work as effectively. Researchers recently determined that the brain forms myelin until midlife, which is much longer than anyone previously suspected. Brain myelination, too, is promoted by life experiences.

Neuronal Pruning

We are born with an excess of brain cells, if you can imagine such a thing. The extra cells and connections in the brain die off when they are not stimulated. "Use it or lose it" is not just a figure of speech. It's important for children to have many kinds of experiences because much of our neural circuitry is put in place in childhood. Later on, we can call upon the connections our brains made while we were reading, running, dancing, swinging, or playing the piano. If we never do any of those things, our silent, unused brain cells will simply die off.

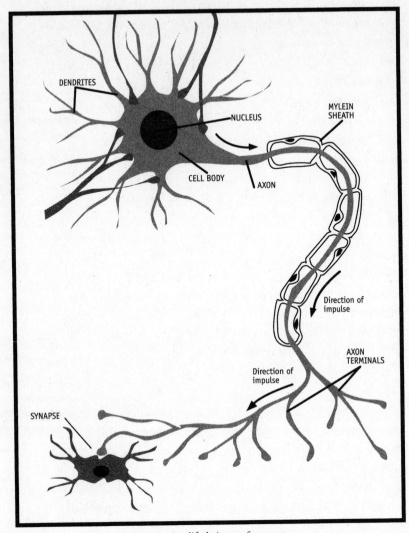

Here is a simplified picture of a neuron.
Neurons communicate with each other across gaps called synapses.

Neurogenesis

For a long time, experts believed that the brain did not make new neurons. It's true that the vast majority of the neurons in our brains are present from birth. However, scientists have discovered that new neurons form in the hippocampus, a part of the brain associated with learning and memory. Research by Princeton psychologist Elizabeth Gould suggests that new neurons may even grow in the neocortex, which is associated with language and other higher functions.

When it comes to neurogenesis, birds in the wild grow more new neurons than birds in the lab, and rats that live with other rats grow more new neurons than rats in isolation. Again, life experiences have a direct affect on the brain. Complex environments promote neurogenesis, while deprived environments appear to inhibit it.

> Children whose neural circuits are not stimulated before kindergarten are never going to be what they could have been.
>
> Sharon Begley,
> "Your Child's Brain"

Neuroplasticity

The brain is considered "plastic" because in response to life experiences, it alters its structure and function. For example, learning to juggle enlarges the cerebral cortex. Cabbies in London who memorize "the knowledge" (as learning how to navigate all the city's streets is called) show changes in a part of the brain associated with memory. Although there are limits, the brain is very adaptable. Children who have had one hemisphere of their brain removed in order to cure intractable seizures have gone on to live normal lives with half a brain. In a somewhat horrifying experiment, frogs were given a transplanted third eye—something for which their brains could not have been innately prepared—and eventually they learned how to see with it. When necessary, areas of the brain can be recruited for new functions.

> Whenever you read a book or have a conversation, the experience causes physical changes in your brain. It's a little frightening to think that every time you walk away from an encounter, your brain has been altered, sometimes permanently.
>
> George Johnson,
> *In the Palaces of Memory*

The Brain's Chemical Soup

The brain is bathed in a constantly changing mixture of sex hormones, stress hormones, neurotransmitters, neuropeptides, and so on. Through magic (OK, it isn't really magic, but it defies explanation) our experiences are translated into memories, and our feelings are transduced into messenger proteins, or what researcher Candace Pert, PhD, calls the "molecules of emotion." Every life experience we have, from making coffee in the morning to holding a new baby, resonates within our brain and causes a cascade of effects in the brain and body.

Lifelong Learning

It would be great if any type of neural connection could occur at any time throughout life, but that isn't the way the brain works. During the brain's development there are windows of opportunity called "critical periods" when neural connections must be formed, or the chance is lost forever. This is true of the connections needed for vision, language, muscle control, and even reasoning. For example, eye problems in babies need to be corrected while the baby's brain is still forming the circuitry responsible for sight. If problems are fixed too late—for example, a crossed eye—the child will be functionally blind, even though the eyes can be made to work correctly. Similarly, a child who is immobilized in a body cast until the age of four will learn to walk, but never without conscious effort. And people who take up a second language after the age of ten to thirteen may learn to speak it fluently, but usually will never grasp the accent perfectly.

> The brain remains a dynamic structure that alters from year-to-year, day-to-day, even moment-to-moment over our lifespan.
>
> Richard Restak, MD,
> *The Secret Life of the Brain*

Still, with new developments in brain-imaging technology, researchers have learned that the brain is a work in progress for longer than previously believed. This has transformed the way experts see adolescent behavior, among other things. "Executive functions" like self-control, planning ahead, and making rational decisions simply aren't possible until the brain is fully developed, which may not occur until age twenty-five or later.

> The brain is a little saline pool that acts as a conductor, and it runs on electricity.
>
> Judith Hooper and Dick Teresi,
> *The Three-Pound Universe*

Happily, a healthy brain is capable of learning and responding to new experiences all our lives. This is such an important topic that I am going to come back to it later in this book when I talk about brain fitness in chapter 11.

Learning from Misfortune

Researchers have learned a great deal about the brain by observing people who have suffered brain illness or injury. One example is Phineas Gage, a railroad worker who had a metal bar driven through his head in an explosion in 1848. The bar went up through his face and out the top of his skull. Amazingly, even though the bar remained in his head, Phineas survived, but he underwent a per-

Brain Scanning Techniques

In the old days, brain research consisted of doing autopsies and observing people whose brains were damaged by injury or illness. With increasingly sophisticated brain-imaging techniques, researchers are now able to observe brain activity in healthy people.

Emergenetics associate Ross Judice, MD, metaphorically compares the current brain-imaging technology to taking pictures of the earth from the moon. We can see mountains, volcanoes, rivers, rain forests, and highways, but we don't really know what is going on down there (on a neuronal or transmitter level). Here are some current scanning techniques:

- EEG (electroencephalogram): Introduced in 1929, the EEG uses electrodes on the scalp to measure the tiny electrical signals produced by neurons in the brain as they fire. Although this technology has been around for decades, it is still useful today.
- CT (computerized tomography): The "CAT" scan, introduced in the 1970s, produces anatomical images by taking thousands of X-ray "slices" of the brain using a scanner that revolves around the skull.
- PET (positron emission tomography): A PET scan, also dating from the 1970s, produces three-dimensional images of brain activity. Patients are injected with a radioactive marker (glucose or certain drugs) and their brains are scanned as the solution is metabolized by active neurons.
- MRI (magnetic resonance imaging): Introduced in the 1980s, an MRI is a three-dimensional computer image that is produced without radioactive injections, using a strong magnetic field and pulses of radio waves. An MRI scan is useful for observing structures, but is not keyed to brain activity.
- fMRI (functional magnetic resonance imaging): A cousin of the MRI that dates from the 1990s, fMRI technology produces three-dimensional maps of brain activity. In this case the marker is deoxyhemoglobin, a naturally occurring byproduct of brain activity. The MRI scan detects minute changes in blood flow as a person performs certain activities, such as visual tasks.
- MRS (magnetic resonance spectroscopy): Commercially available since the 1990s, the MRS scan uses an MRI scanner and specialized software to measure biochemical changes in the brain.
- MEG (magnetoencephalography): This new technique, not widely available as of this writing, measures very faint magnetic fields generated by electrical activity in the brain as it occurs. This supersensitive scan measures neural activity too brief to be recorded by an fMRI or a PET scan.

sonality transformation. Before the accident, he was a quiet and industrious worker. Afterward, he became a surly, combative man who could not keep a job. This was a turning point in understanding the anatomy of the brain because it suggested that key parts of personality are associated with the frontal lobe.

About twenty years later, surgeon Paul Broca identified a speech center in the brain by autopsying brain-damaged patients who had lost their ability to speak. This section of the brain, located in the left, inferior frontal lobe, is now known as Broca's area.

At roughly the same time as Broca, Carl Wernicke was observing stroke victims. His area of interest was not patients who were unable to speak, but patients who had lost their ability to speak correctly. Some could not speak grammatically, while others were unable to retrieve the precise words they wanted. Wernicke pinpointed a different area of the brain associated with language, which today is known as Wernicke's area.

Broca was able to determine that damage to the left frontal lobe produced different symptoms from those caused by damage to the right frontal lobe. Researchers also recognized that damage to the left side of the brain produced symptoms in the right side of the body, while damage to the right side of the brain affected the left side of the body. But the next leap in understanding the different hemispheres of the brain did not occur until nearly a century after Phineas Gage's accident.

> The brain is the last and grandest biological frontier, the most complex thing we have yet discovered in our universe. It contains hundreds of billions of cells interlinked through trillions of connections. The brain boggles the mind.
>
> James D. Watson, MD, PhD,
> in *Discovering the Brain*,
> by Sandra Ackerman

Split-Brain Research

In the early 1940s, William van Wagenen performed the first "split-brain" surgery to relieve catastrophic epilepsy in severely affected patients for whom medications and other treatments were not effective. He reasoned that if epilepsy was an "electrical storm" in the brain, cutting the corpus callosum—the bundle of nerve fibers that connects the two hemispheres—should stop the seizures. These early operations were not very successful because only part of the corpus callosum was severed. Later, more extensive experiments by surgeons Philip Vogel and Joseph Bogen were much more successful in controlling epileptic seizures.

Roger Sperry, neuropsychologist and 1981 Nobel Prize winner, and his associate Michael Gazzaniga performed follow-up testing on the split-brain patients. They found that when the corpus callosum was bisected, the split-brain subjects functioned with two separate minds. The patients were able to walk, talk, read, and play sports, but unfortunately the total breakdown in communication between the two halves of the brain caused some peculiar symptoms, at least for a while. One patient tried to forcibly grab his wife with his left hand, only to be restrained by his own right hand. Another reported that if he held a toothbrush in his left hand, he knew how to use it, but couldn't remember what to call it. However, if he held it in his right hand, he immediately could say "toothbrush." Yet another patient, when asked to write down what job he would like, got a different answer from each hand. His right hand wrote that he wanted to be a draftsman, while his left hand wrote that he wanted to be a racecar driver! These patients seemed to be literally of two minds.

Laboratory experiments with split-brain patients produced groundbreaking information about how the brain is organized and how this affects our behavior and thinking. When researchers showed the patient's right eye (left brain) a picture of a spoon, he could say "spoon." When they showed the patient's left eye (right brain) the same picture, he could not express what he had just seen. However, he could pick out a spoon with his left hand. This suggested that the left brain was verbal, but the right brain was not.

Further experiments were even more fascinating. When a command such as "laugh" was shown to the right brain (left eye), the patient would laugh. However, because the right brain is non-verbal, he would be unable to explain why he was laughing, so when asked to explain, he would give a phony reason. The left brain would simply make something up.

From these experiments, it became clear that the two hemispheres of the brain are responsible for different kinds of thought. Although their functions are normally integrated, they possess different capacities and can operate independently.

SEE *LEFT BRAIN, RIGHT BRAIN* BY SALLY SPRINGER AND GEORG DEUTSCH

LEFT HEMISPHERIC LATERALIZATION ("LEFT BRAIN")	RIGHT HEMISPHERIC LATERALIZATION ("RIGHT BRAIN")
• Symmetrical thinking	• Asymmetrical thinking
• Rational	• Intuitive
• Logical	• Emotional
• Analytical	• Holistic
• Mathematical	• Nonverbal
• Verbal	• Visual
• Linear	• Spatial
• Sequential ordering	• Simultaneous comprehension

The left brain tends to process logical, rational, linear, sequential, analytic, and systematic modes of thought. It absorbs data, analyzes differences, and uses concepts like time and other measurements. The left brain excels at problem-solving, calculations, and search strategies. It seeks order, and will invent it when none is present. It likes explanations, and likes to put things in context. Ask the left brain why it did something, and it will make up a story that sounds logical—even if it isn't true.

> Slight hemispheric differences have been transformed by the popular press into clear-cut, all-or-nothing dichotomies that have been used to account for everything from baseball batting averages to socioeconomic class.
>
> John Pinel, *Biopsychology*

The right brain tends to process intuitive, emotional, nonverbal, holistic, and conceptual modes of thought. It excels at facial recognition, spatial skills, and visual imagery. It has rudimentary language skills, such as matching words to pictures. It lives in the present, sticks to verifiable sensory input, and does not look for deeper meaning. Ask the right brain why it did something, and it won't say a word because it cannot speak.

Two criticisms of Sperry and Gazzaniga's work are worth noting here. First, there is no question that the study of hemispheric differences is one of the most important lines of research in neuropsychology, but it also has led to major distortions over the years.

Second, Sperry's original experiments were performed on small groups of brain-damaged people. Fortunately, researchers now can use modern scanning techniques to peer inside the minds of the healthy. Using these new technologies, they have mapped and observed all types of brain activity. Their results have not only upheld much of Sperry and Gazzaniga's early work, but also have expanded it in a much more sophisticated way.

People generally tend toward one hemisphere or the other. "Left-brainers" are considered more logical and analytical, while "right-brainers" are seen as more intuitive and conceptual. (Handedness appears to be an independent system, so whether you are left-handed or right-handed is irrelevant here.) Obviously the finer points of neurological research have been lost in these generalizations, but people do tend to favor one type of thinking or the other.

The Parts of the Brain

In the 1950s, Paul MacLean, MD developed the concept of the triune brain. His theory was that the human brain consists of three layers, with each layer corresponding to a different stage of evolution, and each being responsible for a different kind of mental processing. MacLean identified the innermost layer as

The Human Brain

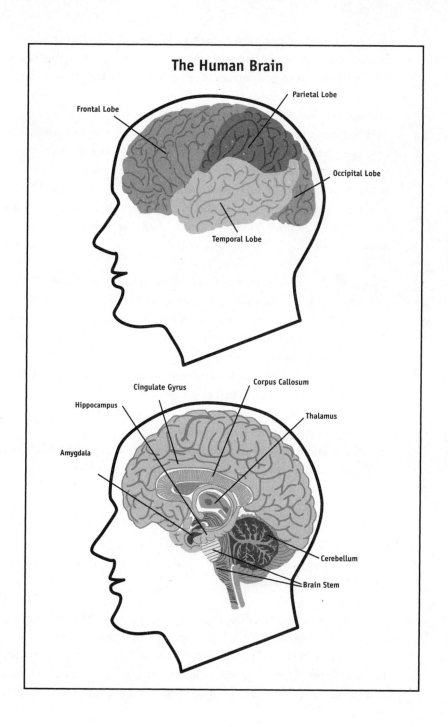

the reptilian brain (the most primitive, dealing with automatic functions like breathing and avoiding danger), the middle layer as the limbic system (which deals with emotions and memory formation and retrieval), and the outer cerebral layer (the most recent to develop, associated with higher functions such as language).

Most cognitive thought processes, planning, and future-oriented thinking take place in the cerebral cortex (also called the neocortex). This is the "gray matter" that covers the cerebral hemispheres with deep fissures and convolutions. The cerebral cortex is divided in four lobes that collectively interpret sensations, control our movements, and enable us to think, speak, write, plan, create, calculate, organize, and do all the other things that make us human.

1. The frontal lobe (at the front of the brain) is associated with judgment, creativity, problem-solving, and purposeful acts. It includes the frontal cortex, which is involved in movement and speech, and the prefrontal cortex, which is involved in the "executive functions" like decision-making and planning.
2. The occipital lobe (at the back of the brain) is associated with receiving and processing visual information.
3. The parietal lobe (across the middle of the brain) is involved with higher sensory and language functions.
4. The temporal lobe (on the left and right sides of the brain) is associated with hearing, memory, meaning, and language.

There is some overlap in the functions of the different lobes, and in fact some researchers today believe the brain works holographically.

From Halves to Quadrants

In addition to favoring either logic or intuition, most people also tend to focus on either the abstract or the concrete. Some people are happy designing gardens, while others need to actually dig in the dirt. Some like to create the picture on the needlepoint canvas, while others excel at the stitchery. Some like to design beautiful buildings, while others want to put mortar to brick. These preferences look like this:

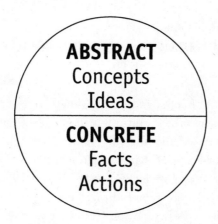

If you superimpose the abstract/concrete model on top of the left brain/right brain model, you create a four-quadrant model that looks like this:

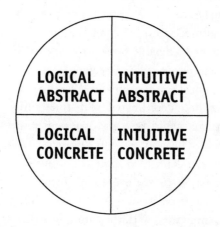

Ned Herrmann is generally recognized as one of the first people to popularize a four-quadrant model of the brain using a metaphorical interpretation of Sperry's and MacLean's research. His work, developed while he was at General Electric in the late 1970s, brought the idea of hemispheric lateralization to training and development. Herrmann originally called these four quadrants left cerebral, left limbic, right cerebral, and right limbic, and he developed a questionnaire for people to use in identifying which kind of thinking suited them best.

BUILDING A BETTER MOUSETRAP:
THE EMERGENETICS QUESTIONNAIRE

Looking at Herrmann's model and several others, it seemed to me there was room for improvement. The assumption in the 1980s was that all "right-brainers" were extroverted and all "left-brainers" were introverted, but I had observed many "right-brainers" who were introverted and vice versa. The psychological tests that were popular in the 1970s and 1980s, including Social Styles and the Myers-Briggs Type Indicator, did not distinguish between behavior and thought processes. I was certain that my colleague Wendell Williams, who at the time was working on his doctorate in applied psychology, and I could do better.

We looked at hundreds of tests, and we found that they were either too simple, too complicated, too focused on thinking styles, too focused on behaviors, and so on. Many tests fail to distinguish thinking styles from behaviors. In addition, they are not normed against the population at large (more about this in chapter 5). We envisioned a flexible test that would yield results that could be normed against the population at large by gender.

We started to develop a test that involved asking people about their behavioral styles, and how these coordinated with their thinking preferences. We originally thought there would be a six-quadrant model of thinking in the brain. As we gathered data and ran our statistics, we discovered the four-quadrant thinking model continued to hold up, but it did not correlate with the expected behaviors. What we eventually identified was a four-quadrant thinking model plus three behaviors. We then set out to determine how the behavioral attributes integrated with the thinking attributes.

While we were developing our model, the nature/nurture debate was heating up. Every parent can tell you that different children of the same parents behave differently from birth. Some babies are sleepers, some are crabby, some are active, some are quiet. For decades, eminent psychologists like Pavlov and Skinner had focused on how environmental conditioning shapes personality, but advances in DNA research now shifted the pendulum to an emphasis on genetics. At first we thought people came into the world genetically wired to think a certain way, while their behavior was influenced by their environment. But fascinating studies on twins who had been raised separately during World War II indicated that behavior was more hard-wired than anyone had previously realized. These findings resulted in a new theory of behavior and learning called *emergenesis,* a term coined by researcher David Lykken. Emergenesis proposes that human beings are wired to process information in certain preferred patterns. Just as we have a biological tendency to share with our forebears our genetic heritage for disease, body type, and facial characteristics, we also have a tendency to think and process information based on our genetic programming. Wendell and I decided to call the constantly emerging combination of genetics and environment Emergenetics—literally, patterns of thinking and behaving that *emerge* from your *genetic* blueprint.

> **The human brain is generally regarded as a complex web of adaptations built into the nervous system, even though no one knows how.**
>
> Michael Gazzaniga, PhD,
> *The Mind's Past*

The Emergenetics Questionnaire

Our first Emergenetics test consisted of 200 questions. Unlike other tests that use "forced choice" questions—for example, choosing whether you are introverted *or* extroverted—the Emergenetics questions do not require you to deny any part of your temperament.

We administered the first Emergenetics questionnaire to 500 people. After analyzing the results, we determined that there were four distinct Thinking Attributes (Analytical, Structural, Social, and Conceptual) and three Behavioral Attributes (Expressiveness, Assertiveness, and Flexibility). Furthermore, there was almost no correlation among them. In other words, a person could be highly Expressive (for example, a motivational speaker) without being Social (friendly), or very Assertive (determined to get her or his own way) without being Analytical (logical). We found that people of any thinking style—not just the Conceptual types—can be creative. We found that people with any behavioral style—not just extreme Assertiveness—can be leaders. Using the four Thinking Attributes and three Behavioral Attributes, we finally could construct accurate Emergenetics Profiles of people. Better yet, people could immediately understand themselves and others without getting into a lot of psychological mumbo-jumbo.

We administered the next test, refined to 100 questions, to 1,000 people. After more fine-tuning, we gave the test to 1,000 men and 1,000 women. This is when we realized that men and women really do think differently, and we developed gender norms for the test. As we continued to gather data, we gave the test to 10,000 people from all walks of life—truck drivers, Junior League volunteers, CEOs, physicians, farmers, you name it. As of this writing, over

250,000 people from all over the world have taken the Emergenetics test, and this data has made it possible for us to create the population and gender norms each test is scored against. Emergenetics is as psychometrically sound as an instrument of this type can be.

De-mystifying Human Behavior

Emergenetics provides a framework for understanding how you operate in the world. It classifies your thinking and behaving into seven preferences that work in harmony to generate your choices.

For an example of how this works, consider humor. We would never say that only a certain brain type is funny. Every attribute in the Emergenetics Profile enjoys humor in its own way. Dick Cavett has a wry and intellectual wit, Robin Williams is wacky and frenetic, Ellen DeGeneres is an affable storyteller, and Jerry Seinfeld makes witty observations of everyday life with surgical precision. Each comedian uses a vastly different style, and perhaps you like one more than another. It's about their style, and the filters of your brain.

It can be frustrating when your friend thinks a certain comedian is hilarious, while you think he is merely average. Your friend may think you lack a sense of humor. You do have a sense of humor, but it is just different from his. Emergenetics will help you understand why these and many other differences exist.

3

Great Minds Do Not Think Alike

The Four Emergenetics Thinking Attributes

I'm sure Einstein had a strong preference for Conceptual thinking, in addition to other preferences. I wish I could have given him the Emergenetics questionnaire! Without access to his answers, I can't say for certain how his brain worked, but I do know that Einstein made incredible leaps of thought, and once declared, "I never came upon any of my discoveries through the process of rational thinking."

Martin Luther King Jr. must have had a lot of Conceptual thinking in his brain, too, as he "had a dream" for the world.

Obviously, Analytical thinking worked fine for some other great minds. Gregor Mendel, for example, probably used Analytical thinking to determine the principles of genetics after years of painstaking observations.

I'm assuming Structural thinking allowed Bach to configure his fugues, and Eisenhower to plan the invasion of Normandy, thus turning the tide of World War II.

The Dalai Lama and Oprah Winfrey clearly tap into their Social thinking. They may have other strong thinking attributes as well, but it is hard to imagine they don't prefer to think from their Social attribute.

Every person possesses, to a certain degree, each Thinking Attribute. No one thinks only in one Attribute. If that were the case, all we'd ever have to do is figure out someone's sole thinking mode, and then we'd be able to communicate with total understanding. But people are not that simple. We have overlays and textures that are not always visible; it's what makes us remarkable and human.

It is the energy you generate around these Attributes that distinguishes your personality. Some people are extremely strong in one Attribute, while others are strong in two Attributes. Multimodal types access three Attributes to about the same degree, while quadra-modal thinkers use all four Attributes to about the same degree. In chapter 5 you will have a chance to read about different kinds of brain Profiles and how common or uncommon they are. But first things first: in this chapter, you will find out about each of the four Emergenetics Thinking Attributes.

> What seems astonishing is that a mere three-pound object, made of the same atoms that constitute everything else under the sun, is capable of directing virtually everything that humans have done: flying to the moon and hitting 70 home runs, writing *Hamlet* and building the Taj Mahal—even unlocking the secrets of the brain itself.
>
> Joel Havemann and
> Stephen Reich,
> *A Life Shaken*

ANALYTICAL THINKING (BLUE)

In God we trust . . .
all others must bring data.

Analytical thinking combines rational thought with a love of abstract ideas.

When the Analytical mind is intrigued, it perseveres until all its questions are answered. In a meeting or learning situation, people with strongly Analytical minds are the ones that make all the non-Analytical thinkers uncomfortable by continually querying the speaker, asking "why?" or "how?" and basically saying "prove it to me."

What's the Key Question for the Analytical Mind?

The Analytical mind asks: "Where's the research?" The Analytical part of your brain immediately looks for verification.

What Is Analytical Thinking?

Analytical thinking is logical and objective. People who show a strong preference for Analytical thinking enjoy math, science, technology, and fields like finance. They have disciplined thought processes, and prefer deductive reasoning that follows a logical sequence. They base their conclusions on facts, not conjecture, and—being naturally skeptical—seek data, evidence, and proof. They do not believe in "cosmic woo-woo." The Analytical mind is comfortable with statistical and technical information, and is able to mesh details with abstract ideas. If you gave strong Analytical thinkers a new technological device, they would find a hundred ways to adapt it to their needs, using all of its capabilities, sometimes in unexpected but nonetheless successful ways.

> *Nick, who has an extremely Analytical Profile, attended one of my seminars that was held in a luxury hotel. "My family always complains that I don't tell them I love them," he told me. "You have inspired me and I am going to change, beginning this minute. I am going into the gift shop to buy some postcards to send to all my children and grandchildren. On the card I shall tell each one of them that I love them. Do you know where I can find a Xerox machine?"*

What Is Good about Analytical Thinking?

The Analytical part of your brain is excellent at rational, clearheaded problem-solving. People who are extremely Analytical are terrific at formulating systems that accommodate lots of important details. They are excellent critical thinkers, always notice inconsistencies, and can spot the fault line in an approach that isn't going to work.

How Does the Analytical Mind Solve Problems?

The Analytical approach is theoretical, but not fanciful. The scientific method—careful observation, use of data, plus a new idea in the form of a hypothesis—is a premier example of Analytical thinking.

How Does the Analytical Mind Learn?

The Analytical part of your brain learns by mental analysis. This is a solitary activity, so people who are highly Analytical often work alone. Analytical thinkers want value for time spent, and they get more out of a learning opportunity if they have some reading material to absorb ahead of time. If you are teaching someone with a very Analytical mind, be prepared for critical questions, and make sure you can defend your information. If you are discussing something interesting about which they know little, strongly Analytical people are happy to consider you the expert—unless they catch you in a mistake. If this happens, you might as well pack your bags and go home.

> Nothing in life is to be feared.
> It is only to be understood.
>
> Marie Curie

What Are Some of the Drawbacks of Analytical Thinking?

People who are extremely Analytical are so logical that they can be perceived as unemotional and uncaring. In fact, they may care a great deal, but they do not let their emotions interfere with their thought processes. Analyzing a problem from every angle is their way of showing that they care. Why bother, otherwise? People with a preference for Analytical thought can be intimidating and somewhat judgmental. Often they are seen as negative and critical, when really they are simply attempting to deeply understand a topic.

Analytical Thinking at Work

Roger's Profile is extremely Analytical. On the first day of a three-day seminar I gave to aircraft engineers, Roger asked, "What happens to the brain as we age?" I responded that the aging brain basically gets better as we get older, and proceeded to support this declaration by quoting several recent gerontology research articles by Yale researchers. Satisfied, Roger had no further questions.

On the third day of the seminar, Roger raised his hand. I called on him, but I mistakenly called him Andrew, the name of another participant. When the group immediately called this to my attention, I laughed and said, "Sorry, Roger. I know your name. My recall just isn't what it used to be."

Immediately eight people with strongly Analytical Profiles jumped up and, in concert, yelled, "But on the first day, you said our brains get better as we get older!"

How much did this simple mistake matter?

At the end of the seminar, the participants filled out evaluations. Under "instructor thoroughly demonstrates knowledge of subject matter," this group's average response for me was "5" on a 7-point scale. These engineers enjoyed the seminar and were already thinking about how to apply Emergenetics concepts at work. But they weren't about to let their overall enthusiasm

Does This Sound Like You?

The following statements describe the **Analytical** brain:

- I like to review new technology.
- I make most of my decisions based on rigorous analysis.
- I like to have reading material prior to any class, lecture, or meeting I'm attending.

cloud their judgment about my performance. A mistake is a mistake, and I had to be held accountable. One of the engineers came up to me at the end of the session and said in a flat, monotone voice, "Thank you. This has been the most significant event of my life." I knew, coming from an Analytical brain, this was high praise. However, on his evaluation form he gave me a "4" out of 7—which for him was as good as it gets.

STRUCTURAL THINKING (GREEN)

Of course I don't look busy. I did it right the first time.

Structural thinking combines sequential thought with a love of practical applications.

Structural thinkers cover all the details and are known for their thoroughness. They go from A to Z and do not skip LMNOP. The Structural mind knows that its results are dependable, which may explain why people with a highly Structural Profile are stressed by trying a new approach unless the new way is proved superior. If the Structural part of your brain is asked to repeat a process, it will do so over and over again perfectly.

What's the Key Question for the Structural Mind?

The Structural mind asks: "How can I apply this practically?" It aims for a workable solution.

What Is Structural Thinking?

Structural thinking is practical and dependable. People with a preference for Structural thought are known for their common sense. The Structural part of their brain gives them a talent for drawing comparisons, looking for connections, organizing the components of a problem, and creating order out of chaos. This part of the brain is precise and good at handling detailed work.

Highly Structural people like to follow guidelines, agendas, procedures, and protocols, and feel comfortable with rules and regulations. They are task-oriented, meet deadlines, and are good organization people. The Structural brain is methodical and orderly to the point of being predictable, and it tends to be cautious of new ideas. If you gave a store-bought daily planner to someone with an extremely Structural Profile, she or he would use it exactly the way it was intended to be used. Why do things differently when a tried-and-true approach works fine?

> *Chris, one of four children, told me, "In my stocking almost every Christmas was an envelope with some money in it. It was usually an odd amount, like $17.23, and never the same amount each year. A couple of years there was no money. When I got older, I finally asked Mother what this was all about. She explained that every Christmas Eve she added up how much money she had spent on each child for Christmas gifts that year, calculated the greatest amount she had spent on any one of the children, then gave the other children their pro rata share."*

What Is Good about Structural Thinking?

When it comes to laboratory analysis, only a Structural mind will do. You don't want a drama student cross-checking your biopsy report. Similarly, if you want a really solid plan, ask someone who is highly Structural. She or he will focus on what is tangible, will remember to include all the important details, and will come up with a workable plan that will solve your problem on time.

How Does the Structural Mind Solve Problems?

The Structural mind uses sequential thinking and a detailed, methodical approach that non-Structural minds find tedious. Structural thinkers love the "cookbook" approach, in which everything is clearly laid out step-by-step.

How Does the Structural Mind Learn?

The Structural part of your brain learns by doing. People who are highly Structural are hands-on learners. If you are teaching someone with a lot of preference for Structural thinking, provide plenty of "how to" information and don't deviate from the subject at hand.

What Are Some of the Drawbacks of Structural Thinking?

Structural thinking is conventional and conservative, not bold or daring. Someone with a highly Structural brain may be plodding and inflexible, and may insist on doing things by the book. This can aggravate visionaries and people who take shortcuts. Structural thinkers believe they can do certain tasks better and faster than anyone else, which makes it difficult for them to delegate to others.

Structural Thinking at Work

When I give presentations during the holiday season, I often put groups together according to their strongest Attribute, then ask them to plan the perfect party. I am no longer surprised at how different these ideal parties are, and I now have many outrageous Structural stories, most of them involving someone's mother.

Buffy's mother has a highly Structural brain. Buffy told her group that her mother always had the Thanksgiving agenda planned to the last second. One year, at the appointed hour she rose to clear the table. However, the family—which was still engaged in a spirited discussion—begged her to hold off on the dishes a little longer.

Does This Sound Like You?

The following statements describe the **Structural** brain:

- I would like a job with a lot of rules and regulations.
- I prefer it when others speak in specific terms.
- I like planning tasks to meet an objective.

"In an agreeable mood," Buffy said, "Mother disappeared into the kitchen and returned a few seconds later to join us in the continuing conversation. Fifteen minutes later, an oven timer that Mother had surreptitiously set jarringly interrupted our talks. We were all very surprised, but headed to the kitchen to attack the dishes."

"That sounds like *my* mother!" interrupted John, a delightful Georgian. "My mother starts setting the table for Thanksgiving dinner in September."

"September?" I exclaimed incredulously. "What about the dust?"

"Dust?" John drawled. "Do you think my mother would have *dust*?"

Miss Faulk, principal of the elementary school where I began my career as a teacher, was a beautiful example of someone whose preference for Structural thought was so strong that it appeared to color her every view of the world. One summer she accompanied her nephews to Disneyland. This was the last place we teachers could imagine her, and we could hardly wait for her to return to tell us her impressions of the place. I was the first to ask, "Miss Faulk, how was your trip? What did you love best about Disneyland? The lights? The sounds? The people? The rides? The entertainment? Mickey Mouse?"

"None of that, Mrs. Browning. My favorite was the lines. You should see how they are organized—in spirals—and even though there were lots of people there, the whole system operates smoothly. It was the most well-designed place I've ever been. Also, it's very clean."

Of all the people for whom I ever worked, Miss Faulk taught me the most about organization, orderliness, time management, and structured thinking. She never worked with more than one piece of paper on her desk at a time so she could focus her entire attention on the task, and she never took on another chore until the one in front of her was completed. If she was interrupted, she simply returned to what she was doing after the interruption ended. She spoke in clear, precise language, and at the end of the day, she swept her desk clean, placing everything in her middle drawer so she could begin the next day with a pristine surface. "A clean space is the sign of an uncluttered mind," she often pronounced.

Kermit the Frog was wrong when he stated it's not easy being green (Structural). Historically, time management rules, banking systems, and, for the most part, schools and large organizations were designed for this preference. Structural thought was the favorite thinking pattern of the Industrial Age. Today, in the Information Age, we have learned that there are other effective systems to manage our lives—but Structural thought is still the standard-bearer of orderliness.

STRUCTURAL THINKING

The key question is:	How can I apply this?
Structural thinking is:	Methodical, conservative, thorough, practical
The Structural mind learns by:	Doing
The Structural mind likes:	Following procedures, planning workable solutions
Predominantly Structural thinkers may:	Appear to lack imagination

When my life feels out of control, I often ask, "What would Miss Faulk do? How would she approach this task? Where would she start?" And the voice inside my head always answers, "Begin with a clean space, Mrs. Browning. It will clear your mind."

The Difference Between Analytical (Blue) and Structural (Green) Thinking

To understand the difference between Analytical and Structural thinking, you have to understand the difference between abstract and concrete thinking. Analytical thinking is abstract thinking. Someone who is highly Analytical has the ideas, but doesn't always know, nor necessarily want to follow, the details to get them implemented. Someone who is highly Structural doesn't think about the big picture. Instead, he will take another's big idea and make it happen. For example, a highly Analytical person wants to know the exact account balance and feels it is important that the checkbook be balanced, but he doesn't want to concern himself with the balancing. A highly Structural person not only wants to know the balance, but also trusts only himself to figure it out.

Walter is a CFO who told me how he and his wife Jennifer balance their checkbook each month. He says they illustrate the difference between Analytical and Structural thinking in how they manage their finances. Walter is a CPA who enjoyed setting up the system. Shortly after getting married, he reviewed the system with Jennifer, who then worked the numbers to make sure they balanced at the end of each month. Her satisfaction is the relief that the job is done and all is in balance for another month. I asked Walter to show me his system, which is as follows:

Procedure for Bank Reconciliations and Financial Understanding

1. Jennifer must balance each bank account and cash management account:
   a. not bank to books
   b. not books to bank
   c. but books to "true" and bank to "true"
   d. not reconciled until "true" equals "true"

2. Make all adjustments in "bank to true" portion of reconciliation as entries in checkbook (e.g., service charges, dividends, interest).

3. Summarize all cash accounts to determine total aggregate cash portion (just do on any bank statement where reconciliations are documented).

   a. This total cash position will be compared to "black book" containing itemized details of cash flows and the aggregate month-end cash position (see steps 4 through 6 below).

4. Use a 12-column ledger book: column #1 (including paychecks, interest/dividends, and other cash) for income, columns #2–11 for expense categories, and column #12 for beginning-of-month and end-of-month "cash numbers."

5. Post each check (and cash withdrawals from ATM) by spreading to appropriate expense column (e.g., food, auto-related, clothes, entertainment, contributions, taxes, household expenses, etc.).

6. Foot each column and then cross-foot column totals to come to an aggregate month-end cash position in lower right corner.

7. Comparison is between "true" in step #1d to lower right-hand number in book (step #6).

8. If step #3 equals step #6, then success (defined as done for another month).

9. If step #3 doesn't equal step #6, then review steps #1 through #7 until errors are found and corrected.

10. Detail and column totals for each expense category in step #5 form the basis for budget planning/goal setting.

SOCIAL THINKING (RED)

I wear my heart on my sleeve.

Social thinking combines intuitive thought with a love of people.

Being extremely Social can be a burden. Those who are dominantly Social suffer from the constant burden of holding so much emotion. They feel things that others don't understand, and—like people who are extremely Conceptual—often have difficulty explaining things they just "know" to be true. The insights of the Social mind are just as valuable as other kinds of thoughts, but translating them to a world that is largely Analytical and Structural can be intimidating, and people with an extremely Social Profile often feel they aren't as intelligent as people whose Profiles are dominated by the other three attributes. Probably no one has ever told them otherwise. Until recently, few teachers or educational institutions validated Social talent. Fortunately, this is changing!

What's the Key Question for the Social Mind?

The Social mind asks: "Who else would enjoy this?" A misconception is that everybody with an extremely Social Profile is animated and extroverted, and that they surround themselves with lots of friends at all times. Some do, but a quietly Social person would be happy sharing an experience with one friend.

> *Margaret is a middle manager at a large corporation. When someone asks her for her opinion in a meeting, she always responds by telling them what she feels and then saying, "the data will follow."*

What Is Social Thinking?

Social thinking is being socially aware and intuitive about people. People with a preference for Social thought in their Profile like to relate and to feel connected. Because they are sensitive, others can find them emotional or "touchy-feely." The Social part of your brain is what makes you empathic and sympathetic—a friend in need. Your Social brain is a team player, and it wants everyone else to be happy. People who are extremely Social are facilitators, willing to listen to everyone and to weigh all solutions equally. They are also in touch with their own emotions, and are introspective and self-aware. Social thinkers feel personally connected to events and ideas, and engage with information through anecdotes and personal information. The Social brain

> I have come to believe over and over again that what is most important to me must be spoken, made verbal, and shared, even at the risk of having it bruised or misunderstood.
>
> **Audre Lorde,** *Sister Outsider*

also is sensitive about environmental changes. If you asked someone with a strongly Social preference to clean up her or his office, chances are she or he would not be able to throw anything away. Half the stuff would have sentimental value, and the other half might be useful someday.

What Is Good about Social Thinking?

People who are very Social thinkers care about the welfare of other people—their self-esteem, their feelings, their personal growth. The Social mind knows how to help disparate people interact with each other.

The Gut Brain

Scientists now know that humans have two brains, one in the head and a second in the intestinal tract. The gut brain, known as the *enteric nervous system*, doesn't look like the brain in your head, and it can be seen only under a microscope, but it plays a major role in human emotions and may be the primary source of "gut intuition."

The gut's brain is located in tissue lining the esophagus, stomach, small intestine, and colon. Just like the brain in your head, it contains neurons and neurotransmitters that zap messages back and forth. The gut brain can learn, maintain a memory, and act independently of the brain in the head, although there is also conversation between the two.

Nearly every substance that helps run and control the brain has turned up in the gut. The neuronal cells of the enteric nervous system produce and respond to more than thirty kinds of neurotransmitters. Until recently, people believed the gut's muscles and nerves were controlled directly by the brain. However, the enteric nervous system has over 100 million neurons—more than the spinal cord. According to Michael Gershon, MD, author of *The Second Brain*, now researchers believe the brain sends signals to a small group of "command neurons" that spread the message throughout the neurons in the gut. Both command neurons and interneurons are spread throughout the gut tissue called the myenteric plexus and the submucosal plexus.

Everyone has an enteric nervous system, but some people rely more on gut instinct than others. Gabrielle, someone with a lot of Social preference in her Profile, is the marketing director of a large university foundation. She always had the possibility of transferring her skills to the private sector, and one day a company offered her such a position. She felt stifled at the university, and the offer was quite attractive. She couldn't make a decision, however, and she eventually came to me for advice. I suggested she spend an hour in quiet contemplation. Then, if she still couldn't decide, she should flip a coin.

Flipping a coin may sound well, flippant, but I assure you it is not. I have used this technique ever since it was recommended to me by Sherry Manning, who holds a PhD in operations research and who wrote a four-hundred-page dissertation on decision making. Sherry said to me, "I know all decisions in the end can be narrowed down to 'yes' or 'no,' and if I flip a coin, my gut tells me if I get the right answer."

Gabrielle thought for an hour and was still undecided, so she took out a coin. If the coin landed heads, she would switch jobs. If it landed tails, she would stay at her present company. She called me the next day and told me the coin came up heads.

"Congratulations on your new position," I said.

"Well not exactly," she answered. "When it came up heads, I felt a little funny. I looked in the mirror, realized I had turned pale, and felt I needed to investigate this matter further. And then I vomited."

When the coin landed heads, the brain in Gabrielle's gut outweighed what the brain in her head was telling her. Gabrielle realized she was not stifled at her current job, but was, rather, upset with her boss. She wanted to stay in the public arena, and just needed to figure out ways to rework her position. Two years later, she is still at the foundation and excelling. She would tell you that listening to her gut was the best decision she ever made.

How Does the Social Mind Solve Problems?

The Social mind doesn't solve problems the way an Analytical or a Structural mind does, but it is expert at using a critical resource: other people. A good first step for this kind of mind is seeking the opinions of others. People who are very Social also rely on visceral or "gut" intuition to guide their choices.

How Does the Social Mind Learn?

People who are dominantly Social are experiential learners, and they like to feel a rapport with others. Because they rely on the opinions of others, it's OK with them if you do the research and just give them the results. If you are trying to teach someone with a very Social Profile, make sure you keep his or her attention, because it will wander away while you aren't looking.

What Are Some of the Drawbacks of Social Thinking?

When the Social brain doesn't feel personally engaged by something, its attention wanders and it gets easily sidetracked. People with an extremely Social Profile can care so much about an issue that they may drive everyone else crazy with concerns no one else has personalized.

Social Thinking at Work

Randy's Emergenetics Profile is extremely Social. The Kenyan Children Foundation, of which I am a board member, is my nonprofit passion. One year I broadcast an e-mail to several business associates inviting them to spend a great deal of money to come with me to Nairobi to perform backbreaking, physical labor building a school for orphaned street children, many of whom are HIV-positive. Part of the deal was to also spend time interacting with the children. Randy answered the call without hesitation, not knowing where he would acquire the money to go. He just had a gut feeling it was the right thing to do, for him and for the kids.

On the first day of our work at an orphanage for physically and mentally challenged children, Randy created a sensation. Within sec-

Does This Sound Like You?

The following statements describe the **Social** brain:

- I like building the self-esteem of people I meet.
- I really care about my coworkers, colleagues, and clients.
- I pick up on the vibrations of people around me.

onds of walking into the schoolyard, this affectionate, sensitive, humorous man drew children to him as if he were a famous celebrity. At first we thought it was his headgear. He was wearing a do-rag emblazoned with a USA flag pattern that made him look like Hulk Hogan. The children were absolutely fascinated. But on the second day he didn't wear the do-rag, and he achieved the same results. As soon as we walked into the schoolyard, hoards of children screaming "Raaaaannnnndy!" flocked to him. This time we thought maybe they were fascinated by his tattoos—they had seen tattoos before, but never on white skin.

> I can intuitively know the solution, but I must present additional ideas in order to show I've done "enough" work. Thinking is the work for me.
>
> Jane Rainwater,
> Graphic Designer

Finally, after several days of Randy creating pandemonium wherever he went, we realized that the children recognized his inner light, his joie de vivre, and his unconditional love for them.

Randy was the catalyst for them and for the sixteen other Americans who traveled with us. If you ever need to assemble and galvanize a group, you want a Randy to be part of it.

SOCIAL THINKING	
The key question is:	How do I feel about this?
Social thinking is:	Personalized, empathic, intuitive
The Social mind learns by:	Being shown, being involved in the process
The Social mind likes:	Team building, taking care of others
Predominantly Social thinkers may:	Be too emotional

CONCEPTUAL THINKING (YELLOW)

I feel like I'm diagonally parked in a parallel universe.

Conceptual thinking combines intuitive thought with a love of abstract ideas.

Perhaps because we live in an Analytical/Structural world, people who use a lot of Conceptual thinking are the most misunderstood. I've never met a person with an extremely Conceptual brain who didn't have an emotional reaction to his or her Profile. I think that even though their goal is to be unique, they are relieved to learn they are "normal" and that there are others like them out there in the world. Sometimes I ponder the possibility of getting them all in one room in order to have a conversation about the uniqueness of their Profiles—but gathering them would be like the proverbial herding of butterflies.

What's the Key Question for the Conceptual Mind?

The Conceptual mind asks: "What's the concept here, and where can I go with it?" This part of your brain immediately grasps essential ideas, and it likes to see where things lead. The goal of the Conceptual mind is to connect the ideas, but only at the cerebral, global level.

What Is Conceptual Thinking?

Conceptual thinking is intuitive about ideas. It is clever, inventive, imaginative, and visionary. The Conceptual mind sees the big picture, and thinks futuristically. People who are predominantly Conceptual thinkers appreciate the aesthetic, are often artistic, and tend to express themselves in diagrams, pictures, and metaphors. The Conceptual mind is energized and intrigued by creativity, innovation, new possibilities, new ideas, and unexpected developments. This part of your brain enjoys the unusual, and likes new techniques and technology. It is theoretical, and likes experiments and chasing options. Conceptual thinkers do not mind digressions. They are independent thinkers, and their thought processes are very individual. If you asked one of them to file a box full of papers, she or he would create a new and unique system. You might come to understand and appreciate it—or you might just be mystified.

> *I have been reflecting on our last session and have to say that for the first time in my life I can see why I am so misunderstood. I had a long conversation with my daughter about my Conceptual brain. I suspect she is an Analytical/Structural thinker. She expressed to me that while she cannot always understand where I am coming from, she always knows it comes from a deep and good place.*
>
> *—P.F.*

What Is Good about Conceptual Thinking?

The Conceptual part of your brain helps you to be an excellent catalyst for change because it allows you to come up with unconventional ideas and enables you to see situations from a different vantage point. People who are strongly Conceptual are terrific at seeing pictures in their mind's eye: the big picture, the global consequences, and the long-term view. They have a special gift for what I call WOW power—Wisdom withOut Words.

How Does the Conceptual Mind Solve Problems?

The Conceptual approach to problem-solving is to take in as much stimulus as possible, mentally explore all the options, and then walk away from the problem until an answer pops up. People describe this as the "aha!" or the "eureka!" effect. People who are strongly Conceptual can be very informal, and often do their best thinking in a casual environment.

> **Grasp the subject, the words will follow.**
>
> Cato

How Does the Conceptual Mind Learn?

The Conceptual part of your brain learns by experimenting, and likes to find things out on its own. It finds details boring, so Conceptual thinkers don't have the patience to read a manual or to stay focused through a two-hour lecture. If you are trying to teach someone who is highly Conceptual, keep things interesting. The worst thing you can do is explain EVERYTHING IN DETAIL.

What Are Some of the Drawbacks of Conceptual Thinking?

Conceptual thinking is not linear, not logical, and not step-by-step. The only thing predictable about Conceptual thinking is its unpredictability. People who have an extremely Conceptual brain may not appreciate what a plan requires for execution or what their suggestions actually would entail. They can be perceived as idiosyncratic, unrealistic, and undisciplined. Sometimes they jump to the wrong conclusions. They are quick to decide whether they are interested in something or not—and if they decide they're not, you've lost them.

Conceptual Thinking at Work

Jim has a highly Conceptual brain. I encountered Jim early in my research when, out of curiosity, he filled out an Emergenetics questionnaire after hearing a coworker describe my seminar. I was dumbfounded when I saw Jim's Profile, not only because of his strong preference toward Conceptual thought, but also because he said he was a computer analyst. In those days, I didn't yet understand that all kinds of Profiles perform all kinds of jobs. I thought a computer analyst should prefer lots of Analytical and Structural thinking, not Conceptual. I decided to investigate. I called Jim and invited him to lunch.

At the restaurant, we sat across from each other in a booth while I went through a basic explanation of his Profile. As I was bringing my remarks to an end, I noticed his head was bowed and large tears were dripping off his cheeks into his chicken Caesar salad. Horrified, I said, "Gosh, Jim, I'm sorry if I've said something to offend you!"

And he replied, "No, no, you don't understand. These are tears of relief. You make me sound normal."

"Well," I laughed, "I'm not certain 'normal' is the right word, and in fact, I'm sure you secretly pride yourself on being unusual. But if you mean that, to a certain degree, we can quantify and explain your quirky thinking, then you can feel relieved."

"Tell me more," he said.

From then on, Jim and I established a relationship that continued to help me understand someone whose primary Thinking Attribute is Conceptual. Whenever something important happened in his life, he would call. His calls always began without the usual introductory fanfare. For example, after our initial meeting, the phone rang and a deep male voice said, "Let's do lunch again."

Does This Sound Like You?

The following statements describe the **Conceptual** brain:

- I see new projects as new opportunities.
- I search for new ways to solve old problems.
- I have a clear vision of where my industry should go.

"Who is this?"

"Jim, from Boulder."

By the time our third lunch rolled around, Jim had decided that being a 75 percent Conceptual thinker was not a good thing (his words, not mine). I did my best to suggest that his Profile represented an incredible gift, and that he should be proud of his abilities. Undaunted, he insisted that he wanted to expand his Analytical thinking, and asked what I recommended.

"Well," I said, "why don't you go back to college and take an advanced math course?"

He folded his arms across his chest and mumbled, "I don't do math."

"You don't do math? How is this possible? You *are* a computer analyst?"

This was the beginning of my learning about what I call Wisdom withOut Words—or WOW—power, an intuition that allows you to know things without knowing *how* you know. Whereas visceral intuition is accompanied by a gut feeling, with WOW power, ideas simply come. It seems that Jim never went to college because he never graduated from high school. He claimed he flunked high school math because while he was able to give the teachers the answers to the questions, he couldn't show how he arrived at the answers. The teachers, who were certain he was cheating, gave him a failing grade on every test.

Eventually I took Jim to a laboratory where a researcher hooked him up to a machine called a "mind mirror" that measured brain wave output. (This was in the days before PET scans.) We then gave Jim complicated statistical formulas to solve, and he did so with alacrity. He could only give the answers, had no idea how he got them, and the mind mirror machine showed brain activity mostly in his right hemisphere.

Later, I read studies that confirmed what happened with Jim. It's a little tough to explain WOW power, but if you have it, you know what I am speaking about. If you don't, you might want to read this section so you can understand your significant others and value their sense of "knowing" even though they can't explain to you how they know what they know. I suspect we all have this gift, but most of us don't pay attention to it, as there is no rational explanation for how it works. I believe we all posses WOW power, but the Conceptual mind taps into it most strongly.

Folks who prefer Conceptual thought tend to have tons of books lying around their spaces, yet one rarely sees them actually reading. That is, they seldom read a book from cover to cover, starting at page one and moving sequentially through the book as we were taught to do in school. Instead, they *grok,* a word coined by Robert A. Heinlein in his book *Stranger in a Strange Land.* Roughly translated, it means to mind-meld, or to learn and comprehend without the usual intellectual steps involved.

So how does this work? I'm not sure, but I suspect that right before they go to bed each night, predominantly Conceptual thinkers run the tips of their fingers over the books and, by some mysterious process of osmosis, information infiltrates their brains during the night. They always seem to know a little bit about a wide range of subjects. While the Analytical and Structural minds prefer to have a narrow but deep knowledge base, the Conceptual and Social minds tend to have a wide but shallow knowledge base. They seem to capture snippets of information and then fill in the blanks.

My friend Carol, a brilliant neuropathologist and former chancellor of the University of Nebraska Medical Center, once gave a lecture on "Bringing Spirit to Leadership." With a subject like that, most of the people in the audience probably had Conceptual and Social Profiles. Carol began by saying, "I went into my library, stood in front of the bookshelves, and said, 'Will the books I need to prepare for this lecture please fall off the shelves?' Of course they did, and they even fell open to the exact pages I needed for this lecture." Most of the audience, also grokkers, chortled—but those who didn't are probably still wondering what kind of drugs she was on at the time.

When I reviewed this story with Carol, hoping to obtain her permission to use it for this book, she had one correction. "Actually, I would describe this as synchronicity through books. That is, the ones I need are always there when I need them. The books I need don't fall off the shelves, they *thrust* themselves at me," she noted.

I wonder about other kids who, like Jim, could be failing in school at this very minute because they can't explain their answers. Increasingly, however, educators are beginning to gather the information they need to understand students like Jim. One principal of a large high school brought me in to demonstrate to his staff the viability of different learning styles. He himself had graduated from college with honors and holds a masters degree, yet has never read a book from cover to cover, and he wanted his teachers to understand that many of their students could also have this gift.

People who are highly Conceptual can make others uncomfortable with their unconventional thinking. The one thing I know for sure about strongly Conceptual minds is that while they appear to love risk, live life on the edge, and make snap decisions, they almost always can creatively get themselves out of any mess they get into. I have learned to trust the extremely Conceptual people in my life who say, "Come on, take a chance. It will work out!" It always does, for them—and in the end, they always take my thinking to a new level.

The Difference Between Social (Red) and Conceptual (Yellow) Thinking

The Social brain prefers to deal with people, while the Conceptual brain does not. People who are highly Social consider how their decisions will affect others before making a choice. A Social person who is very EXPRESSIVE typically enjoys being the life of the party. This individual may send out 200 holiday cards to "nearest and dearest" friends with a short note written in each one. Social people who are *Expressive* still think of others first, but they are much more reserved. They feel no need to outwardly express their thoughts about others. They may send out only a few holiday cards to their best friends, containing long, personalized notes.

> We are an intelligent species and the use of our intelligence quite properly gives us pleasure. In this respect, the brain is like a muscle. When we think well, we feel good.
>
> Carl Sagan, *Broca's Brain*

People frequently assume that Conceptual thinkers enjoy working with people. However, this is not the case. Since Conceptual thought is abstract, a Conceptual brain is drawn to ideas. Thus, Conceptual thinkers do not need people and do not really care whether people are involved or not. One time I asked an extremely Conceptual thinker how she chooses to lead. She replied, "I don't cultivate loyal soldiers. I want them to connect to the values and goals rather than connect to me." To her, dealing with people was a burden she did not need, unless it was for the progression of her goals.

We have done marketing studies asking people how they prefer to take vacations. People with predominantly Social brains usually note that they do not care where they go, as long as it is with a group or with significant others. People with predominantly Conceptual brains often come up with unusual and spectacular trip ideas. These ideas, however, rarely involve the inclusion of others.

DISCOVERING YOUR THINKING PREFERENCES

You've probably already recognized how your brain works. Remember that all of us possess all four Thinking Attributes, so you will probably relate to each one to some degree. To find how much energy you have around each preference, look at the chart on page 53.

Your Thinking Attributes, which you have evaluated in this chapter, are tempered by your Behavioral Attributes. In the next chapter you'll have an opportunity to find out just how Expressive, Assertive, and Flexible you are—and how others see you!

Your Thinking Attributes

Certain words best describe how you prefer to think most of the time. Select all the words below that best describe you. You may select few or many. Select only words that identify your preferences, not necessarily your skills or how others see you. As you circle more words in a certain area, this is a clue that you have a preference in this area. Your choices may reflect more than one Thinking Attribute. Your results provide a visual representation of your Thinking Attributes at a glance.

Analytical

Reasoned	Critical thinker
Intellectual	Investigative
Objective	Inquiring
Questioning	Rational
Follows logical thinking	

Conceptual

Inventive	Unconventional
Original	Innovative
Seeks change	Bored easily
Imaginative	Global
Intuitive about ideas	

Structural

Detailed	Disciplined
Methodical	Predictable
Rule follower	Traditional
Organized	Practical
Follows process	

Social

Sensitive	Empathic
Giving	Supportive
Friendly	Feeling
Compassionate	Caring
Intuitive about people	

How Others See You

The Three Emergenetics Behavioral Attributes

Foster is a tall, likeable-looking scientist who says little. When you meet him, you don't know what he is thinking. You can tell, however, that he is a quiet, mild-mannered individual.

Foster was a participant in one of our excursions to Kenya for the Kenyan Children Foundation. This particular year we were helping to build a school in a slum area outside Nairobi where there was neither indoor plumbing nor running water. It was too far to return to our sleeping quarters for a midday meal, and certainly there were no restaurants to visit for lunch, so we ate in one of the partially finished buildings and washed whatever dirty dishes we collected in a bucket of water that someone toted up from the village.

Each day I assembled a different team, gave them a small amount of money, and challenged them to figure out how to acquire lunch for the rest of us. Every day each team got more creative as they attempted to outdo the lunch from the day before. One team discovered a way to provide a tablecloth. The next day another team acquired a tablecloth and candles. The next day another team served ice cream for dessert. By the time it was Foster's team's turn, we thought every creative idea had been taken. Wrong! Foster's team provided, in addition to candles, tablecloths, and ice cream, after-lunch entertainment. Foster wrote a poem whose lyrics contained a vignette about each person on the trip. As he read it, his team performed a dance behind him. It was hysterical, and we loved it. We also had no idea that Foster, Dr. Senior Scientist and one of the quietest members of our group, was so clever.

> Cherish forever what makes you unique, 'cuz you're a real yawn if it goes.
>
> Bette Midler

After lunch when the rest of us went back to work, Foster excused himself from the afternoon's work schedule. He didn't show up for dinner and was also not ready to work the following morning. That evening, as we were reflecting on the day's events, he apologized to the group for not helping and then explained that the writing and performance of the poem had totally exhausted his inner resources and he had needed some time away from the crowd to regroup. Poetry writing and reading were not part of his everyday life, and while he could muster all of his resources to perform, it left him exhausted afterward.

Foster's preferred Thinking Attributes are Social, Structural, and Conceptual, in that order. You might assume, looking at his Emergenetics Profile, that he'd be right at home performing for a group. But this is where the Behavioral Attributes come into play. Foster is at the reserved end of the spectrum for *Expressiveness,* and providing the lunchtime entertainment was very difficult for him.

The Behavioral Attributes indicate your behaviors in three areas: Expressiveness (your level of participation in social situations); Assertiveness (your interest in controlling results); and Flexibility (your willingness to accommodate others). Your Behavioral Attributes are what people notice about you. They can't see how you think, but they can observe how you behave. In addition, to refine this process even further, the Behavioral Attributes are described along a spectrum.

In chapter 5, you'll find more information about the way the Thinking Attributes and Behavioral Attributes tend to combine. However, I have learned that people are infinitely variable. One of the reasons people enjoy Emergenetics so much is that the attributes can be mixed and matched to accurately describe any individual.

Another Note about Language

One of the themes throughout this book is that there are many ways to be, and none is right or wrong. Every attribute brings valuable assets to any project, so it is important not to promote any negative stereotypes. In my seminars, I always use the words "first-third," "second-third," and "third-third" when describing an individual's Behavioral Attribute in order to avoid using the value-laden words of "low" and "high." For example, describing someone as "first-third Expressive" allows me to avoid using language like "not very Expressive" that makes it sound as if this person is missing something. Similarly, describing someone as "first-third Flexible" allows me to avoid using a word like "inflexible" that has negative connotations. However, terms like "second-third Expressive" take some getting used to, so I have taken some liberties in this book.

As I mentioned earlier, people who are in the first-third of a particular Behavioral Attribute spectrum are described in italics (for example, *Expressive, Assertive,* or *Flexible*), while those who fall in the third-third are described in uppercase letters. When you see the words EXPRESSIVE, ASSERTIVE or FLEXIBLE, you will intuitively understand that this means third-third Assertiveness or Flexibility!

THINKING IN THIRDS

We can place people along a spectrum representing the strength of each Behavioral Attribute. We can divide the strength of behavior into the first-third of the population (0–33% of the population), second-third of the population (34–66%), and third-third of the population (67–100%). For example, if you are in the first-third for Assertiveness, most people are more Assertive than you (the exact amount depends on your score). If you are in the third-third of the population, you are more Assertive than most people.

Your responses to the Emergenetics Questionnaire will place you on a particular point on the spectrum for each Behavioral Attribute. This point illustrates what percentile you are in. If there are 100 people in a room representing the population at large, and you are at the 6th percentile of Flexibility, 5 people will report themselves as less Flexible than you, while 94 will report themselves as more Flexible than you.

Your point on the spectrum is very important in helping you understand how long you prefer to operate in any one mode. Although you are capable of behaving out of character, your behavior generally hovers around the first-third, second-third, or third-third, whichever is the norm for you. Some days, for example, you may be at the 6th percentile point and some days at the 32nd percentile point, but your comfort level is first-third. It's rare that you will jump from the 6th percentile point to the 95th percentile point. If you do, like Foster, you will be exhausted later.

In this book we will mostly discuss the behaviors that are at the first-third and third-third ends of this spectrum. If your scores fall in the second-third percentages, we assume you can adapt to any situation. That is why this is called the "it depends" group.

EXPRESSIVENESS

The opposite of talking isn't listening.
The opposite of talking is waiting.

—FRAN LEBOWITZ

Your degree of Expressiveness indicates the amount of your participation with others and the world around you. Expressiveness is not what you experience inside, but what you share with the outside.

Expressives

We refer to those who fall in the first-third (0–33%) as *Expressives. Expressives* don't waste words, and think before they speak. They are seen as quiet and reserved, and are perceived as less emotional (which may or may not be the case). In fact, *Expressives* are sometimes so quiet that they may not realize other people cannot readily understand what they are thinking. *Expressives* tend to avoid participating in large group situations, and can appear thoughtful and shy. *Expressives* usually enjoy working with things more than people. They hope they won't be singled out in group situa-

> *Judy, who is EXPRESSIVE, went on a meditative retreat that required her to be in solitude for two days. "It was wonderful," Judy told me, "and when I got back, I phoned everyone I knew to tell them what it was like to be in solitude for so long!"*

Does This Sound Like You?

The following statements describe the *Expressive* individual:

- I keep my feelings to myself.
- In a meeting, I listen more than I talk.

The following statements describe the EXPRESSIVE individual:

- I enjoy being admired by others.
- I am happy to share information about myself.

tions, and are less dependent on others for their own amusement. If they must spend prolonged periods of time with people, they will eventually need to retreat to privacy.

EXPRESSIVES

Folks who are more outgoing and animated than others are EXPRESSIVES and score on the third-third of the scale (67–100%). In general, EXPRESSIVES openly communicate affection for others, easily start conversations with strangers, and are comfortable attracting attention to themselves. They learn by talking, and are energized by interacting with others. EXPRESSIVES are excellent at getting things going, although they need to be careful about being overbearing. They can be quiet, but if they engage in long periods of quiet time, they need to be reenergized by others.

Expressiveness

MY THOUGHTS ARE MY BUSINESS	I CAN'T WAIT TO TELL EVERYONE!
Tell a friend	Tell the world
Quiet, reserved	Gregarious, performer
Pensive	Spontaneous
Energized by solitude	Energized by people
Facial expressions are stoic	Facial expressions are animated

Expressiveness at Work

My colleague Wendell and I have been doing business together for many years. We are at opposite ends of the Expressiveness spectrum. Wendell is *Expressive,* while I am EXPRESSIVE. We live in different cities, and meet about two times a year, typically for three days at a time. At the end of our meetings, I am usually exhausted. Why? Because Wendell never talks and I feel like I have to start every conversation. I ask him a question, and then we can begin an exchange of ideas. When we have finished addressing one topic, I have to ask another question for the conversation to continue.

If you ask Wendell how he feels after our meetings, he will also tell you he is exhausted because he has to answer my barrage of questions. After I drop him off at the airport, he gets on the plane loaded down with reading material, a laptop, and earplugs so he doesn't have to talk to the person sitting next to him. He says it takes two days to reenergize himself after one of our sessions.

> **"Do you think before you speak?"**
>
> **"No, I like to hear it at the same time as everyone else."**
>
> From the TV show *Becker*

One time I asked him how he processes information when we are together. He said, "When you ask me a question, I put it into my mental elevator. The question goes down to my solar plexus region and searches for an answer. Usually I am cogitating about the answer when you ask *another* question, which starts the whole process over again. The constant movement of this elevator causes me to be fatigued at the end of our meetings."

Even though we have our differences in Expressiveness, Wendell and I work very well together as long as I understand that when I ask him a question, I have to wait for his Expressiveness to kick in. When I get a response, it is brilliant and well thought out. And Wendell has to understand that when I am articulating my thoughts, it is my way of "thinking out loud."

EXPRESSIVENESS	
The key question is:	How much emotion do I show toward others and the world around me?
Expressives learn by:	Being alone
EXPRESSIVES learn by:	Talking with others
Expressives like:	Thinking before they speak
EXPRESSIVES like:	Sparking the conversation
Expressives may:	Not realize people do not understand what they are thinking
EXPRESSIVES may:	Be too overbearing

ASSERTIVENESS

*Have you ever noticed anybody going slower than you is
an idiot, and anyone going faster than you is a
maniac?*

—GEORGE CARLIN

Your degree of Assertiveness reflects the amount of energy you invest in expressing thoughts, feelings, and beliefs. Assertiveness is about your control regarding tasks.

Assertives

People who fall in the first-third (0–33%) are *Assertives,* and may be viewed as peacemakers. They are genial, easygoing, and supportive. They are often inclined to go along with decisions, and do not voluntarily express their opinions.

They are not necessarily passive, but they don't put a great deal of energy into sharing their ideas and in fact can get lost in the crowd. *Assertives* learn by listening and reflecting.

A seminar attendee once called and spoke with my assistant Karen, and proclaimed that she did not think she was as ASSERTIVE as her Profile stated. She said, "At Geil's seminar, she said an ASSERTIVE person constantly hits the elevator button, thinking it will arrive faster. Well, that is absurd. I only hit the button once, because I know it won't come any faster."

"Okay," Karen said, "Where do you position yourself during the ride?"

"Oh, that's easy," she said, "I stand right in front of the doors, so the second they open, I can be the first one off the elevator and on my way as quickly as possible!"

ASSERTIVES

ASSERTIVES are the third-third of the population (67–100%) at the other end of the spectrum. They try to convince other people of their point of view and are competitive, driving, and "telling." ASSERTIVES learn by debating. They don't mind handling uncertain situations, and enjoy being direct, confrontational, challenging, and in charge.

Stress has a significant influence on Assertiveness. Under extreme stress, some people drop exceptionally low on the Assertiveness scale while others go exceptionally high. However, everyone has a comfortable range of assertiveness, which can be recognized in everyday interactions.

Assertiveness

**NO NEED TO
GET EXCITED**
Keep the status quo
Amiable
Peacekeepers
Complete tasks at own pace
Voice usually remains even-toned

**LET'S GET THIS
DONE NOW!**
Set a goal
Competitive
Hard charging
Complete tasks at all costs
Voice often becomes louder

Assertiveness at Work

Assertiveness is clearly seen on the Interstate highways. When an *Assertive* gets caught in a traffic jam, he is tolerant and patient. He realizes there is little he can do. He will put in a CD, listen to the news, or quietly reflect on the day's events. An ASSERTIVE considers a traffic jam as war. Whoever gets to his destination first is the victor. He will shift lanes, cut off other drivers, and prematurely exit the highway in attempts to find a quicker route.

Tom and Bill ride together to work. One day when they arrived at my seminar, Tom was as white as a ghost, but said nothing.

"What's wrong?" I asked Tom, an *Assertive* who exhibits vehicular patience.

"Bill crossed the solid white line while merging onto the highway," Tom answered in a monotone. "He boxed in the driver in front of us, prevented him from merging, ran him off the road, and nearly got him killed."

Does This Sound Like You?

The following statements describe the *Assertive* individual:

- I will go to almost any lengths to avoid confrontation.
- I am easygoing.

The following statements describe the ASSERTIVE individual:

- I voice my opinions and concerns willingly.
- I prefer a fast pace.

Bill, an ASSERTIVE with several speeding tickets on his record, replied rather loudly, "That guy was fine! If I hadn't crossed the white line, I would have missed the opportunity to run the yellow light at the exit, which would have caused us to be two minutes late."

Although Tom was horrified by his brush with death, he showed little animation describing this event. Bill, on the other hand, raised his voice, gestured with his hands, and wanted me to understand that he had made the best possible judgment call.

Why do Tom and Bill continue to ride to work together? Bill doesn't mind Tom because Tom doesn't criticize his driving, whether he approves of it or not. Tom, having agreed to carpool with Bill, doesn't want to make waves by backing out, so he continues to suffer in silence.

ASSERTIVENESS

The key question is:	How much energy do I invest in expressing thoughts, feelings, and beliefs?
Assertives learn by:	Reflecting
ASSERTIVES learn by:	Debating
Assertives like:	Supporting
ASSERTIVES like:	Plowing ahead
Assertives may:	Get lost in the crowd
ASSERTIVES may:	Appear too competitive

FLEXIBILITY

Plan to be spontaneous tomorrow.

Your degree of Flexibility measures your willingness to accommodate the thoughts and actions of others. Flexibility is a measurement of your willingness to create an environment that encourages others to become comfortable. People who are comfortable are more inclined to communicate information about important ideas. Flexibility involves a broad range of interpersonal skills because it requires you to anticipate the needs of others.

Flexibles

People who fall within the first-third (0–33%) are *Flexibles.* They may prefer and learn best in defined situations. *Flexibles* are focused, have strong opinions, and have a strong agenda. Because they are not known for being willing to change their mind, *Flexibles* may be perceived as stubborn.

FLEXIBLES

FLEXIBLES are those who fall within the third-third (67–100%). They are typically easy to get along with, remain cheerful and even tempered in most situations, and are patient with difficult people. A FLEXIBLE person is usually open to suggestions from others. This makes them pleasant to work with, but FLEXIBLES do need to be careful about appearing too bland.

Sally is in the first-third of Flexibility, with Analytical and Structural thinking. She has worked with me since the beginning of my company. During the early days, we used to score Profiles by hand. I never knew her to make a mistake.

When we wrote a new computer program that automatically scored Profiles, Sally had a hard time moving into this new technology. She prided herself on her ability to score those Profiles perfectly and as fast as any computer. She saw no need to be "replaced by a machine." But as she became more familiar with the program, she began to appreciate the fact that she could focus her attention on other tasks.

One day the computers went down and Sally had to go back to scoring Profiles individually. I knew we had turned a corner when she asked how soon the computers would be up and running again!

Many people think having lots of Flexibility is the optimum behavior. However, when working in teams, it isn't efficient to have a room full of FLEXIBLES, since everyone will be happy to accommodate each other and nothing will get done. Having all behaviors represented is important for productivity.

When they are forced to change, *Flexibles* need time to assess new procedures and ideas. People with more Flexibility need to understand that this process can't be hurried. Keep in mind that once they are on board with a new idea, *Flexibles* will be your best ally!

People who are FLEXIBLE often have difficulty with time management and closing in on decisions. FLEXIBLES would rather think about the different options and wait to make a decision. There are so many great choices that they prefer to ponder and leave them all

> The difference between perseverance and obstinacy is that one often comes from a strong will, and the other from a strong won't.
>
> **Henry Ward Beecher**

open. This can be extremely frustrating for those who are *Flexible* and need a decision immediately.

Flexibility

IT'S MY WAY OR THE HIGHWAY!	YOU CAN DO WHAT YOU WANT
Prefer defined situations	Don't mind ambiguity
Have strong opinions	See all points of view
Prefer being in control of others	Put needs of others first
Have a strong agenda	Don't mind interruptions
Stay on track	Open to suggestion

Flexibility at Work

John and his son Devon run a boutique financial consulting firm and hired me to help with their business relationship. John was FLEXIBLE, while Devon was *Flexible.* John's plan was to retire within five years and hand over the business to Devon. Devon was frustrated because he felt the succession plan was not running smoothly. Even though they thought alike and shared a common vision for the business, they had problems realizing their goals because of the flexibility factor.

The three of us sat down to air concerns and work toward a solution. Devon noted there were several office management decisions that needed attention, but he could not make decisions without John's approval.

"Whenever I need John's authorization on a business decision, I can't seem to get his attention long enough to talk it through," Devon said. "So then I make an informal lunch appoint-

Does This Sound Like You?

The following statements describe the *Flexible* individual:

- I work until I believe the job is done perfectly.
- I know I'm right.

The following statements describe the FLEXIBLE individual:

- I don't mind changes and transitions.
- I communicate well with diverse coworkers, colleagues, and clients.

ment, but he always cancels or is late due to a client 'crisis' that requires his immediate action."

John looked puzzled and said, "We talk all the time in the hall outside your office or on the way to the garage at night. You are just not listening. Furthermore, our clients are the most important part of our business, and I must take care of them first."

John's FLEXIBLE nature is such that he is always trying to squeeze as much as possible into his day. Because Devon is *Flexible,* he required John's full attention when discussing the business, and conversations on the run were not sufficient. Devon needed to understand John's FLEXIBLE makeup and communicate his own needs more emphatically.

Be patient, I'm processing.

Ian, a *Flexible,* in the middle of a heated exchange with her boss, a FLEXIBLE

John was more than happy to give Devon his full attention, but he assumed that Devon was FLEXIBLE like him, and that the quick conversations were sufficient. John had to realize that his FLEXIBLE nature made him hard to pin down, and that he cannot always sacrifice his coworkers' needs for those of the client.

I suggested that Devon and John meet at the same time, once a week, in their conference room where they could be free from distractions. Furthermore, their staff had to know the importance of these meetings and never interrupt them during this time. Finally, John had to solidify the appointment by scheduling it in his PDA and vowing to be on time to every meeting for the rest of the year. John was able to harness his FLEXIBILITY, and Devon was at ease because the office decisions received the attention they required.

FLEXIBILITY

The key question is:	How much am I willing to conform and flex with the interpersonal needs of others?
Flexibles learn by:	Defined situations
FLEXIBLES learn by:	Accepting all ideas
Flexibles like:	Focusing
FLEXIBLES like:	Handling ambiguous situations
Flexibles may:	Appear stubborn
FLEXIBLES may:	Appear too wishy-washy

DISCOVERING YOUR BEHAVIORAL PREFERENCES

Below you'll find an easy way to estimate your Behavioral Attributes at a glance. They can be mixed and matched to describe anyone and everyone. Behavioral preferences are combined with each other and with Thinking preferences to create an infinitely variable rainbow of individual Profiles. Your Emergenetics Profile results are uniquely yours, just like your fingerprints, and are the key to self-awareness and success.

> The only normal people are the ones you don't know very well.
>
> Joe Ancis

Your Behavioral Attributes

Certain words best describe how you prefer to behave most of the time. Select all words below that best describe you. You may select few or many. Select only words that identify your preferences, not necessarily your skills or how others see you. As you circle more words in a particular area, this is a clue that you have a preference in this area. If you select an equal number of words from the left (first-third) and right (third-third) ends of a spectrum, you probably fall in the "it depends" group in the middle. Your results provide a visual representation of your Behavioral Attributes at a glance.

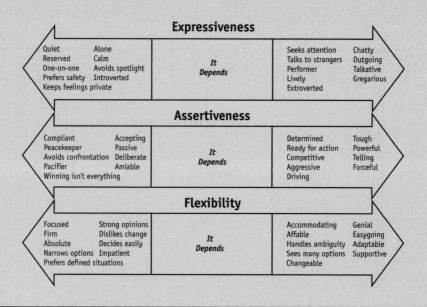

Expressiveness

Quiet	Alone	*It Depends*	Seeks attention	Chatty
Reserved	Calm		Talks to strangers	Outgoing
One-on-one	Avoids spotlight		Performer	Talkative
Prefers safety	Introverted		Lively	Gregarious
Keeps feelings private			Extroverted	

Assertiveness

Compliant	Accepting	*It Depends*	Determined	Tough
Peacekeeper	Passive		Ready for action	Powerful
Avoids confrontation	Deliberate		Competitive	Telling
Pacifier	Amiable		Aggressive	Forceful
Winning isn't everything			Driving	

Flexibility

Focused	Strong opinions	*It Depends*	Accommodating	Genial
Firm	Dislikes change		Affable	Easygoing
Absolute	Decides easily		Handles ambiguity	Adaptable
Narrows options	Impatient		Sees many options	Supportive
Prefers defined situations			Changeable	

5

Putting It All Together

The Complete Guide to Emergenetics Profiles

As you have already seen, different people combine different aspects and degrees of the seven Emergenetics Attributes. Most of us use more than one Attribute, depending on the situation before us.

The Emergenetics Profile graphically illustrates each individual's unique combination of Thinking and Behavioral Attributes and makes their strengths instantly understandable. This chapter explains Emergenetics Profiles, outlines the basic combinations of Thinking Attributes, explains the different possible combinations of Behavioral Attributes, shows interesting Profiles of real people, and ends with a lighthearted quiz to see how comfortable you have become with Emergenetics concepts.

THE EMERGENETICS PROFILE

The Emergenetics Profile contains three important parts:

1. A pie chart colored in blue, green, red, and yellow illustrates how your Thinking preferences compare to each other. Your pie chart reflects, in percentages, the extent to which you rely on Analytical, Structural, Social, and Conceptual thought. Our data analysis concluded that any percentages 23 percent or greater indicated a preference in that attribute.
2. Bar charts in blue, green, red, and yellow show your Thinking preferences in percentiles. These bar charts show how your answers compare to those of the population at large for your gender.
3. Bar charts in purple illustrate your Behavioral Attributes in percentiles as compared to the population at large for your gender.

Emergenetics Associate Peter McLaughlin compares preferences to boiling water. Generally water boils at 212°F, just as an Emergenetics preference starts at 23 percent. At 211°F, water is simmering, just as at 22 percent a preference has not fully declared itself.

Here is a real Emergenetics Profile for Barbara, an owner of a construction company, whose Thinking percentages are:

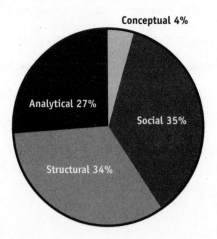

This pie chart helps clarify Barbara's strengths in relation to one another. For example, it's clear that she prefers to think Analytically, Socially, and Structurally, while Conceptual thinking is her least-preferred Attribute.

Next are bar charts for Barbara's Thinking Percentiles. Based on data from over 250,000 completed Profiles, these percentiles show how Barbara compares to the general population of women. When you complete an Emergenetics Profile, it is statistically normed against the entire population by gender to produce the Thinking percentiles. In Barbara's case, her results look like this:

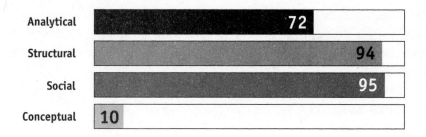

What do these bars mean? When it comes to Conceptual thinking, Barbara scores at the 10th percentile of all women. That means in a room full of 100 women, who perfectly represent the population of women at large, 90 of them prefer Conceptual thinking more than Barbara does. At the same time, she prefers Analytical thinking more than 71 of them, Social thinking more than 94 of them, and Structural thinking more than 93 of them.

Finally, there are the bar charts for Barbara's Behavioral percentiles. Barbara is in the 45th percentile of women in Expressiveness, the 95th percentile of women in Assertiveness, and the 5th percentile of women in Flexibility. Her percentiles looks like this:

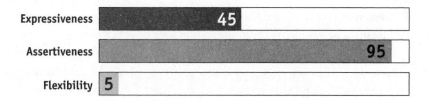

Looking at Barbara's complete Emergenetics Profile, you can predict a number of things. Since she has a tri-modal brain (with three Thinking preferences over 23%), she tends to ruminate about things longer than some people because she has to process information from three points of view. Since Structural thinking is one of her favorite Thinking Attributes and Conceptual is one of her least, you can safely assume she likes to go by the book. Her Social thinking helps her be friendly with customers, but her Assertiveness and Flexibility scores denote an unrelenting style that intimidates her counterparts during negotiations.

MIXING AND MATCHING THE THINKING ATTRIBUTES

People are endlessly complex and fascinating. They become a little less mystifying when you are able to view them in terms of their Thinking Attributes. The basic combinations of Thinking Attributes can be broken down into four categories:

1. Uni-modal,
2. Bi-modal,
3. Tri-modal (sometimes called multimodal), and
4. Quadra-modal.

Our studies have shown that 5 percent of the population is uni-modal, meaning they prefer to think in only one Thinking Attribute (Analytical—1%, Structural—2%, Social—1%, Conceptual—1%). For these people, you can assume they think along the same categorical lines as discussed in chapter 3. The other 95 percent of the population fall within one of the eleven combinations of thinking preferences explained below.

We have asked hundreds of people to describe themselves and their work. We have synthesized their statements and written summaries for each combination.

Please remember that a Profile represents how people would describe themselves. Having a preference for certain types of jobs does not mean they actually have the skills to do these tasks. However, a preference for these tasks may help them, as it is easier to do work you enjoy. It would be easy to tell you which types of occupations fit in each category, but I avoid doing this because I don't want to stereotype. All kinds of people can be successful at all kinds of work. Just remember, if someone has a Social/Conceptual brain and works in an occupation that is generally considered Analytical/Structural, she or he will do the work differently from other people and might be weary at the end of the day.

Bi-Modals

Bi-modals possess two Thinking preferences. These two preferences may come from the same half of the brain, or they may be diametrically opposite.

The combinations of attributes from the *same half* of the brain are:

- Symmetrical thinking, or Analytical/Structural
- Asymmetrical thinking, or Social/Conceptual
- Abstract thinking, or Analytical/Conceptual
- Concrete thinking, or Structural/Social

The combinations of attributes that are *diametrically opposite* are:

- Analytical/Social
- Structural/Conceptual

Analytical (Blue) and Structural (Green)
"Make a plan and follow it."

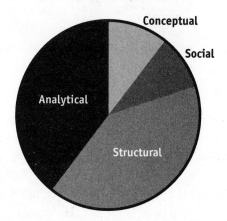

The Analytical/Structural combination is found in 17 percent of the population at large. This is the most prevalent Profile in our database. These kinds of thinkers dive instead of skim the surface. They prefer to study a subject in depth and look at learning vertically, from a deep, narrowly focused point of view. Because their Profile favors symmetrical thinking, they like math, enjoy guidelines, are clear thinkers, are predictable and methodical, are cautious of new ideas, and approach problems logically. They describe their work as organized, technical, detailed, efficient, results-oriented, and structured. They usually enjoy financial analysis, projects that have parameters, and making continuous progress in established processes.

Because Social and Conceptual thinking are their least preferred attributes, people with this Profile see teamwork as a means to accomplish work, rather than a means of socializing with others. They understand that business is not personal, and run the risk of being perceived as cold. Their idea of looking into the future means setting goals that are attainable within three years.

Social (Red) and Conceptual (Yellow)
"Let's create this together."

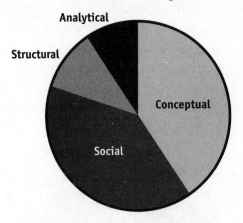

The Social/Conceptual Profile is found in 12 percent of the population at large. People with this Profile prefer to learn from many viewpoints, and intuitively explore subjects without background information. Because their Profile favors asymmetrical thinking, they know what is happening without opening a book. They describe themselves as imaginative, intuitive about ideas and people, visionary, socially aware, and empathic. They like to learn by experimenting and interacting with others. People with this Profile say their work usually involves sharing, connecting with others, making new products, developing theoretical concepts, doing projects that involve finding relationships between different items, gathering information from different sources and putting it into another form, finding new solutions to a problem, and using details in a creative way. They are good at seeing what is coming before others do.

People with this Profile may experience a conflict between their desire to be liked and to make everyone happy, and their desire to do what needs to be done to implement their vision. Because their thinking is intuitive, they may feel out of step with other people in their organization, which is difficult for them because they are so Social. They also run the risk of being perceived as space cadets. They do not typically enjoy processes or number-crunching, so once they have an idea, they need to team up with someone who is Analytical/ Structural or their great ideas can be lost.

Analytical (Blue) and Conceptual (Yellow)
"I see the forest."

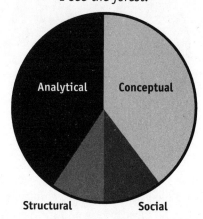

Analytical

Conceptual

Structural

Social

The Analytical/Conceptual Profile makes up 11 percent of the population. People with this Profile see the forest instead of the individual trees. They excel at abstract thinking, although their Analytical thinking (logical, analytical, clear) argues with the Conceptual part of their brain (imaginative, visionary, and intuitive). Their work involves big-picture thinking that is grounded with facts. Since the Analytical attribute can translate to the outside Analytical world what the Conceptual attribute is thinking, this can be a powerful thinking style.

People who are both Analytical and Conceptual can run into trouble balancing both kinds of thinking simultaneously. They are very good at grasping the vision of a company, but can get mired in the details of implementing it. People with this Profile also can have a difficult time relating to other employees. More often than not, they believe they are "smarter" than the average person. Others tend to agree and may find them intimidating. After one of my associates offered this description to an audience at a seminar, several people from the audience with Analytical/Conceptual Profiles came to him and said, "We take umbrage at your statement. We do not *think* we are smarter than most people, we *know* we are!"

Structural (Green) and Social (Red)
*"I'd love to share the experience with you,
but please make an appointment first."*

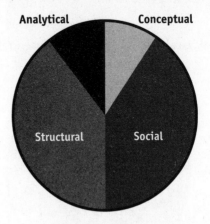

The Structural/Social Profile makes up 11 percent of the population at large. People with this Profile excel at concrete thinking. They like guidelines and structure, but can also be sympathetic and fun-loving, so sometimes their Structural and Social Attributes are in conflict with each other. They take pleasure in getting the task accomplished while simultaneously working with other people, and enjoy helping others develop their skills. They are very effective at organizing and planning, meeting due dates with high-quality results, letting you know what is expected while successfully collaborating with and coaching other teammates, and making sure clients and business partners are satisfied.

While the Analytical/Conceptual thinker can see the forest, the Structural/Social thinker likes to count the trees. People with this Profile run the risk of being unable to see the big picture, and also can be hindered by their avoidance of technical issues. Because of their Social thinking, they can worry about the impact of certain decisions on other people. They also may focus on how other people are doing their work, which may be perceived as micromanaging them. Because of their Structural thinking, they have a tendency to first turn to solutions that have worked in the past instead of trying to come up with something new and different.

Analytical (Blue) and Social (Red)
"An informed head with a warm heart."

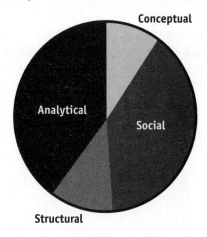

The Analytical/Social Profile represents 6 percent of the population. People with this Profile often appear competent and friendly. However, what you see is not always what you get. Their Social, fun-loving, devil-may-care aspect may suddenly be usurped by their Analytical, critical preference, and they will ask the most exacting questions. People with this Profile may find themselves in the awkward situation of working alongside highly Analytical colleagues who don't have a Social preference and who don't mind being solitary. In this case, they will feel lonely because they don't have anyone to talk to.

Structural (Green) and Conceptual (Yellow)
"Nailing Jell-O to the wall."

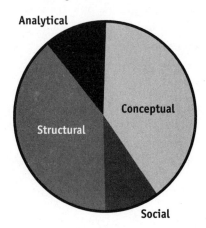

The Structural/Conceptual thinker represents less than 2 percent of the population. People with this Profile have an inner tennis game going on all the time. When the ball is in its court, the Structural part of their brain wants to clean its desk. When the Conceptual part has the ball, it wants to fly a kite. Since the Structural and Conceptual Thinking Attributes are diametrically opposed to each other, the Conceptual attribute can come up with great ideas, but the Structural attribute will dismiss them just as quickly. However, when individuals with this Profile harness both aspects, they are powerful because their Conceptual preference can create, imagine, and look into the future, while their Structural preference can sort out the crazy or weird ideas and implement the plan.

People with this Profile can encounter great difficulty in choosing a profession. They cannot decide whether they want to be a bookkeeper or a dolphin trainer.

Tri-modals

The Tri-modal Profile combines three Thinking Attributes. The gift of a Tri-modal thinker is the ability to empathize with other ways of thinking. People with this Profile can be catalysts in a group and help promote understanding among the team members. One of my associates was once called a "universal donor" because of her ability to relate to different thinking styles. The stress of this Profile, however, comes from being a Jack of all trades, but master of none.

Tri-modals are not always able to sort out their thoughts or feelings about an issue, since to them all sides of the issue makes sense. Tri-modals often tell us that making a decision is difficult. As one Tri-modal explained, "My brain needs to weigh all sides of the question. It's like the committee has to meet, and sometimes the committee fights with itself." This tends to cause the Tri-modal thinker to take a longer time in arriving at a decision than a Bi-modal or Uni-modal thinker.

Tri-modals fall into two categories:

1. "Tri-left" thinkers have two Thinking Attributes from the "left brain." They combine symmetrical thinking from the Analytical and Structural preferences with either Conceptual or Social thinking.
2. "Tri-right" thinkers have two Thinking Attributes from the "right brain." They combine asymmetrical thinking from the Social and Conceptual preferences with either Analytical or Structural thinking.

Tri-Lefts

Analytical (Blue), Structural (Green), and Social (Red)
"Efficiency with feeling."

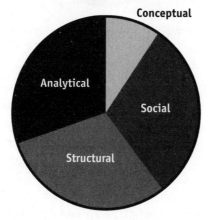

The Analytical/Structural/Social Profile represents 13 percent of the population. People with this Profile think before they act or speak, let you know what is to be expected, and tell you in a sympathetic manner.

Because their thinking is so symmetrical and concrete, people with this Profile do not view new work as opportunity and may create an environment that stifles innovation. They already have a proven way of doing things, so why change it?

Analytical (Blue), Structural (Green), and Conceptual (Yellow)
"Ideas are for doing."

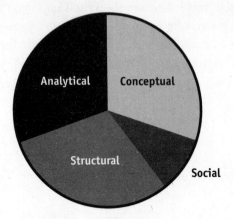

The Analytical/Structural/Conceptual Profile represents 5 percent of the population. People with this Profile are able to use their abstract preferences (Analytical and Conceptual) to invent ideas, and then use their Structural thinking preference to make a project work. Individuals with this Profile do not have a Social preference. While they are busy creating and following through on ideas, they have a difficult time relating to people. They are at risk of neglecting or even warding off others along the way.

Tri-Rights

Analytical (Blue), Social (Red), and Conceptual (Yellow)
"What do you think of this global idea?"

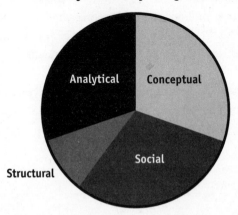

The Analytical/Social/Conceptual Profile represents 13 percent of the population. People with this Profile combine very asymmetrical thinking with abstract, Analytical thinking. They are great at listening to others empathically, while reasoning out new solutions to move their company into the far future.

Because Structural thinking is not their favorite, people with this Profile tend to do many things, all at the same time, and never really feel organized. They can confuse and annoy team members who prefer to work in a more organized environment.

Structural (Green), Social (Red), and Conceptual (Yellow)
"Creative thinking with controlled emotions."

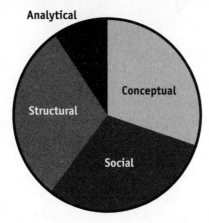

The Structural/Social/Conceptual Profile represents 4 percent of the population. People with this Profile combine asymmetrical thinking with concrete, Structural thinking. They can inspire people and put together a process to see that the inspiration is completed.

This Profile does not prefer Analytical thinking. It does not like contemplating technical issues or engaging in critical thought. In a meeting, people with this Profile can be confusing because one minute they are brainstorming, and the next minute they are putting on the brakes.

Quadra-modal

The Quadra-Modal Profile makes up just 1 percent of the population. All the Thinking preferences are nearly even. People with this Profile tend to be either

Quadra-modal (Blue, Green, Red, Yellow)
"Fair and balanced."

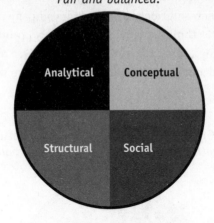

very successful or very bland. When they are successful, they have learned to relate to all kinds of minds while still being able to make firm decisions. When they are bland, it is because they don't have any strong tendencies in any particular direction, tend to second-guess decisions, and can appear wimpy.

These people tend to communicate very well with others (depending on their Behavioral Attributes) since they can relate to how others think. The challenge for people of this Profile is that they do not stand out from the crowd. If you have this Profile, you will probably rise in your organization quickly (assuming you are competent) because you have been able to take on many kinds of jobs. However, after rising your career may stagnate because you have not become expert in any one area.

MIXING AND MATCHING THE BEHAVIORAL ATTRIBUTES

As you saw in chapter 4, there are three Behavioral Attributes: Expressiveness, Assertiveness, and Flexibility. These Attributes influence our outward dispositions toward each other. Your degree of preference for each Behavioral Attribute is expressed as a first-third, second-third, or third-third percentile.

Of the population at large, 35 percent report that they are a uniform combination of either all first-third behaviors, all second-third behaviors, or all third-third behaviors. The remaining 65 percent of the population report different thirds for each behavior. It would take a very long time to describe every possible combination of all the possible percentiles of every Behavioral Attribute. The task becomes a lot simpler if we narrow the choices to one end of each spectrum or the other. In this section I will discuss seven combinations, six of which highlight the differences between the first-third and third-third behaviors (people in the second-third [the "it depends" group] can go either way).

1. *Expressive, Assertive,* and *Flexible*
2. EXPRESSIVE, *Assertive,* and *Flexible*
3. *Expressive,* ASSERTIVE, and *Flexible*
4. *Expressive, Assertive,* and FLEXIBLE
5. EXPRESSIVE, ASSERTIVE, and *Flexible*
6. EXPRESSIVE, ASSERTIVE, and FLEXIBLE
7. The "it depends" group

My associate Chris Cox illustrates these differences with a scenario. Imagine that you are among a group of coworkers who each have different Behavioral Attributes, and you are all trying to decide where to have lunch. The initial idea is for Italian food at Strings, but another option is Chinese food at the South Garden instead.

1. *Expressive, Assertive,* and *Flexible*

This person does not feel like eating Italian food, but will give no outward indication of this. She is very concerned about not making waves, and will go out of her way to keep the peace. She may end up going to Strings to be with the group, but she will order very little from the menu. She still very much wants to go to the South Garden. She may make an excuse about why she cannot go to lunch and will end up ordering take-out. In either case, she will do her best to not draw any attention to herself or cause a disruption among the group.

2. EXPRESSIVE, *Assertive,* and *Flexible*

Expressiveness	
Assertiveness	
Flexibility	

Like the person above, this person desperately wants Chinese food but doesn't want to make waves. However, since he is EXPRESSIVE, he feels the need to give some insight into his preferences. Therefore he will offer several, subtle clues to try to politely sway the group. He may ask, "Has anyone read the latest negative review on Strings?" or "That drive will take at least thirty minutes—are we sure that we can get back in time?" Each question is offered in hopes that a group member will pick up the message that he doesn't want Italian. In the end will he go to lunch with the group? Of course. The appeal of conversation with the crowd will make up for the meal.

3. *Expressive,* ASSERTIVE, and *Flexible*

Expressiveness	
Assertiveness	
Flexibility	

This person has no problem being direct with the other members of the group, but will not go to great lengths to do so. She will firmly make the point that she wants Chinese food, and then remain silent. She is a person of very few words, but she usually will get her way. You would never want a person with these Behavioral Attributes to drive to Strings, because she will probably end up driving to the South Garden instead, and the group will have no idea what happened until lunch is over and everyone is back at work!

4. *Expressive, Assertive,* and FLEXIBLE

Expressiveness	
Assertiveness	
Flexibility	

This person will give no outward sign that he does not want Italian food and will go along with the group decision. The problem is, he still wants Chinese food. After the final decision to get Italian food has been made, he is thinking of different ways to get Chinese food in the immediate future. Maybe he can swing by the South Garden for dinner.

5. EXPRESSIVE, ASSERTIVE, and *Flexible*

Expressiveness	
Assertiveness	
Flexibility	

This person can and will dominate the entire decision-making process. She wants Chinese food and will let the group know this fact. She will start from the beginning of the conversation and repeat her desires until someone agrees with her. This type of behavior can often be seen as bullying, because she will say things like, "You will go to South Garden if you want this group to be together."

6. EXPRESSIVE, ASSERTIVE, and FLEXIBLE

Expressiveness	
Assertiveness	
Flexibility	

This person will dominate the decision-making conversation, but is willing to defer to group consensus. If you have two of these people in the group, the lunch conversation could go on for twenty minutes, as each will give his comprehensive list as to the pros and cons of each restaurant. They don't really care which one is chosen, but while at Strings, they will feel compelled to give their observations of the restaurant and how it compares to the other suggested restaurants.

7. The "It Depends" Group

Expressiveness	
Assertiveness	
Flexibility	

People in the second-thirds of Expressiveness, Assertiveness, and Flexibility (the "it depends" group) can swing to either the first-third or third-third of each Behavioral Attribute, depending on the scenario. Their decision may be swayed by their overall desire for Chinese food, or by the arguments promoted by the people involved in the decision.

MIXING AND MATCHING THE THINKING ATTRIBUTES WITH THE BEHAVIORAL ATTRIBUTES

I never get tired of looking at Emergenetics Profiles. The different combinations of percentages are endlessly variable and, like fingerprints for the brain, are as unique as the individuals they represent. This enormous flexibility is one of the great advantages of Emergenetics. No one is forced into a "canned" Profile, and each Profile is generated separately.

I'd be happy to discuss all the permutations of Thinking and Behavioral Attributes from here until the next millennium, but the level of detail would make your eyes glaze over. My objective in this chapter is to give you enough information to understand yourself and other people in terms of the seven Attributes. The more you use Emergenetics concepts in your daily life, the more you will begin to see the subtleties.

How the Thinking and Behavioral Attributes
Relate to One Another

Are the seven Attributes linked to one another? You'll remember that when we first began developing the Emergenetics Profile, it was assumed that certain kinds of thinking and behavior naturally went together. Emergenetics has shown that this is not the case.

Actually, it makes me happy that the Thinking and Behavioral Attributes are, in general, so independent of each other. This means the Emergenetics Profile has successfully identified traits that do not overlap. There are a few exceptions. For example, Social thinking and Flexibility often appear together. In some cases, there is a *negative* relationship between Attributes, meaning they are less likely to appear together. For example, Structural and Conceptual thinking are sometimes mutually exclusive—but not always!

In each case, the relationship is the percentage of the variance accounted for (see Appendix for more information). This is a statistical term used to describe the strength of a relationship between two variables. When all the data are examined, the relationships between the Thinking and Behavioral Attributes are as shown on page 86.

REAL PEOPLE, REAL PROFILES

Here are the Emergenetics Profiles of several people who are all successful in their fields. I interviewed them so you can understand how they describe the gifts and drawbacks of their Profiles. Their words give invaluable insight into the different thought processes of each Profile.

Please know that Emergenetics Profiles are completely confidential and I *never* reveal them without permission. These individuals all permitted me to share this information with you.

How the Emergenetics Thinking and
Behavioral Attributes Are Related to One Another

Analytical:
- Minimal relationship with Structural (1%)
- No relationship with Social (0%)
- Minimal relationship with Conceptual (0.1%)
- Minimal relationship with Expressiveness (0.1%)
- A little relationship with Assertiveness (5%)
- No Relationship with Flexibility (0%)

Structural:
- Minimal relationship with Analytical (1%)
- No relationship with Social (0%)
- Very strong *negative* relationship with Conceptual (54%)
- Strong *negative* relationship with Expressiveness (26%)
- Strong *negative* relationship with Assertiveness (25%)
- Slight *negative* relationship with Flexibility (4%)

Social:
- No relationship with Analytical or Structural (0%)
- A little relationship with Conceptual (5%)
- Strong relationship with Expressiveness (30%)
- A little relationship with Assertiveness (2%)
- Very strong relationship with Flexibility (64%)

Conceptual:
- Minimal relationship with Analytical (0.1%)
- Very strong *negative* relationship with Structural (54%)
- A little relationship with Social (5%)

- Strong relationship with Expressiveness (27%)
- Strong relationship with Assertiveness (24%)
- A somewhat strong relationship with Flexibility (14%)

Expressiveness:
- Minimal relationship with Analytical (0.1%)
- Strong *negative* relationship with Structural (26%)
- Strong relationship with Social (30%)
- Strong relationship with Conceptual (27%)
- Very strong relationship with Assertiveness (64%)
- Strong relationship with Flexibility (44%)

Assertiveness:
- A little relationship with Analytical (5%)
- Strong *negative* relationship with Structural (25%)
- A little relationship with Social (2%)
- Strong relationship with Conceptual (24%)
- Very strong relationship with Expressiveness (64%)
- Minimal relationship with Flexibility (1%)

Flexibility:
- No relationship with Analytical (0%)
- Slight *negative* relationship with Structural (4%)
- Very strong relationship with Social (64%)
- Somewhat strong relationship with Conceptual (14%)
- Strong relationship with Expressiveness (44%)
- Minimal relationship with Assertiveness (1%)

JAMES

James is an Analytical/Structural thinker. He is the CEO of a 300-million-dollar business with over 2,600 employees.

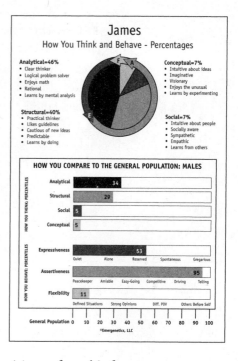

James
How You Think and Behave - Percentages

Analytical=46%
- Clear thinker
- Logical problem solver
- Enjoys math
- Rational
- Learns by mental analysis

Conceptual=7%
- Intuitive about ideas
- Imaginative
- Visionary
- Enjoys the unusual
- Learns by experimenting

Structural=40%
- Practical thinker
- Likes guidelines
- Cautious of new ideas
- Predictable
- Learns by doing

Social=7%
- Intuitive about people
- Socially aware
- Sympathetic
- Empathic
- Learns from others

HOW YOU COMPARE TO THE GENERAL POPULATION: MALES

HOW YOU THINK: PERCENTILES					
Analytical	34				
Structural	29				
Social	5				
Conceptual	5				

HOW YOU BEHAVE: PERCENTILES					
Expressiveness	53				
	Quiet	Alone	Reserved	Spontaneous	Gregarious
Assertiveness					95
	Peacekeeper	Amiable	Easy-Going	Competitive	Driving	Telling
Flexibility	11				
	Defined Situations	Strong Opinions	Diff. POV	Others Before Self

General Population 0 10 20 30 40 50 60 70 80 90 100
©Emergenetics, LLC

I always take my job from the Analytical/Structural perspective first. I maintain organized, detailed lists to keep myself on track. I'm a detail person, so one of the hardest things I've had to give up is checking the fine print on everything that involves my business. If I could, I would read every page of every contract myself, but now I have people to do that for me, so I just make sure every contract crosses my desk before it gets signed.

Sometimes I have to make tough calls. That's what I get paid to do. I would say I'm definitely a logical decision maker. I'll do what's right for the business. If I have to restructure people out of a job, I'll make the transition as favorable for them as I can, but I can't worry about their feelings. They should know it isn't personal.

I phone my finance people every hour of every day to see how much money is coming in. People are always calling me "anal," but it doesn't bother me. I mean, they rely on me to be that kind of person. I'm the one who is accountable. And people like working for me because I tell them exactly what I want them to do, and then make sure they've done it. I inspect what I expect. You can't always guarantee everything, but if you cover your bases, you can at least keep uncertainty to a minimum. If I tell my people something is going to happen, it's going to happen.

My team established a hotel in a location that everyone said could not be viable, and now it's under construction. We were determined to make the location work, and it did. I think my Assertiveness probably helped me with that. I also use my Assertiveness to force myself to be more Social at work. There are always people issues I have to deal with. I realize that my job is predominantly about motivating people, so interacting with others is a very important part of my success. I have to wake up in the morning and talk myself into being more

Social. Even though I don't want to, at points during my day I have to take a deep breath, smile, and interact with others because it is such a key part of my job. If I am poring over financial statements, I never get tired, but on those days that I have to heavily use my Social preference, I get really drained. My wife can always tell when I've had a particularly talkative day.

I know hundreds of people, but I don't have a lot of close friends. This doesn't bother me. My closest friends are all from grad school and college because we had four years to build relationships. I don't do small talk well, although I don't mind listening. One of my friends is really Social and EXPRESSIVE, and we both like sports, so we'll watch the game on TV together. Since he likes to talk a lot, I don't have to worry about maintaining the conversation. Every now and then, I'll throw out a stat or two, and then my friend will just keep talking.

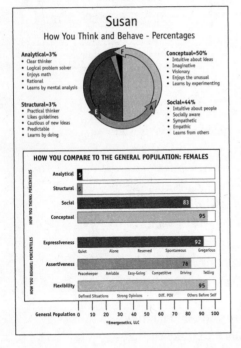

SUSAN

Susan is a Social/Conceptual thinker. She is vice president of human resources at a large telecommunications company.

I think the biggest gift of my Profile is being able to see things that other people don't see and being able to adapt to change quickly. In telecommunications there are lots of mergers and acquisitions, and I was always able to be a little bit ahead of the learning curve rather than be jolted or surprised by it. I was always the one from the old team to progress with the new team. I quickly networked and made new friends, and I was able to get along with new ideas and innovations.

Sometimes I would be kind of puzzled by other people's behavior, and I would feel like the odd one out. I had not yet learned to go with my intuition. In fact, when I really started on that journey, the Emergenetics Profile helped me validate who I was, and see that I was OK, and that my Profile was not something to overcome—which is something I had tried to do in the business world.

Because I am very Social, I tend to be concerned about how people are accepting something, rather than just making a decision and going with it. I want people to be happy, and I also want to be liked and approved of.

It always tickled me to see myself or others coming up with a new way of organizing or structuring the organization in a way that would help us work and perform better. On the other hand, sometimes I am in a different realm than some of the other people in the organization. Many times I would find myself feeling out of step. I would feel like, what is wrong with these people? Why don't they hurry up? Why are they messing around with flow charts and all of that when it is clear where we need to go?

The most exhausting thing in the world for me is preparing a budget or doing any kind of financial analysis. I can remember the excruciating pain of sitting through day-long financial reviews, letting my body stay there, but my Conceptual brain was drifting far, far away.

I have a lot of Expressiveness and Assertiveness so I'm not afraid to speak my mind. The combination of these two behaviors comes with no fear. I have been able to address large groups, small groups, give presentations, facilitate large meetings, you name it. I think this helped me advance, because when promotions or new projects were being discussed, my name was always in play.

I like to have fun discussions with those around me. I used to be too quick to speak. That can rub people the wrong way, so I have learned not to be the first one to talk, and to let those around me have their say. Sometimes I am so "out there" with ideas and words that it is overwhelming to other people because they don't have time to catch up. My brain is click, click, clicking, and I'm out with it immediately and ready to move on. I think this is not something that helps a group of people. Everybody has to come to their own conclusions in their own way.

Being really FLEXIBLE has helped me move from environment to environment. I've had several different careers in different industries and different companies. But where being FLEXIBLE does not serve me well is appearing kind of wishy-washy. It's like there is a push/pull with my Assertiveness. I'll blurt out how I feel at the beginning, and after hearing three other options, I can understand them, too. So people are thinking, where do you stand on this? The temptation is to sit there all day and listen to every viewpoint, but that isn't good for the group. Sometimes you just need to move on. I'm not one to say "this is THE way and the ONLY way." But when you are in a leader's role, people are looking to you to do that.

Talking helps me think. If I really want to think about something, I find someone I can talk to.

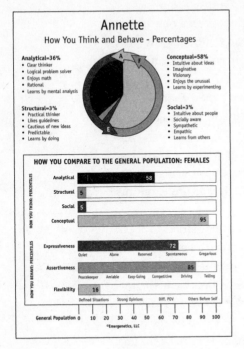

Annette
How You Think and Behave - Percentages

Analytical=36%
- Clear thinker
- Logical problem solver
- Enjoys math
- Rational
- Learns by mental analysis

Conceptual=58%
- Intuitive about ideas
- Imaginative
- Visionary
- Enjoys the unusual
- Learns by experimenting

Structural=3%
- Practical thinker
- Likes guidelines
- Cautious of new ideas
- Predictable
- Learns by doing

Social=3%
- Intuitive about people
- Socially aware
- Sympathetic
- Empathic
- Learns from others

HOW YOU COMPARE TO THE GENERAL POPULATION: FEMALES

HOW YOU THINK: PERCENTILES

Analytical	58
Structural	5
Social	5
Conceptual	95

HOW YOU BEHAVE: PERCENTILES

Expressiveness	72
	Quiet Alone Reserved Spontaneous Gregarious
Assertiveness	85
	Peacekeeper Amiable Easy-Going Competitive Driving Telling
Flexibility	16
	Defined Situations Strong Opinions Diff. POV Others Before Self

General Population 0 10 20 30 40 50 60 70 80 90 100
©Emergenetics, LLC

ANNETTE

Annette is an Analytical/Conceptual thinker. She is the CEO of a technological corporation and has been nationally recognized with many outstanding entrepreneurial business awards, including the Hispanic Business Magazine Entrepreneur of the Year Award.

The Conceptual part of my brain helps me to be visionary. I think I'm one of the most creative people in my organization. Information technology is a strategy business. You need to apply creativity to solve problems and set a vision. My Conceptual thinking helps me do this in a way that makes it fun for me and brings energy to the organization.

I like any processes within the business that are about building something new, or defining strategy. Setting direction and vision is really fun for me. And because I like Analytical thinking, I also enjoy the process of sitting down once a month and doing nothing but running the numbers. I call it my Inner Geek. I'm probably the strongest person in my company, besides the CFO, in doing this.

When I make decisions, I look to the future first, and then analyze my decision. Even though I like to think outside the box, I always look at the data. The Analytical part of my brain helps me interpret information around problem-solving. It's the part of me that gets me in a place where I'm not just floating around in big ideas, but also am grounded in data and information, and have a framework to understand what it all means.

My Profile has practically no Structural thinking, so I have to really focus on being organized. Even setting the time aside on a weekly basis to get organized is hard for me, but I know it's important. And although I know exactly where I want to go, figuring out how we are going to get there is not as interesting to me. When people complain to me about process, right away I get irritable. Can't these people just go deal with it?

The president of my company has a highly Social brain. I do not have a preference for Social thinking, so my style is quite different from the president's.

However, our two Profiles complement each other. In my heart I care about the people who work for me, but my employees tell me I have to get better at having regular, consistent communication with people. I feel like I'm pretty open. If you just ask me, I will tell you. But people don't ask, or I don't make myself available. When people have to vent emotionally, it is really hard for me to listen. Come to me for guidance, or decisions, but not for emotional support. Being a therapist would be a life in hell for me.

I see teamwork as completely critical. When we don't work in teams, things don't work. When we do work in teams, there is so much direct benefit that it is pretty obvious. Teamwork has to be effective, or I wouldn't spend my time doing it. But the teamwork is not about being with people, it's about effectiveness. Being with teammates is not why I engage in teamwork.

Because I am ASSERTIVE and EXPRESSIVE, you always know what I am thinking. Also, once I have made up my mind, that is my final decision.

I'm really quite simple. I'm honest, straightforward, and collaborative, and I don't have a big ego about things.

MARK

Mark was formerly the CEO of a large Canadian advertising company, and today is a consultant. He is a Structural/Social thinker in a predominantly Conceptual occupation. When I asked him how he has been so successful, he stated that he figured out how to take others' creativity and sell it.

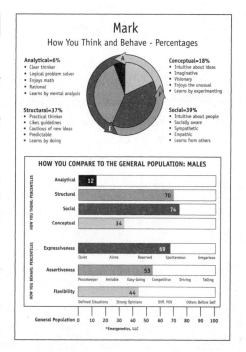

I spend a lot of time thinking about how to make things work. If someone is presenting something to me and I know something isn't right, I'll try to figure out how to make it right.

The strength I brought to my early job [at a major agency] was my ability to figure out structurally what was right for the company. One of the things I had to do was look at the account managers who make up the client contact group, figure out who the leaders were, and how to structure departments around those people. When I came on board, there was 50 percent turnover in management. That was unacceptable. How do you replace 50 percent of your account group every year and remain stable? I put in place a process where we provided that group with the education they would need to progress in their careers. I like providing opportunities so people can succeed. We put together job descriptions so that they would know what was expected of them. We included an understanding of how they could get promoted. They understood the ground rules and the values, and we turned that 50 percent turnover rate into 12 percent the next year. I think both my Structural and my Social thinking allowed me to make that happen.

Because I'm so Social, I need people. I need to be around them. I miss not working with people every day in my job now. When I get into a project with a client, and I get into working with their staff, my energy level goes way up because I get excited. There is a bit of lonely existence being a consultant because you are not with clients every day.

When I was CEO, I never stayed in my office. I would walk down the halls, I got to know people, I sat in their offices and talked to them about their challenges. We looked at the work together, appreciated the work together, and celebrated our victories together. I think I brought a much more communicative style to the agency, so people were much more aware of what was going on and why it was going on. And that helped us achieve the goals we were trying to achieve. This was real "take your boots off and lets get our feet wet" type of leadership. I think the staff felt they could walk into my office. Even though they still respected the CEO's office, they knew the door was open and if they needed to talk with me they could come and speak to me.

I was around brilliant, highly Conceptual people, and I didn't feel able to contribute at that level. But I knew how to appreciate great work, and how to create a prosperous environment where people were motivated and properly compensated, a place where people would want to stick around. I made sure we had the right talent because I could recognize great work. I knew how to get people in the right place, and how to create an environment that allowed them to do what they did best.

I'm EXPRESSIVE, so I don't have any hidden agenda. It's all out there. I tend to speak my mind, and I have a lot of integrity and honesty. I think the strength of my relationships is based on these values. People know that they can count on me, that my word is my word and that I express my word. There is nothing to fear, as I tell it like it is. Of course, that also gets me into trouble, as I will go into a relationship trusting before I distrust. I have been let down. In business you can't necessarily extend trust if it has not been earned, and I often would. Now I am a bit more reserved, because I have to be.

I'm an extremely competitive person and I take that into all walks of life. If I see conflict, I won't avoid it because I want it to be corrected, I want to fix it. If people provide me with strong rationale for a different point of view, I will listen to it, but if they don't, I won't. My father was like that. He would be of the mindset that if you are going to express a point of view, you better be prepared to back it up with something. Personally, I don't have the facts. I rely on my gut, on a feeling, or a point of view supported by others. But when people are presenting me with a strategy or a structure or something like that, I'm looking for rational support.

JIAN

Jian spent thirty-four years as a senior lawyer at a law firm in Taipei. He is Social, Conceptual, and Analytical. In addition, his Behavioral Attributes are all third-third. Jian is outgoing and mischievous, as well as self-confident and firm.

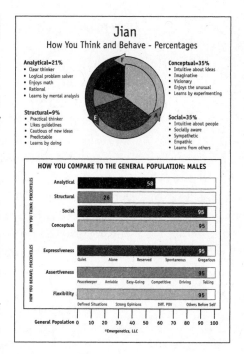

My priorities are different from those of most lawyers. My main interest is coming up with innovative ideas, whether they are about legal work, or business situations, or social issues, or politics. At the next level, I'm interested in public policy and corporate strategy. And then, as the value chain goes down, the next stage would be legal work.

Having three preferences means I juggle a lot of balls in the air at once. I don't like working on just one thing at a time. Recently I have decided to focus on innovations in public-policy advice. I help the government and businesses in the private sector change their thinking with regard to policy, laws, and regulations. To help people come up with innovative strategic thinking, I started an independent consulting business. I also am a professor teaching law, and the business school at the same university has asked me to teach courses there as well. On the side, I'm very much involved in a nonprofit foundation that encourages entrepreneurship in startup companies.

One of the things I enjoy about being a lawyer is that you can change professions a lot. A lawyer can become a politician, or a marketing person in a big corporation, or a businessman. It looks like I have changed my field, but deep down in me, I think it is not changing fields, it is upgrading my legal skills into thinking about how law is made.

I don't really enjoy the detailed, technical aspects of legal work, so I outsource it to younger lawyers. I also would not be a good criminal lawyer, working in a narrow field all my life. I think a good lawyer should be creative, and I teach my law students to think creatively. The creative part of legal work used to be confined to litigation and resolving legal problems, but I think lawyers could play a bigger role in thinking about economic and social structures. I also believe I can be more valuable to clients by getting involved in different aspects of their work.

Because I am Social and Conceptual, I enjoy thinking in the grand, strategic sense. I enjoy finding partners with whom to work. I think being FLEXIBLE allows me to be involved and uninvolved at the same time. I'm not likely to be too disturbed by a differing opinion, so that makes me an observer. Because I am EXPRESSIVE, I toss out a lot of ideas and see what happens. I enjoy brainstorming.

When you are doing something you are extremely interested in, time is not a concern. You find the time. Or something that normally takes an hour, you do in five minutes. I look for the most effective way of conveying ideas. With some high-level people, all you need is three minutes and an executive summary.

I may be criticized for not focusing. I also get bored when people are discussing financial issues. I like to have other people who understand finance just tell me the result. Are we making money, or not making money? I probably could not work alone, because I need a lot of logistical support. I'm constantly figuring out how to form the most efficient team to do a job, and then I put them on the payroll.

JANICE

Like Jian (above), Janice is a lawyer. She is a partner in a prestigious law firm in her city. This is one of the most interesting Profiles in my databank. Besides being very Structural, Janice is first-third in all her behaviors. When Janice attended an Emergenetics seminar with a group of leaders, I hardly knew she was in the room. After the seminar I commented to her that I thought her Profile was unusual and asked her to talk about it. Janice said, "I went to law school in 1967. I was one of four females, and the first African-American female—how do you think I survived?" I answered, "I get it. You never made any waves, and then you overwhelmed them with your brilliance." Janice, however, is exceptionally modest and doesn't see it this way.

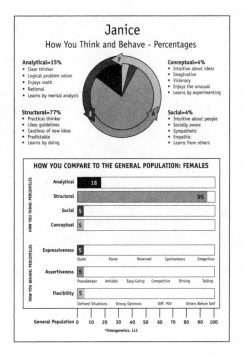

I consider my Structural thinking to be the biggest plus, in both my job and my life. It enables me to be in touch with reality and not pie in the sky. I think, if this is step A, where is it going to lead us? If I go from A to C, what will be the ramifications?

I learn by doing, and I think that is an advantage, too. I know if I can do it once, if I can master something the first time, then hopefully I can do it a second time without making the same mistakes. I find that in life, although the circumstances change, the situations are similar. If you learn from experience, it should serve you well.

A drawback is that I am cautious about new ideas. I know I have missed opportunities because I don't really like change. For example, I had two chances to invest in long-shot ideas, and my cautious nature would not allow me to do that. In one case, I made the right decision because it was a flop, but the other one . . . well, there was money to be made by those who did invest.

As for my *Expressiveness,* I prefer not to be the first person to talk. I'd rather take in opinions and ideas from the people who speak before me. And I prefer not to be the first person up at the podium.

I am just not an ASSERTIVE person. If I think you are wrong, I will try to get that point across, but I'm not going to continue to try to show you the error of your ways. There are times, over the years, when I recognize I should have been more Assertive.

Lawyers are usually ASSERTIVE and EXPRESSIVE, and often they are very Social. None of those fit me. But I do estate planning and probate work, and within my realm, I don't need to be those things. I can survive without them. People who are very Social and EXPRESSIVE tend to bring in more clients, but in terms of the ability to perform the work that I do, I can do it just as well because I deal mainly one-on-one. I get my clients mostly by referrals— people who know me.

I'm not good at delegating. I give some things to a paralegal to do, but I do most of my own stuff. I would not make a good office manager. If someone doesn't get it done quite right or on time, I don't make a big commotion about it. I just don't have that strong personality.

I was the first African-American woman at my law school, but I didn't see it as anything out of the ordinary. For four years in undergrad, I was one of three African-Americans in the whole school. When I went to law school, it wasn't any better. I didn't feel out of place. I was just one of the law students, and I was there to get an education. I did feel at a disadvantage because I did not come from a family of lawyers. I didn't even know any lawyers.

I didn't overwhelm with brilliance, I survived. First year wasn't easy, but when the grades came out, I realized I had done better than I anticipated, and my GPA gave me an invitation to be on law review. I spent a lot of time with that small group over the next two years. I'm hoping over the years that I have changed to include a little more Social involvement. It may be up to 6 percent now, from 4 percent. As I move into my later years, I realize there is more to life than being a practical thinker.

YOUNG-JU

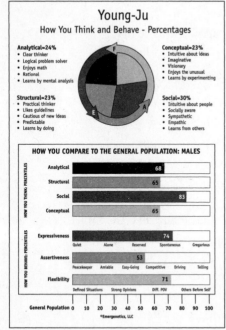

Young-Ju is the CEO of an industrial corporation in Seoul. He started the company himself thirty-one years ago. Young-Ju has a Quadra-modal brain and is on the second-third of Assertiveness and the third-third of Expressiveness and Flexibility.

Half my business is cultivating timber, and the other half involves windows, doors, floorings, and furniture. We have plantations all over the world, and factories as well.

I have always thought I was given a special gift from God. My thinking was always very positive. Whenever I had any kind of tough time, I never really minded it very much. I know I can handle it. I always thought about the long-term and wide view. I never thought about short-term things.

Because I'm Social, I'm very good with people. Most of the people in my company have been working with me for twenty-eight to thirty years. Although I'm Analytical, I'm not the best at figures and numbers. I'm better than others, but I've found that I'm a little bit more artistic than realistic. Because I'm Structural, I very much like to put things into structures, and I am always on time. People think I am conservative, but actually I'm very FLEXIBLE. I'm just very practical as well.

I think I have been successful because (1) I work hard, and (2) I know what is important. I have a sense of what is important, and what is less important.

I have a tendency to think through every possibility, and that can make me slow. I can't decide quickly. Until I am sure, I don't know. I always believe there is a better way, which is tough for me and my people I work with.

I have many different kinds of friends. I have friendships that have lasted forty years. I still communicate with business partners I haven't worked with since the 70s. Sometimes we see each other. One of them retired, then joined us as president of our American operations. My friends from high school and college play golf with me, and have fun with me, but they seem to feel I am older than they are. That sometimes annoys me.

I am a good communicator, and I respect other people. I will talk to anyone. I find most people very interesting, but I don't like people who talk too much, or who talk only about themselves. It takes too long, and there's no important meaning in their words. I like people who listen carefully, who are wise. I used to be more explosive when I was young, but now I know how to give constructive criticism to others. I write memos about problems, and accumulate them for six months to a year, and then review what I wrote. I typically find the things were not that important. If there are one or two important things, I talk to the person over coffee. I'm very strict about this. I try to maintain good relationships with people.

I usually don't argue with others. If tempers are hot, I wait, and think things over. Sometimes I find I am wrong. If I think the other person is wrong, I will approach him at another time and try it again more peacefully. I always try to think of his position.

Somehow I am able to persuade people better than others. Why? I don't know. I never lie to others for my own short-term purpose. I always tell the truth. I think that is very important. You can only lie once; you cannot lie twice.

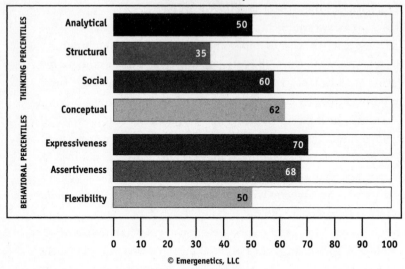

Emergenetics Mean Scores
USA CEOs Group

THINKING PERCENTILES

Analytical	50
Structural	35
Social	60
Conceptual	62

BEHAVIORAL PERCENTILES

Expressiveness	70
Assertiveness	68
Flexibility	50

0 10 20 30 40 50 60 70 80 90 100

© Emergenetics, LLC

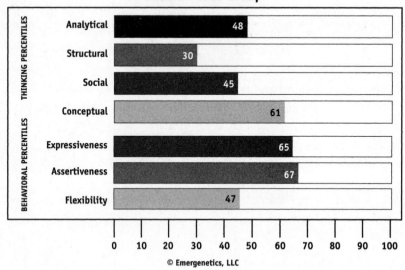

Emergenetics Mean Scores
Swedish CEOs Group

THINKING PERCENTILES

Analytical	48
Structural	30
Social	45
Conceptual	61

BEHAVIORAL PERCENTILES

Expressiveness	65
Assertiveness	67
Flexibility	47

0 10 20 30 40 50 60 70 80 90 100

© Emergenetics, LLC

EMERGENETICS AROUND THE WORLD

Whenever I do a seminar, I obtain in advance Emergenetics Profiles of everyone who will be attending. Using these Profiles, I then generate a chart that shows the mean scores of all the attendees by attribute. One of the things I've discovered is that people are people, everywhere. If you put together a composite chart of all the employees in an organization, you'll see all kinds of brains represented. If you compare charts across cultures, you'll see similar results.

When we work with managers in Moscow, or Kenya, or Vietnam, or Singapore, their charts look like those of managers in the United States. I had an opportunity to address two groups of CEOs, all of whom were members of Young Presidents Organization, a worldwide association. One group was from Sweden, while the other was from the United States. Interestingly, although the Swedes have no word for "Assertiveness," their Emergenetics Profiles were almost identical to those of their American counterparts, as you can see from the charts on page 98.

PREDICTING PEOPLE: TEST YOUR KNOWLEDGE

Here are some descriptions of people with different kinds of Profiles. Can you predict how they will behave?

1. Catherine is a middle-aged woman who is Structural and AS-SERTIVE. One day her coworker Irene, who is slightly older than Catherine, came into Catherine's office and said, "I can tell I'm getting older because my height must be shrinking. I went into the storeroom to pull out some paper and I could not reach the top shelf the way I used to. What should I do about this?" Catherine replies:
    a. "Oh, it's so frustrating when things happen and we are forced to comprehend that we are getting older. I also know you must feel like you don't want to bother anyone else to get the paper for you."
    b. "Get a stool!"

2. David is an architect with his own small firm. He is an Analytical/ Structural thinker, and is *Expressive, Flexible,* and ASSERTIVE.

David has noticed that one of the draftsmen in his office, Damian, has been slacking off. Even worse, Damian's behavior is starting to rub off on the rest of the staff. David tackles this problem by:

 a. Calling Damian into his office and giving him a six-point plan for improvement.

 b. Scheduling a special lunch with Damian, gently inquiring if everything is OK, and offering to help in any way he can.

3. Lynn, a Social/Conceptual thinker who is *Expressive,* is standing near the corner of the room with a friend during a lively party. Alex, also a Social/Conceptual thinker, but who is EXPRESSIVE, approaches the two and says, "I noticed the two of you have been by yourselves all night. I hope you are not miserable. Why don't you come over and join the group?" Lynn replies,

 a. "Oh yes, thank you Alex, we've been waiting for someone to come over and invite us into the Conga line."

 b. "Thank you for thinking of us, but we've been quite all right on our own. We enjoy watching the others make fools of themselves."

4. Brad is an Analytical/Social thinker, who is EXPRESSIVE and ASSERTIVE. Before his colleague Sandy gives a presentation, he approaches her with a big hug, smile, and words of encouragement. During the presentation, Sandy's logic appears flimsy to John. How does he handle this?

 a. Lets it slide and concludes to himself that Sandy has no idea what she is talking about.

 b. Mercilessly fires one question after another at her until she has shorn up her logic.

5. Julie has a Structural/Conceptual Profile and is *Flexible* and *Assertive.* She is an excellent tax attorney but is bored with her occupation. Ideally, she would like to leave her job and become a musician. She goes to a career consultant for advice, and he tells her to follow her dreams. What is her final decision?

 a. She dismisses her dream as crazy and impractical, and remains a lawyer. She will always think of new occupations, but she never will follow through.

b. She listens to the consultant, leaves her job, and now plays at Johnny's Tavern.

ANSWERS:
1. b
2. a
3. b
4. b
5. a

In the previous two chapters, you evaluated your Thinking and Behavioral Attributes. To refresh your memory, you may want to turn to "Determining Your Thinking and Behavioral Attributes at a Glance" in Part III, The Emergenetics Toolbox. Then, to see how your preferences influence your reading style, look at "How Will Different Minds Read This Book?" on the following page.

How Will Different Minds Read This Book?

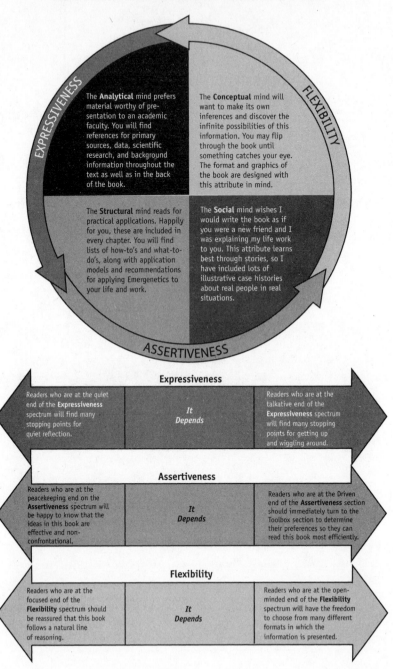

EXPRESSIVENESS

FLEXIBILITY

The **Analytical** mind prefers material worthy of presentation to an academic faculty. You will find references for primary sources, data, scientific research, and background information throughout the text as well as in the back of the book.

The **Conceptual** mind will want to make its own inferences and discover the infinite possibilities of this information. You may flip through the book until something catches your eye. The format and graphics of the book are designed with this attribute in mind.

The **Structural** mind reads for practical applications. Happily for you, these are included in every chapter. You will find lists of how-to's and what-to-do's, along with application models and recommendations for applying Emergenetics to your life and work.

The **Social** mind wishes I would write the book as if you were a new friend and I was explaining my life work to you. This attribute learns best through stories, so I have included lots of illustrative case histories about real people in real situations.

ASSERTIVENESS

Expressiveness

Readers who are at the quiet end of the **Expressiveness** spectrum will find many stopping points for quiet reflection.

It Depends

Readers who are at the talkative end of the **Expressiveness** spectrum will find many stopping points for getting up and wiggling around.

Assertiveness

Readers who are at the peacekeeping end on the **Assertiveness** spectrum will be happy to know that the ideas in this book are effective and non-confrontational.

It Depends

Readers who are at the Driven end of the **Assertiveness** section should immediately turn to the Toolbox section to determine their preferences so they can read this book most efficiently.

Flexibility

Readers who are at the focused end of the **Flexibility** spectrum should be reassured that this book follows a natural line of reasoning.

It Depends

Readers who are at the open-minded end of the **Flexibility** spectrum will have the freedom to choose from many different formats in which the information is presented.

Why Real Men
Don't Ask for Directions

Emergenetics and Gender Differences

Alice, a strong Social/Conceptual thinker, is CEO of a medium-size public relations firm. She used to date Mark, a strong Analytical/Conceptual thinker. Shortly after their relationship began, they embarked on a two-week road trip. Mark often remarked, "Alice, for someone who is as smart as you are, I can't figure out why you can't logically find your way from point A to point B!"

Alice admitted to me that her navigational skills once caused her to drive fifty miles in the wrong direction before she realized her mistake. "But at least I acknowledge it when I'm lost," she said to me somewhat sulkily. "And when someone gives me proper directions, I don't have any trouble."

I laughed. "Does 'proper directions' mean 'turn left at the Dairy Queen, go through two stop signs, and look for a green house with red geraniums'?"

"Exactly," Alice continued. "Mark used to say things like 'go two miles south, then one block west, and pick up Route 22 north.' What kind of person gives directions like that?"

I explained to Alice that actually lots of people use directions like that—particularly men. Because men and women generally have different spatial abilities, men are often more comfortable with abstract directions, while women usually prefer to navigate using landmarks. Both kinds of directions are valid, but for different types of brains.

> Sometimes I wonder if men and women really suit each other. Perhaps they should live next door and just visit now and then.
>
> Katharine Hepburn

When working with the opposite sex—and who doesn't?—it's helpful to know how the other half thinks. As you saw earlier, genetics and life experiences help determine who we are. As you'll see in this chapter, so does gender.

WARNING: STEREOTYPES ARE SIMPLISTIC

Researchers have discovered differences between the brains of women and men, which I'll discuss later in this chapter. I am intrigued by these differences, and the implications they have for gender-based behavior. On the other hand, I really don't like stereotypes of any kind. Broad, group-based averages don't describe the characteristics of any one individual. For example, although women like Alice prefer landmarks, other women prefer to read maps.

Still, when researchers look at women and men as a whole, there are small but significant differences. Certainly there are exceptions to the generalizations, and there are cultural shifts that occur over time that change the way women and men think and behave. But there are observable gender-based differences in the brain that contribute to the way people characterize the sexes.

I believe that women and men's general Emergenetics preferences have to do with both their gender and environment. However, people seldom fit into tidy little boxes. Usually there is at least an arm or a leg sticking out somewhere. You can tell whether or not someone's Profile fits the gender research by the way she or he communicates.

For the last twenty-five years two colleagues, Carol Hunter and Tim Rouse, and I have conducted two gender-based executive development programs: *Influence* for women, and *Focus* for men. Every six weeks we meet for two days. The curriculum is designed to involve every Emergenetics Attribute, and the content is exactly the same for each group. We have found that a group made up exclusively of women, or of men, will have different kinds of discussions than a group of men and women together. (In a teaching situation, the gender of the leader eventually is not an issue.) When both are together, the research tells us that they are inclined to engage in gender-typed behaviors (posturing, flirting, humor, power displays). When you bring one man into a group of women, the women start acting differently, and when you put one woman into a group of men, the men start acting differently. This is why we continue to keep these programs separate. But when it comes to communication differences between men and women, Carol, Tim, and I believe individual Emergenetics Profiles explain more than broad gender theories.

An airplane engineer once told me, "My wife and I have been married for thirty-two years. The day we got married, I told her, 'I love you, and unless something changes, you can assume I will feel the same way in the future.' " This quote always gets a laugh in my seminars. But from my years of working with single-gender groups, I know this engineer's approach to romance is not based on gender, but on his Thinking Attributes. I have worked with women who also have a strong Analytical preference with a small sliver of Social thinking, and they say similar kinds of things to their partners.

When I think about how people learn, make decisions, and communicate, I always think in terms of Emergenetics attributes instead of gender differences. So are gender stereotypes useful at all? Actually, yes, they are—because they dovetail with the Emergenetics data.

EMERGENETICS GENDER NORMS

As I mentioned earlier, the Emergenetics data are gender normed. The sexes are closer than you might think, but there are statistical differences. These differences are not good or bad—they are just differences. Females score themselves significantly higher in Structural and Social thinking, as well as in Expressiveness and Flexibility—attributes typically associated with verbal skills, sensory awareness, social awareness, and relationships. Males score themselves higher in Analytical and Conceptual thinking, and in Assertiveness—attributes typically associated with mathematical and spatial concepts, aggression, competition, and self-assertion. Remember these are group comparisons. They do not represent a comparison of one person to another.

Because of these differences, the final score in each Profile for each attribute is reported in relation to others of the same sex. To compare female scores with male scores or vice versa would be like comparing oranges to apples.

Since its inception in 1991, Emergenetics has been periodically re-normed to reflect changes in the culture. Social standards change all the time. Re-norming allows us to go back and establish new means and standard deviations for the Thinking and Behavioral calculations, so that Emergenetics Profiles reflect current trends. Revisiting the norms every two years prevents the Profiles from dragging too far off course in terms of the general population.

Through the years, the norm numbers as a whole have not shown substantive changes, with the exception of two years: 1995 and 2002. When we examined the data from those years, we found there have been gradual shifts in the means and point differences in some of the attributes, as the Gender Gap chart reveals.

Perhaps the most interesting modification, at least in terms of the culture, is the change in Assertiveness over the last decade between women and men. In 1991, males' preference for Assertiveness was 5 points higher than that of females. In 2002, males' preference for Assertiveness was only 2 points higher. So what happened to narrow the gap? In my opinion, the evolving nature of women's professional lives has caused them to rate their Assertiveness in stronger terms.

In the 1995 re-norming process, men's Social thinking, when compared to women's, increased 1 point, and Flexibility increased 2 points. Why did the gender gap close a little? Were women becoming less Social and Flexible, or were men becoming more Social and Flexible? It turns out men were answering the questionnaire from a more Social and Flexible perspective. In the 1990s, I coincidentally began to notice more men becoming the primary caregiver, taking their children to the grocery store, or even hugging each other. In 1996, a *Focus* participant, a thirty-four-year-old lawyer, humorously recapped the events of his weekend for his male colleagues. His wife went out of town, and without any prompting from her, he decided to potty-train his son. He didn't necessarily see this as a woman's task or a man's task, but rather just a

Emergenetics Gender Norms for the Thinking Attributes*

- Men report themselves more Analytical by 5 points.
- Men report themselves more Conceptual by 2 points.
- Women report themselves more Social by 6 points.
- Women report themselves more Structural by 2 points.

Emergenetics Gender Norms for the Behavioral Attributes*

- Women report themselves more EXPRESSIVE by 2 points.
- Men report themselves more ASSERTIVE by 2 points.
- Women report themselves more FLEXIBLE by 3 points.

* These are t-scores. The comparisons are statistically significant at the P = <.01 level (a t-score is a measure of statistical difference between the means of two populations).

GENDER GAP

Attribute	Mean	1991	1995	2002[1]
Analytical	Males Higher	5 points	4 points	5 points
Structural	Females Higher	2 points	2 points	2 points
Social	Females Higher	7 points	6 points	6 points
Conceptual	Males Higher	3 points	3 points	2 points
Expressiveness	Females Higher	1 point	1 point	2 points
Assertiveness	Males Higher	5 points	3 points	2 points
Flexibility	Females Higher	5 points	3 points	3 points

Over the years, the Emergenetics gender norms have changed slightly. For example, since 1991 the gap between men and women in Assertiveness has narrowed from a difference of 5 points to a difference of 2 points.

[1] We are not reporting the 2004 numbers here, as they did not change significantly from the 2002 data. Before we report a change in means, we first assure that numbers are statistically significant.

task that needed to be accomplished. This was also a time when I noticed that men began to reevaluate their roles professionally and personally. Over this decade, the sons of the mothers who protested for change in the 1970s were now starting to say that they could potty-train their child just as much as the women. And you can see this trend continuing today.

HOW GENDER STEREOTYPES WORK . . .
AND DON'T WORK

In his book *Executive Instinct,* author Nigel Nicholson, an expert in evolutionary psychology, compares the ways in which all-female and all-male groups tend to work. The men generally take turns making and disputing suggestions. One individual will assume a leading role in sorting out a compromise. An individual who disagrees with the strategy that has been adopted is likely to be simply overridden. Then the men assign roles and divide the work. They are usually very efficient, unless they get locked in a power struggle of some sort. During this process there is spirit of competitive camaraderie, or what Nicholson calls

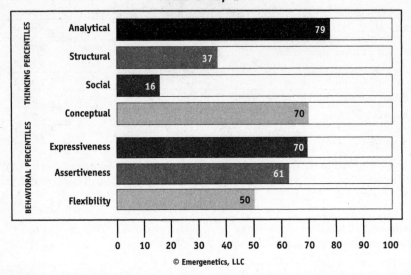

Emergenetics Mean Scores
Focus Group #1

THINKING PERCENTILES

- Analytical — 79
- Structural — 37
- Social — 16
- Conceptual — 70

BEHAVIORAL PERCENTILES

- Expressiveness — 70
- Assertiveness — 61
- Flexibility — 50

0 10 20 30 40 50 60 70 80 90 100

© Emergenetics, LLC

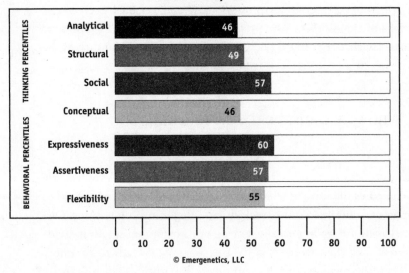

Emergenetics Mean Scores
Focus Group #2

THINKING PERCENTILES

- Analytical — 46
- Structural — 49
- Social — 57
- Conceptual — 46

BEHAVIORAL PERCENTILES

- Expressiveness — 60
- Assertiveness — 57
- Flexibility — 55

0 10 20 30 40 50 60 70 80 90 100

© Emergenetics, LLC

"mildly aggressive joking, a kind of rough playfulness in which sharp exchanges seem quickly forgotten."

In my experience with gender-based groups, the behavior Nicholson describes is evident when the men in the group have the "typical male" Profile: Analytical, Conceptual, and ASSERTIVE. But a group of men who are highly Social behave differently when they are together.

On page 108 there are two bar charts representing two of my *Focus* groups (an executive development program for men). As you can see, Group #2 happened to have a greater preference for Social thinking. They were more emotionally available to each other than the men in Group # 1, spent more time talking about their families, and at the end of the year gave a donation to a charity in recognition of the instructors.

According to Nicholson, women spend more time soliciting and discussing one another's opinions. They express support for one another, and are more tolerant of an individual who disagrees with the group. They will reach a better solution than the men, provided they aren't so accommodating that they try to use absolutely everyone's ideas. There is more cooperation about getting the task done, and less assigning of roles. In general, the group behaves more warmly than the male group. However, if there is any conflict, it cuts deeply and is not quickly forgotten.

Again, I find that this behavior is apparent as long as the women in the group have the "typical female" Profile: Structural, Social, EXPRESSIVE, and FLEXIBLE. When the group is made up of women who are Analytical and Conceptual, as on page 110, the gender stereotype is much less likely to apply.

One year we had a particularly dynamic group of women with Analytical, Conceptual, and ASSERTIVE attributes in our *Influence* group (an executive development program for women). They asked for Profiles of their significant others. I was eager to profile their partners because it would add to my database on committed relationships. At the next meeting, as I prepared to hand out their partners' Profiles, I instructed the women not to open the sealed envelopes because of confidentiality issues. They all solemnly swore to behave. Within seconds of getting the envelopes into their hands, they literally tore them open and started showing them to each other, saying things like, "Oh, look at this! Can you believe my husband's *Flexibility?*" These women could not be contained. To this day, whenever I see one of them, she will ask proudly, "Are we still the most ASSERTIVE group you've ever had?"

Most air traffic controllers are men, and most nurses are women. But the gender stereotypes do not always apply. Many men are uncomfortable with the

SEE *EXECUTIVE INSTINCT: MANAGING THE HUMAN ANIMAL IN THE INFORMATION AGE* BY NIGEL NICHOLSON

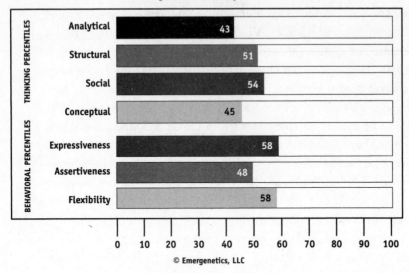

Emergenetics Mean Scores
Influence Group #1

THINKING PERCENTILES
BEHAVIORAL PERCENTILES

Analytical 43
Structural 51
Social 54
Conceptual 45
Expressiveness 58
Assertiveness 48
Flexibility 58

0 10 20 30 40 50 60 70 80 90 100

© Emergenetics, LLC

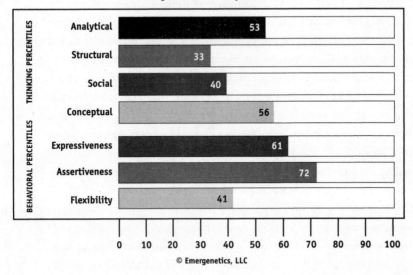

Emergenetics Mean Scores
Influence Group #2

THINKING PERCENTILES
BEHAVIORAL PERCENTILES

Analytical 53
Structural 33
Social 40
Conceptual 56
Expressiveness 61
Assertiveness 72
Flexibility 41

0 10 20 30 40 50 60 70 80 90 100

© Emergenetics, LLC

"guys' locker room" culture, and many women are more systematic than nurturing.

Even though stereotypes don't always apply, they don't entirely disappear, either. Each time we re-norm Emergenetics, the gender gaps in our test results remain. Sometimes the gaps widen and sometimes they narrow, but the gender-based trends within men and women's Thinking and Behavioral Attributes do not go away. On average, men remain Analytical/Conceptual and more Assertive, while women remain Structural/Social, more Flexible, and slightly more Expressive. When I meet a man whose Profile is Structural/Social, EXPRESSIVE, and FLEXIBLE, I know he probably works well with women and has lots of women friends. Similarly, when I meet a woman who is Analytical, Conceptual, and ASSERTIVE, I can predict that probably she is quite comfortable working with a group of men.

GENDER DIFFERENCES

Women and men are different. No surprise there. And this isn't just because little girls and little boys are raised differently.

The brains of female and male fetuses start out the same. At around nine weeks in utero, hormones begin to affect both the brain and body development of girl babies and boy babies in different ways. By the time we can observe their differences, girls and boys pick different games, play with the same toys in different ways, and respond differently to social situations.

Why do the gender differences remain? For answers, we turn to the latest research regarding the differences between women and men in brain structure and brain function, as well as evolutionary differences that have developed over thousands of years. It seems like every two years or so, studies come out that talk about the differences in gender. I'll discuss some of the prevailing research that may correlate with how women and men respond to the Emergenetics questionnaire.

It is generally easy to tell whether someone is male or female. But what about our brains? Are male brains different from female brains? "At a glance, no, but let's look again," reports Mary Case, MD, neuropathologist and Emergenetics Associate. "While we are all familiar with what hormones, especially sex hormones (predominantly testosterone in the male, and progesterone and estrogen in the female) do to the body, we are less familiar with their effect of the growing brain. In fact, the presence of sex hormones causes groups of neurons and their characteristic functions to migrate to certain areas of the brain. For example, they influence the different standard locations for speech and language processing in male and female brains. By birth, a baby's brain is genetically hardwired for these functions, although it is not apparent. Basically the testosterone hormone, produced by the male fetus, masculinizes the organizing brain and sets up the circuitry for standard male thinking and behavior. If the fetus is female, the absence of significant amounts of testosterone and the presence of estrogen and progesterone will mean the brain is hardwired as female."

Differences in Brain Structure

In women the areas of the brain associated with language, judgment, and memory are more densely packed, with 18 percent more neurons. This may be why women outperform men on verbal tasks and are better at matching games. Women are also generally better at noticing small differences. This ability to appreciate details may correlate with their Structural responses on the Emergenetics questionnaire.

In the female brain, the corpus callosum—the band of synapses and neurons that connects the two hemispheres of the brain—is wider at the back and also 23 percent thicker than in the male brain. This means the "pipeline" between women's hemispheres allows more rapid interaction than men's, with more activity in multiple brain regions at the same time. This may explain why women are generally better at multitasking and making intuitive connections. The ability to use both hemispheres also may help explain why women's responses to the Emergenetics questionnaire tend to be more Flexible.

Differences in Brain Function

Current imaging techniques reveal that the brains of women and men have different patterns of activity while engaged in the same tasks.

> If a man is shaving and you talk to him, he'll cut himself.
>
> Barbara and Allan Pease,
> *Why Men Don't Listen and Women Can't Read Maps*

When men and women underwent brain imaging while listening to a passage from a novel, the majority of men showed activity exclusively in the left hemisphere, meaning they were processing language only in their left hemisphere. Women, on the other hand, showed activity in both sides of the brain. Women tend to hear better with both ears—and if you want a man to hear you, turn off the radio, ask him to stop what he's doing, and speak into his right ear. This is another example of women's ability to access both hemispheres, which may contribute to their responses to the Emergenetics questionnaire regarding Flexibility.

In men, one area of the brain lights up at a time. This may help explain why men tend to put information into mental "bins." In women, several areas often light up at once. For example, when women talk, six to seven language centers light up at once. This may explain why women use a random format for memory. Using several parts of the brain at once also may give women an edge in Social thinking, which requires making connections.

Numerous studies have shown that men are superior at tasks that involve spatial reasoning, such as judging speed, parallel parking, reading blueprints, or mentally rotating a three-dimensional object (see below). There are, in general, more male engineers, architects, air traffic controllers, and race-car drivers. Because they are superior at grasping geometric relationships, men outperform women in navigational challenges when landmarks are removed. It also may contribute to men's greater degree of Analytical and Conceptual preferences.

> There is simply more neural activity in general in the female brain at any given time. In fact, there is 15 percent more blood flow in the female brain than in the male, with more brain centers lit up in the female brain at a given moment than in the male.
>
> **Michael Gurian, PhD**
> *What Could*
> *He Be Thinking?*
> (citing the research
> of Ruben Gur, MD)

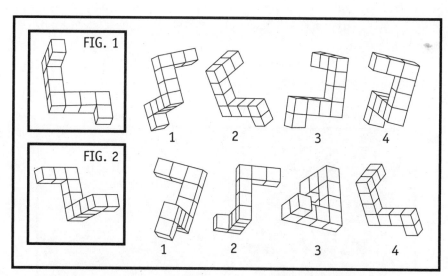

The task here is to determine which two figures on the right match the figure on the left when it is rotated into different positions. In general, men find this easier to do than women. (Figure 1 matches #1 and #3; Figure 2 matches #2 and #3.)

Men outperform women in mathematical reasoning, and boys outscore girls on the math SATs by 7 percent. Dr. Julian Stanley, who has studied mathematically precocious youth at Johns Hopkins for many years, and Camilla P. Benbow found that for every exceptional girl there were more than thirteen exceptional boys. This superior mathematical ability may contribute to men's Analytical/Conceptual preferences.

On the other hand, as mentioned above, women outperform men on verbal tasks. Physiologically, their verbal and spatial functions are more widely distributed. For example, damage to either the front or back of the left hemisphere affects speech in males, but female speech is rarely affected. Studies have shown that women recall words better, which helps explain why they may never forget what you said during an argument. This ability may also correlate with women's greater Expressiveness.

Women are much faster and more accurate at picking up emotions on faces. In one study, men were able to identify happiness in female faces with 90 percent accuracy, but they were less able to detect distress. "A woman's face had to be really sad for men to see it," says neurologist Ruben Gur, an expert on sex differences and the brain. Women's ability to rapidly notice subtleties in facial expressions gives them an edge over men when it comes to social cues.

Women really are more sensitive than men. Their skin is more sensitive, their sense of smell is better, they have wider peripheral vision, they see better in the dark, and they hear better with both ears. This heightened sensitivity and increased perceptual skill may help explain the phenomenon known as "women's intuition."

Current research has demonstrated that females, on average, have a larger deep limbic system than males. This may explain why women are more in

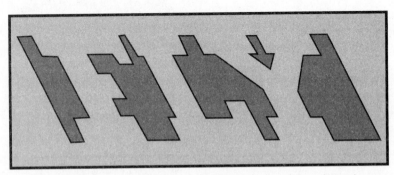

What does this image look like to you? Most men's brains are so busy analyzing the geometric shapes they do not recognize the word "FLY."

touch with their feelings, and they are generally better able to express their feelings than men. They have an increased ability to bond and be connected to others. This correlates with their Social responses to the Emergenetics questionnaire.

Women respond with stronger brain activation than men when they are both shown evocative photographs. In a study conducted by Turhan Canli, women and men responded very differently to the same pictures. Men, for example, would rate the picture of a gun, neutral, while women would rate it as highly negative. In addition, after three weeks, women remembered the pictures better. While men had about 60 percent recall, women had about 75 percent. This study suggests that women's brains are wired to feel and remember emotions more keenly. This may help explain why women tend to be more Social.

> The typical teenage girl has a sense of hearing seven times more acute than a teenage boy. That's why daughters so often complain that their fathers are shouting at them. Dad doesn't think he's shouting, but Dad doesn't hear his voice the way his daughter does.
>
> Leonard Sax, MD, PhD
> *Why Gender Matters*

Evolutionary Differences

The Thinking and Behavioral Attributes of women and men are influenced not only by hormonal and physiological differences, but also by evolution. Eons ago, men were the hunters, while women bore children and gathered food. Today women and men are no longer locked in these primitive roles, but this does not erase the effect of thousands of years of evolution.

The differences between the spatial abilities of women and men have been widely studied and discussed. It's not that women have inferior spatial skills, but that women and men have different abilities. For decades, studies have shown that men excel at such spatial activities as map reading, learning mazes, and mentally rotating three-dimensional images. These tasks are all associated with abstract thinking. Women, on the other hand, are superior at learning and remembering the location of objects. Some experiments done in mock offices have shown that women are 70 percent better than men at remembering the location of items found on a desktop. This task is associated with concrete thinking.

It's possible that this difference in skills is a result of "spatial evolution." As humans evolved, males were the primary hunters. They developed an ability to navigate long distances without losing their way. They often had to pursue prey and maintain their orientation at the same time. Women, conversely, were primarily gatherers. Successful gatherers were required to seek out and locate edible plants that were scattered sparsely among inedible ones. They were also required to remember these locations over successive growing seasons. Generations of prehistoric evolution further widened this cerebral divide.

In an interesting study, mothers and fathers were shown ten-second video clips of babies fussing, with the sound turned down. Using visual cues alone, most mothers were able to detect a range of emotions in the babies, from tiredness to hunger to pain. However, less than 10 percent of fathers could identify more than two emotions. This study may have been culturally influenced, because back in 1978, when the study took place, men were typically less involved in childrearing than they are today. However, it is possible that even though fathers today are generally more responsive to babies, they still find infants somewhat mystifying. It seems logical that over time, the forces of evolution have guided women—the primary caregivers—in the direction of being more responsive to social cues.

> What was especially interesting was that although men's and women's brains functioned differently, their comparable ability was very similar, indicating that there are potentially many different ways that the brain performs the same task.
>
> Bennett A. Shaywitz et al.,
> "Sex Differences in the
> Functional Organization of
> the Brain for Language"

Women and men will never be the same, and they don't need to be. On the other hand, they are not as far apart as we used to think. I have found that although there are inescapable differences between the sexes, the chasm between women and men is modulated by individual preferences.

In my lifetime, attitudes about what it means to be male or female have changed dramatically. In the future, I hope research about gender differences will be used not to create confining cliches that limit self-expression, but to allow both women and men to appreciate their innate capabilities—and each other.

COMMUNICATING WITH THE OPPOSITE SEX

A large part of Emergenetics is learning how to value others for who they are and how to appreciate their strengths. The same rules apply, whether you are talking about individual Profiles or gender differences. Create an inclusive team, and go with each other's strengths. Offices with a roughly equal number of women and men are healthier, and provide opportunities for mutual learning and respect.

According to the gender stereotypes, men report themselves more Analytical, Conceptual, and Assertive, while women report themselves more Structural, Social, Expressive, and Flexible. Because people are so complex, gender stereotypes do not always apply. As I've mentioned before, as soon as you start trying to put someone in a tidy little box, you'll see a hand waving outside. However, to the extent gender stereotypes *do* apply, keep in mind the following:

- Women and men can do the same things, but they will do them differently. Women and men can take completely different routes to the same conclusion. For example, women generally solve math problems by talking them through, while men generally solve them by thinking them through.

> Astronaut Sally Ride, upon being asked the question, "Did you get your brain from your father?" said, "Yes, my mother still has hers."

- Since women tend to prefer written directions and men tend to prefer maps, include both written directions and a map.
- Women tend to be more sensitive, and they might appreciate it when men honor their feelings.
- Men tend not to be as articulate or fluent in expressing their thoughts and feelings. This trait may require patience on the part of women.
- Men find long explanations tedious, so communicate efficiently. In an argument, as emotions escalate, men tend to become more rational and more aggressive. Women, on the other hand, tend to become more emotional and talkative.
- Many men are more Analytical and ASSERTIVE, so they are less likely than women to back down in an argument. Women, who often are more Social and FLEXIBLE, are more likely to back down or find another way out of an unpleasant situation. When a woman backs down, it doesn't necessarily mean she has conceded defeat. She may simply value keeping the peace more than winning.

Now it's time to take a look at your brain at work. In Part II we'll see how Emergenetics principles apply to the workplace.

PART II

Applying Emergenetics

You Can Change

But Why Would You Want To?

Can anyone really change?

"I could never speak in front of all those people. Public speaking isn't my thing."

"My assistant is late for work every day, and it drives me nuts when she isn't here. Is she ever going to get it?"

"I know I need to stick up for myself more, but I just freeze and the words won't come out of my mouth. Then afterwards I'm furious—at myself!"

"My wife says I never tell her that I love her. I don't understand why this is a problem, but it seems to bother her a lot."

Everybody has room for improvement. In fact, doing new things—or learning to do old things in new ways—is excellent for your brain, and will keep your mind sharper longer. But is it likely you, or your assistant, or your significant other, will change spontaneously? Not according to our research.

Test/re-test analyses show that people who completed the Emergenetics profile a second time, up to ten years later, tended to answer the questions in much the same manner as they did the first time. Conceptual scores increased slightly between the first testing and the second testing. We think this might be due to an Emergenetics "workshop effect" where participants learned that being Conceptual can be a "good thing." As we age, we do smooth our edges. However, we don't change drastically.

Imagine what would happen if people were different each day they came to work. What holds us together as a society is consistency in behavior. It is very rare for people to shift from the first-third to the third-third of the population, or vice versa, unless they deliberately decide to change their Profile, or they experience a significant life event that changes them.

Does this mean people act the same in every situation? Of course not. People are incredibly adaptable. Their display of Thinking and Behavioral Attributes depends in part on their environment. Often the way they act at home is vastly different from the way they act at work. However, this does not mean they have a different Profile for home and for work.

Luke received his Profile, which was primarily Analytical and Structural, at one of my workshops. He came up to me after the seminar and proclaimed, "My profile is accurate for how I am at work. However, it would not be the same for me at home. If my family were to fill out the questionnaire for me, they would answer these questions differently. I answered the questions when I was at work. If I were answering them at home, my answers would have been different."

Luke has four children, and when he is at home, he keeps his mind on his family and not on his work. I suggested that he fill out the questionnaire at home.

One week later, his results were very similar. How was this possible? Well, it's possible that he used his Social brain, which was 18 percent of his Profile, more at home than he did at work. He wasn't a different person. He was simply exercising different Attributes for different purposes.

It's true that the way you answer all the Emergenetics questions will not be 100 percent consistent every time. As is the case with any test, your answers will be affected by how you feel at that particular moment. If you're in a great mood you may answer a few questions a point or two higher. However, if you're feeling less expansive, you may answer a few questions a point or two lower. This may mean the difference between results in the 95th percentile or the 80th percentile—but is highly unlikely that your score would change from the third-third of the population to the first-third.

Each Emergenetics Attribute is like a rubber band. Most of the time you operate with the rubber band at rest. Occasionally, the rubber band is required to stretch, depending on the situation, but when the job is finished, it returns to its original shape.

When you "stretch" your Attributes, you'll find that you tire more quickly. Remember Foster, who performed our lunchtime entertainment in Africa— and afterward disappeared for twenty-four hours to recover? He was able to expand his Expressiveness for his performance, but it wore him out. One way to avoid running out of gas because you are operating out of a less-preferred Thinking or Behavioral Attribute is to use your strongest Attribute as leverage.

WORKING THROUGH YOUR STRENGTHS

You don't have to fundamentally change your Profile to accomplish tasks that your brain is not wired to perform. You can work through your strengths to do what you need to do, without permanently shifting your Thinking Attributes.

Let's say you have to attend an annual conference for your industry that involves listening to presentations, meeting clients, attending lunches and dinners, and going to late-night parties. This is a marathon event that requires lots of energy over several days. How are you going to handle it?

- If **Analytical** thinking is your strongest preference, then your Analytical brain will get you through. If you have a choice of presentations, do some research and find out which presenters are the most focused and well informed. Try to determine ahead of time who will be at which lunch or dinner or party so you will be able to meet up with specific people and accomplish something at each event. If you are *Expressive* or *Flexible,* expect that you might be tired afterward.
- If **Structural** thinking is your forte, list the clients with whom you need to meet. Rank them from "essential" to "if there's time," and write down three key questions you need to discuss with each one. To make the best use of your time, set up appointments in advance.

- If **Social** thinking and EXPRESSIVE behavior are your greatest preferences, you will be in heaven. People for you to talk to are everywhere!
- If **Conceptual** thinking is your strongest attribute, leave your schedule open and wander from event to event, so you are sure to pick up new ideas and trends.

The following sections contain guidelines for working through your strongest Thinking Attribute to succeed. Exactly how you do this will be influenced by your Behavioral Attributes. I could go into all the permutations of Thinking and Behavioral Attributes, but it would take until next Sunday and I don't think you have that much time.

WORKING THROUGH YOUR ANALYTICAL BRAIN (BLUE)

Using Your Analytical Brain (Blue) to Be More . . .

Structural (Green)
- Write a structured poem, such as a haiku, a sonnet, or verse in iambic pentameter.
- Organize your books in alphabetical order.

Social (Red)
- Like Stuart, use your PDA to remind you to be more Social on particular days. This could mean encouraging your staff, doing something nice for your partner, or giving someone a hug. I know one techie who programmed his computer to remind him on random days to send flowers to his girlfriend.
- Read a book about interpersonal skills.

Conceptual (Yellow)
- Play classical music (Mozart, Bach, Vivaldi) while you work.
- Listen to someone who has "far out" ideas without passing judgment.

Stuart and I shared a platform together as we were lecturing to a bunch of CEOs of advertising firms. He went first. Stuart told our audience that there were ten ways to make a successful advertising company. Number ten on his list was as follows: "Since we don't pay people in our agency much money, and they all have big egos, it is necessary to compliment them on a regular basis." As I listened to this, I was astounded, because I had Stuart's Profile in my folder and I knew he was an Analytical/Conceptual thinker with a lot of Expressiveness and Assertiveness, but no Social preference to speak of. How had he come up with the importance of compliments?

Afterward, I commented on this to Stuart, and he said, "I've read Tom Peters's books, and I know that I am supposed to compliment people in order to help them perform better."

I suggested that he didn't come into the world wired this way, and that for him to even remember to compliment his team was amazing.

He then pulled out his day planner (this was before PDAs) and showed me that on the 27th day of every month he had written down a reminder to go through the agency and hand out compliments.

Stuart understood the significance of working through his Analytical preference to shore up his Social attribute, and since he had one of the most successful advertising agencies, I guess it worked. Stuart hadn't fundamentally changed his Profile, nor did he want to. Rather, he chose to accomplish his Social tasks by using his Analytical preference, drawing also on his Expressiveness and Assertiveness to help him. On the 27th day of the month, he allowed his sliver of Social thinking to emerge.

WORKING THROUGH YOUR STRUCTURAL BRAIN (GREEN)

Margie is a Structural thinker who is *Expressive* and *Assertive.* She was always annoyed in brainstorming meetings because she felt as if she could not think fast enough. She would have an idea, but be unable to articulate it fully, or she would come up with a great idea after the meeting ended. I encouraged Margie to do some private brainstorming before these meetings and to write down some ideas ahead of time—or if that wasn't possible, to submit her ideas the following day. She certainly was *not* stupid. She just needed time to filter her ideas through her Structural preference, weighing concepts and thoughts about different alternatives.

Using her Structural preference to write down her brainstorming ideas prior to the meetings made it much easier for Margie to express her thoughts when the time came. Her comments were always well received, and she began to feel more confident. Soon she did not have to "pre-brainstorm," and her sliver of Conceptual thinking was able to freely come out in meetings.

Using Your Structural Brain (Green) to Be More . . .

Analytical (Blue)
- Compose a step-by-step plan for a work project. Turn it into a flow chart with diagrams, arrows, and so on.
- Read something you would never have considered reading, and make an outline of what you learned.

Social (Red)
- Keep a list of interpersonal questions by the telephone and use at least one in every conversation.
- Put an agenda together with brainstorming help from another.

Conceptual (Yellow)
- Take down the clocks in your office.
- Delegate a project, and do not inquire about it until the due date.

WORKING THROUGH YOUR SOCIAL BRAIN (RED)

Griffen was a strong Social thinker who was *Expressive, Assertive,* and FLEXI-BLE. She was one of the first women officers of a large corporation. She had almost no preference for Analytical thinking in her Profile, and her level of Assertiveness did not allow her to self-promote the way many successful executives often do. I followed Griffen's career through the years as she ascended from management jobs to vice president of finance. It took Griffen many years to understand that she kept getting promoted because she understood the importance of other people's jobs and how to make them feel good about what they did. Griffen underestimated her gift, and kept thinking she wouldn't be promoted again because she wouldn't know anything about the responsibilities of the next job. Yet she kept getting higher-level positions, and each time she did well.

Griffen did not need to know how to do everyone else's job because she was good at drawing information out of people. Even though she did not have a preference for Analytical thought, Griffen usually knew the numbers because she excelled at getting and remembering the information she needed. She also could "feel" the numbers, and responded to them from her gut intuition (remember the "second brain"?). In fact, her employees were amazed to learn at an Emergenetics seminar that Griffen had no Analytical preference in her Profile.

People loved working for Griffen because she was so appreciative of what they did. She made them feel that their efforts were important, and that they played a key role in the big picture. While other managers struggled with issues like productivity and company morale, Griffen was very successful at keeping her people highly motivated.

Using Your Social Brain (Red) to Be More . . .

Analytical (Blue)
- Read stories about people—but choose a business publication like the *Wall Street Journal* or *Forbes* magazine.
- Program your cell phone with the numbers of all your friends.

Structural (Green)
- Enlist the help of your Structural friends to make sure you're on time. Ask them how long it will take to get where you need to go, and leave when they tell you to.
- Put the names of people you need to call on a list. You must call them at the end of the day after you have completed your other work.

Conceptual (Yellow)
- Replace your usual greeting with, "Have I got an idea for you!" Then have one.
- Take a friend to a movie with subtitles.

WORKING THROUGH YOUR CONCEPTUAL BRAIN (YELLOW)

Scott Halford, one of my Associates, is a huge Conceptual thinker who is also EXPRESSIVE and ASSERTIVE. His bar percentage for Structural thinking registers at the 5th percentile. He describes the 95 percent blank area left over as the "great white sucking space."

While Scott has little preference for organized, detailed, administrative tasks, most people would never know it. If you invite him for dinner, his thank-you note will be in the next day's mail. If he is sent an invoice, the check arrives within three days. When I expressed some amazement about this, Scott said, "I have lots of Assertiveness, and I know I have to take care of these tasks. So I rise every morning at 5 a.m. and work on all my Structural tasks for one hour. At that point the great white sucking space takes over and I have no energy for Structural thinking for the rest of the day."

Scott used his Conceptual thinking to come up with an excellent plan of attack for his Structural duties. However, from time to time his little sliver of Structural sabotages him. In January, we received a check that he neglected to sign, and a note that read, "For invoice 1928 and whatever else seems to be outstanding."

Using Your Conceptual Brain (Yellow) to Be More . . .

Analytical (Blue)
- Do your budget in pictures.
- String some ideas together and fill in the blanks between concepts.

Social (Red)
- Tell your significant other that you couldn't do your job without her or his support.
- Compliment the person who had an idea that jazzed you.

Structural (Green)
- Create a meeting agenda with artistic designs on it.
- Make a game out of doing a Structural task. For instance, number your essential tasks and do each one in order every Friday. Then reward yourself with a massage.

As you can see from these examples, everyone has the ability to accomplish tasks that are associated with a non-preferred attribute. Since each person's Profile is an extraordinary gift, there is no need to change. If you insist on making a permanent change, however, the next section explains the best way to go about it.

IF YOU INSIST ON CONSCIOUSLY CHANGING, HERE'S THE WAY TO DO IT

Beth was an actuary of an insurance company located in the Midwest. At the time Beth attended my seminar, she had the highest Analytical preference I had ever seen in our database, backed up by a preference for Structural thinking. Beth's Flexibility was in the first-third, which suggested she could be definite in her opinions.

After the seminar was over, Beth asked if she could change her Profile. I informed her that her brain was well suited for her job, and also told her it is difficult to change. She insisted, however, that she wanted to develop other parts of her mind. Her profile represented 1 percent of the population, and she did not believe that being in this minority was a gift. She wanted to relate more closely to other points of view and to other people. "You don't know me very well," she said. "Once I put my mind to it, I can do anything." I was sure this was true, especially since her profile indicated a preference for Assertiveness.

Beth called me three months later and admitted that getting out of her Analytical brain had been harder than she expected. "Here are three things I have done that have been particularly difficult," she told me. "First, I signed up for piano lessons. By circumstance, I found a piano teacher who does not teach piano in the traditional way. I went to my first lesson with my new big red music book, but the teacher suggested I simply put my hands on the keys and make noise. I was flummoxed by this and thought it was a waste of time. However, being a good student, I put my hands on the keyboard and music occurred. I was astounded.

"The second thing I did was ask Ted, a man in my department who I believe is quite Social and Conceptual, if he would have lunch with me every Friday. I always avoided Ted because he seemed so strange, and so I thought it was a good idea to have lunch with him once a week. We would go up to the executive dining room, sit next to the window overlooking the city, and have a conversation. I could never figure out what he was saying to me. It seemed to me that we spent a lot of time talking about the clouds.

"The third thing I did was the most difficult. I made a decision to be *late* to three meetings. My Analytical self still made me show up early for these meetings like normal, because this is what I was supposed to do. After I got there, however, I would hide out in a bathroom stall until the meeting had been going on for ten minutes. The first time I did this, perspiration beaded on my forehead, and I entered the room nervous that someone would scold me for being late. The meeting had not even begun. By the third meeting, I was still perspiring and nervous about being late, but I was getting the impression that no one seemed to care. No one ever mentioned my tardiness."

Two months later, Beth called again with big news. She said she was noticing significant changes in her thinking. "Today, Ted and I had lunch," she said, "and this time he actually made sense."

Over the next year, I watched Beth's Profile change from highly Analytical with some Structural, to Analytical, Structural, and Social (a Tri-left), while her behaviors stayed the same. She said, "You told me in your research that opposites attract, and my husband, Kent, has lots of Social and Conceptual in his profile. When I first met him, I was thrilled with his devil-may-care attitude. But after many years of marriage, there were things that annoyed me. Now I understand more how he thinks."

Another year later, Beth decided to take a course on writing poetry. Before the course ended, the professor told her that her writing was clearly publishable. Over the following months her profile changed again, from a Tri-left to mainly Analytical and Conceptual. In addition, her Flexibility had moved into the second-third.

The end of this story is that eventually Beth realized the insurance corporation was too stifling for her. She quit her job and moved to another city. Using her actuarial skills and her new willingness to take risks, she became a consulting career actuary, one of the few in the country.

Beth admits that changing her Thinking Attributes was a great struggle for her. However, since she was so motivated to do so, she was able to persevere. I have stayed in contact with her through the years, and to this day she mentions that even though she likes her new Profile, there are times when she wishes she could go back to her original Analytical self. "There is safety in numbers, and in the Conceptual world, I don't always know if I am right," she said.

Beth started me thinking about how difficult it is to change your Profile. This caused me to look at the brain research about the neurobiology of change—or, more correctly, the neurobiology of why it is so hard to change.

Why Changing Your Profile Is So Difficult

The brain creates a neural pathway each time you learn something new. At birth an abundant amount of basic circuitry is in place. In the first few years, neuron growth proceeds at an amazing rate, allowing us to learn, remember, speak, and move. Beginning with puberty, the growth rate slows down. During adolescence, the brain makes stronger connections between the circuits that are used regularly. In time the circuits and neurons that are seldom (or never) used are eliminated through neuronal pruning.

Efficient neuronal circuitry makes it easier to do some things "automatically." On the other hand, part of the reason bad habits are hard to break is that the brain has become hardwired to perform them without thinking.

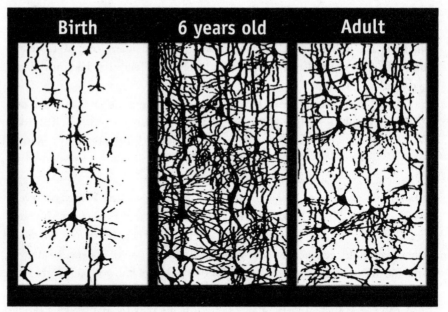

These drawings show what neurons in the brain cortex look like at different stages of life. When we are young, our life experiences cause connections to occur between neurons in the brain. Later, the neurons and circuits that are seldom or never used are pruned away. "Practice makes perfect" because doing the same thing repeatedly strengthens neuronal circuitry. On the other hand, ingrained habits can be hard to break because they no longer involve conscious effort.

Here is an easy way to see how powerful our habits really are. Set this book aside and write the following sentence *without crossing any "t's" or dotting any "i's":*

Ten different times I told you to
write the word timber.

How did you do? If you are like most people, probably not too well. If you think you did well, show someone else your paper, because if you wrote the sentence wrong, chances are you also read it wrong.

My point is not that you can't do this. You are a human being. You can do anything you want. If you practiced, you would get better. However, it is extremely difficult to change a habit once the neural pathways are ingrained. Young children don't have nearly as much trouble with this exercise because their brains are still fresh.

As the brain matures and becomes more specialized, neurons are recruited and reinforced through repetition. In order to learn a new skill, you must engage in repetitive motions that set up and sharpen new neural pathways. New habits must supersede the old ones.

When we want to make a change, it takes repetition and time to rewire the conscious and unconscious synaptic circuitry to form a new habit. When you're trying to form a habit or skill, it takes conscious effort until the new behavior goes into your unconscious mind.

Leslie G. Ungerleider, chief of the Laboratory of Brain and Cognition at the National Institutes of Health, carried out weekly functional magnetic resonance imaging (fMRI) on volunteers while they learned a sequence of finger movements. Ungerleider was able to observe changes in activity patterns of the brain. During the first week, while the activity is new and different, Ungerleïder speculates that neurons are "recruited into the neuronal network" that controls the movement sequence. Over time, as the movements are further practiced and ingrained, more neurons are recruited and involved in the performance of the sequence. Furthermore, the brain changes were detected a year later, even though training had ceased. This is why you often hear statements like "It takes twenty-one days to change a habit."

As You Think, So Shall It Be

The placebo effect is well documented. People who are given a sugar pill, believing it is a powerful medication, feel better. Clearly, beliefs can be self-fulfilling. If you decide you want to change your Profile, then a good place to begin is by believing you will be successful.

While logical thought is obviously important, emotions also play an enormous role in determining our success. Some emotional, subconscious cues that come straight from the amygdala aren't even processed by the more rational cortex. This explains how we can undermine and sabotage ourselves without recognizing it. On the other hand, when all the parts of our brain are working toward the same purpose, we are unstoppable.

The amygdala's automatic responses represent habits built on our perception of past experiences. These beliefs and values can, in turn, be consciously modified. When we repeat certain assertions, they eventually sink into the amygdala and influence our behavior. This process helps align our subconscious with our conscious ideals.

Conscious affirmations—positive statements like "I'm acing this exam!" or "I feel happy and energetic today"—really do make a difference. Martin Seligman, author of *Authentic Happiness* and other books on positive psychology, did a study involving freshmen at the University of Pennsylvania, and found that the students who earned grades that were significantly better than predicted used "optimistic self-talk" that helped them keep their goal in the forefront of their minds. On the other hand, Seligman cautions that simply repeating a positive thought does not affect achievement very much, unless it is connected to your coping style. Seligman's approach to positive thinking includes consciously disputing our negative thoughts and beliefs, and paying attention to our "explanatory style," or how we talk to ourselves about setbacks. For example, if you suffer a business reversal, the message you send to yourself is "I am able to fix this."

As you set about changing your Profile, you can help ensure your success by visualizing the outcome you desire in as compelling a way as you can. This is effective because your brain can't tell the difference between what is real and what is vividly imagined. In a study at MIT, volunteers were shown photographs, then asked to recollect them. The same region in their brain was activated whether they were looking at actual photographs, or seeing them in their mind's eye. Similarly, when you visualize your future—preferably with all the emotions, sights, sounds, and smells associated with it—you program your brain to make it real.

You have undoubtedly seen world-class athletes—golfers, divers, skiers—visualizing their next move. At the Olympics we have an opportunity to witness the best athletes in the world rehearsing in their mind what they are about to do with their body. Studies have shown that executing the moves mentally has a positive effect on executing the moves physically.

If you keep the image, dream, or goal in mind while incorporating new information along the way on a conscious and unconscious level, you will reach or even leap to a different place. Being able to see, hear, and feel what it will be like to be successful in your task helps ensure your success.

Watch your words, because your brain is listening. For example, saying "I *try* my best" is not the same as saying "I *do* my best." There's a difference between "I can't remember" and "I haven't remembered *yet*." In addition, intentions are more powerful when they are expressed in the present tense ("I am ASSERTIVE") instead of the future tense ("I will be ASSERTIVE").

> I'm a great believer in luck, and I find the harder I work, the more I have of it.
>
> **Thomas Jefferson**

We all maintain a running mental commentary. When our inner voice says negative things, it takes a terrible toll on our energy and enthusiasm. Imagine a little troll on your shoulder all day long who critiques your every move with a snide remark. "Why are you so stupid?" "You stink at math!" "You just aren't Social." "You're so boring." I'm sure you would knock him senseless.

You can fight the troll of negativity not only with positive words, affirmations, and visualizations, but also with positive facial expressions. Dr. Marco Iacoboni at the University of California did a study that revealed a connection between facial expressions and activity in the amygdala. Make an angry face, and you will start to feel mad. Make a big smile, and you will feel optimistic.

> The greatest discovery of my generation is that human beings can alter their lives by altering their attributes of mind.
>
> **William James**

Do it. It works.

Four Steps to the New You

Each individual mind carries great gifts and strengths, and adds valuable insight to a group project. You are who you are. However, if you want to shift one of your Thinking or Behavioral Attributes, it requires the following:

1. *Choose a positive motivation.*

Motivation is the key to any change. It's like the old joke: "How many psychologists does it take to change a light bulb?" Answer: "One, but he has to *want* to change."

If someone tells you NOT to think about pink elephants, what is the first thing you think about? Right—pink elephants. The brain is always positive. It attempts to place thoughts in context. Positive goals can be linked to positive behavior, but negative goals are without context. If you say, "I do NOT want to be inflexible!" all your brain hears is "inflexible." On the other hand, if you say, "I want to be Flexible!" your brain hears "Flexible." Now you have something to work toward—not against. When we say, "Don't drink and drive," what our brains actually hear is "Drink and drive." The better slogan is "Drink responsibly." To be successful, turn a negative motivation ("I don't want to be so rigid") into a positive one ("I am FLEXIBLE").

Suppose you want to be more Assertive. Place a note that says "I AM AS-SERTIVE" in a place where you will see it every day—the bathroom mirror, your refrigerator, the dashboard of your car, your computer screen, or all of them. This is your story, and you're sticking to it.

2. *Imagine your goal.*

You may wish to change because you want to develop a wider repertoire of behaviors that allow you to operate in the world at large. Changing may be important in order to take advantage of opportunities at work. It even may be part of your plan to keep your brain sharp well into old age. Whatever your long-term purpose may be, try to capture a vision of where you want to be in the future. Use your strengths to really see yourself in the context of having met your goal, and take a moment to enjoy this vision. If visualizing isn't your thing, use your other powers of imagination to feel, hear, smell, or sense what your success will be like. The abstract (Analytical/Conceptual) part of your brain desires a broad goal. It needs to see the forest before it counts the trees.

3. *Make a 21-Day Plan.*

The concrete (Structural/Social) part of your brain wants to count the trees. Here you focus in and decide which small step of the broad vision you want to work with first. To make any kind of lasting change, you must engage in 21 sequential days of activities that are directly tied to your desired transformation. Connect your goal to taking action every day. If you happen to skip a day of your 21-Day Plan, guess what? You must start all over again from Day 1!

Take time to write down the chronological steps. If you are ASSERTIVE, you will be pleased with this list because you know it will help you achieve your goal as quickly as possible. If you are *Assertive,* this list will solidify your commitment.

If you are FLEXIBLE, you may make adjustments to your list as you go along. Perhaps you'll find a different activity that works better for you. If you are *Flexible,* you probably will not deviate from your 21 steps once you have established them. You already know they are the best possible steps for you.

4. *Enlist others to help you.*

Identify people who will help you achieve your goal, or who will benefit from your success. When you tell others, it makes you accountable for your success. The number of people you involve in your quest depends on your level of Expressiveness. If you are in the first-third of Expressiveness, you may want to tell one friend. If you are in the third-third of Expressiveness, you may want to tell the world!

> My friend Carol Hunter called me shortly after Amazon.com was launched and said, "It's so great to have the ability to buy books online that I ordered books for 21 days straight. Now it's the 22nd day, and I feel the urge to order another book. How do I stop?"

21–DAY PLANS FOR CHANGING
YOUR EMERGENETICS ATTRIBUTES

Steve is a manager who was motivated enough to make a 21-Day Plan and stick with it, and he saw big changes. Although Steve is physically imposing, he used to describe himself as "5'18" tall," and he felt he was being held back by his *Assertiveness.*

Below is the 21-Day Plan Steve developed and meticulously followed. In the end, he not only changed his Assertiveness, but also his Conceptual, Structural, and Social thinking. Because the Attributes work together, Steve changed other things he wasn't planning to change.

Today Steve is happy to be in the business development advisory group, the business management consulting group of his bank. Steve says that it is better to be ASSERTIVE when he is developing business for the bank, and he also notes that his increased Social nature has helped in his home life as well.

STEVE'S 21-DAY DIARY OF BECOMING MORE ASSERTIVE

DAY 1   I belong to a group that builds business skills. Today I had my group address my project *first.* Ordinarily, I would have waited for others to do theirs before mine, but I wanted to make sure we didn't run out of time or ideas before we got to mine.

DAY 2	I delegated a project upward when it became apparent that I had a time conflict with two projects scheduled for the same time.
DAY 3	I snuck out of a meeting to personally deliver wedding anniversary flowers to my wife at her place of work. I kissed her in front of her boss and several high school students, quite an open display of affection for a Russian-German like me.
DAY 4	I picked out a restaurant where I wanted to eat rather than taking nominations from the floor.
DAY 5	I appropriated the best TV in the house for watching the Broncos in their Super Bowl-winning effort.
DAY 6	I wore my Bronco colors to the bank even though it was not an official casual day.
DAY 7	I invited a coworker I didn't know very well out to lunch.
DAY 8	The receptionist from my eye doctor's office called to remind me of an appointment for later in the day. I reminded her that my appointment was really for tomorrow. She acknowledged her error. In the old days, I never would have said anything.
DAY 9	I called the *Denver Post* to point out that my newspaper was not delivered by 6:00 a.m. as advertised and that I really did need it by that time.
DAY 10	My daughter requested an advance on her allowance even though she had not repaid her last advance. I told her no advances until she cleared up her arrears.
DAY 11	I talked to my younger brother about a discussion I had with a friend about how our father shaped our lives. Although talking about this sensitive subject initially caused awkwardness, as we continued to compare notes on our father, we reached an understanding we had never achieved before.
DAY 12	I left the office on time in order to get in a workout at the gym, even though a coworker was lobbying for more of my time and I habitually acquiesce to these requests.

DAY 13 I stuck to my guns on a contract proposal and the other party agreed to my terms even though historically they would have expected me to compromise.

DAY 14 I volunteered a marketing idea in our staff meeting.

DAY 15 I volunteered to do an impromptu speech at the Toastmaster's meeting even though I had done no preparation for it in advance.

DAY 16 I asked a pointed question at an annual stockholders' meeting, where I have traditionally blended in with the woodwork.

DAY 17 I sent food back to a restaurant kitchen because it wasn't prepared the way I had requested. I have never done this before.

DAY 18 I grounded our oldest daughter for violating her curfew. It is getting easier all the time to be more Assertive in an effective and non-threatening way.

DAY 19 I volunteered to be in charge of passing the collection plate at church even though I had never done this before or paid attention to how it was to be done.

DAY 20 I approached a senior manager about taking over a project that was assigned to him but that I thought really belonged in my division. I didn't know this exercise would be as much about managing conflict as about being more Assertive.

DAY 21 Today I delivered a speech to one of the bank's larger operating units (about fifty employees) concerning the market research efforts underway. I took this opportunity to relate to this group some of my own personal philosophy about what working for this bank is really all about, beyond just drawing a regular paycheck.

In the pages that follow, you'll find 21-Day Plans with ideas to help you change some of your Thinking or Behavioral Attributes. These plans are designed to help you become:

- More Analytical
- More Structural

- More Social
- More Conceptual
- More Expressive
- More Flexible
- Less Expressive
- Less Assertive
- Less Flexible

I have not included a plan for becoming more Assertive because you have just read Steve's diary.

A 21-Day Plan for Becoming More Analytical

1. Read an analysis in the *New York Times.*
2. Program your cell phone with all your important telephone numbers.
3. Plan a food budget for a year.
4. Cut the same budget by 10 percent.
5. Run your finances through a computer budget program.
6. Figure out your grocery bill before you reach the checkout line.
7. Play a mind game like Scrabble.
8. Put together a personal financial statement.
9. Help a child with math homework.
10. Read a technical journal about your work.
11. Read a business magazine like *Fortune, Forbes,* or *Business Week.*
12. Calculate the miles per gallon on your next tank of gas.
13. Write a 250-word essay, analyzing your work environment.
14. Read the *Economist* and compare it with an American publication's viewpoint.
15. Wear a digital watch that is set to the most accurate time.
16. Thoroughly research the latest technical gadget, such as a computer, camera, or cell phone, comparing data from several Web sites.
17. Purchase this item and figure out how to use or program it.
18. Go to an art museum and read a book about the works within an exhibit and figure out which one is most valuable to you.

19. Engage a friend in an intellectual conversation about a current event.
20. Watch a movie with a complicated mystery plot.
21. Read the *Wall Street Journal*.

Things to do every day:

- Do the brain teasers in the newspaper.
- Take flying lessons.
- Follow your company's stock price.

A 21-Day Plan for Becoming More Structural

1. Prepare a schedule for the day and stick to it.
2. Divide your tasks into essential and nonessential categories and only do the essential items.
3. Number your essential tasks and do each one in order.
4. Set the automatic timer on the coffee pot before you go to bed.
5. Organize your junk room and throw away anything you have not touched in a year.
6. The next day, do the same for your closet.
7. The next day, do it for your kitchen's "Murphy drawer."
8. Organize your wardrobe so all of your same-color shirts are hanging in the same direction.
9. Arrive seven minutes early to every meeting of the day.
10. Wear an analog watch that is set to the most accurate time.
11. Prioritize your grocery list to correspond with the layout of the store.
12. Create a project list.
13. Read an instruction manual from cover to cover before you begin a project.
14. Write a letter that details the events of your day and the times they occur.
15. Meticulously edit every e-mail you send.
16. Be initially hesitant of others' ideas for a day.
17. Observe the speed limit for the entire day.

18. Make dinner using a recipe, and follow it exactly.
19. Sit at your desk and work at your computer the entire day.
20. Buy a Franklin Planner and use it exactly how you are instructed.
21. File and alphabetize the instruction manuals for your office machines.

Things to do every day:

- Lay out your clothes for the next day every night before you go to bed.
- Meticulously save all receipts and record your expenditures.
- Read a "how to" book from cover to cover.

A 21-Day Plan for Becoming More Social

1. Host a dinner party.
2. Call a friend to "just talk."
3. Bake and deliver cookies to your neighbor.
4. Seek the opinion of four friends with different brain types on a personal problem.
5. Hug one person.
6. Begin a business conversation by inquiring about the other person's family and personal health.
7. Ask the store clerk about his life.
8. Send a note of recognition and appreciation to an employee.
9. Tell a personal story using the pronoun "I."
10. Listen carefully to your friend's story.
11. Send flowers to somebody.
12. Ask someone to explain a task to you.
13. Before acting upon a decision, consider how it will affect others.
14. Encourage another's ideas with positive words.
15. Flip a coin to make a decision.
16. Wear a watch that lights up with different colors.
17. Place a picture of your family on your desk.
18. Donate money to a charity.
19. Hug two people today.
20. Call two friends to "just talk."
21. Volunteer at a soup kitchen.

Things to do every day:

- Call, write, or e-mail a friend.
- Enroll in a listening-skills class.
- Read a romance novel.

A 21-Day Plan for Becoming More Conceptual

1. Rearrange your office furniture.
2. Leave your wristwatch at home.
3. Bring in a new office decoration.
4. Hang an abstract picture in your home or office.
5. Go to lunch at an ethnic restaurant.
6. Take a different path at a different time to work.
7. Assemble a project by only looking at the pictures.
8. Play jazz music in your office.
9. Do something "just for kicks."
10. Wear something outrageous to work.
11. Make dinner from scratch and use no recipe.
12. Make a new outfit from the clothes you already possess.
13. Take an unplanned vacation, and maybe pack a suitcase.
14. Eat breakfast for dinner.
15. Go for a walk or jog with no goal in mind.
16. Buy something unusual, with no notion of what to do with it.
17. Make a broad, twenty-year personal future plan.
18. Make up a new way to solve an old problem.
19. See pictures in the clouds.
20. Do five minutes of interpretative dance.
21. Figure out a way to do a task differently.

Things to do every day:

- Take an art class.
- Daydream.
- Take up a cultural activity, for example, tai chi or yoga.

A 21-Day Plan for Becoming More Expressive

1. Tell a significant other how you feel.
2. Stand up in front of an audience and make a presentation.
3. At a group meeting, be the first to volunteer your opinion.
4. Plan a party and take credit for the success.
5. At a mealtime, volunteer what you learned today.
6. Compliment a stranger.
7. Tell a joke.
8. Voluntarily teach others about something you know.
9. Answer questions out loud in a meeting.
10. During a discussion, feel free to break in on another's remarks.
11. Tell someone your ideas on a new project before you have fully thought them through.
12. Ask a coworker to explain unfamiliar aspects of his job.
13. Tell another about your weekend.
14. Ask two questions at the upcoming meeting.
15. Incorporate exaggerated hand gestures in your conversations.
16. Stand up to make a point.
17. Talk with a loud voice.
18. Call a long-lost friend.
19. Wear something particularly loud or vibrant to the office.
20. Join a Toastmaster's Club.
21. Talk to the cashier at Starbucks.

Things to do every day:

- Say "hooray" every time you are happy about something.
- Initiate and sustain a dinner conversation.
- Attend an Outward Bound program.

A 21-Day Plan for Becoming More Flexible

1. Let someone else choose the paint color for your office.
2. Change your favorite brand just for the sake of change.

3. Act on advice given to you that would completely be out of your comfort zone.
4. Drink tea all day instead of coffee, or vice versa.
5. Write with a different pen or different color of ink.
6. Sleep on the opposite side of the bed.
7. Change the direction of your toilet paper rolls.
8. Brush your teeth with the other hand.
9. Have your partner plan the weekend and go along with it.
10. Agree with friends on a movie without offering your opinion.
11. Ask someone else to order your dinner—and then eat it all.
12. Go to a restaurant someone else has selected.
13. Upon request, stop what you are doing when you are in the middle of a work project.
14. Invite someone from another culture to dinner.
15. Get rid of all the clocks in your office.
16. Operate one whole day with no agenda.
17. Tell every person, for an entire day, that you can see their point.
18. Procrastinate.
19. Provide several options in a meeting, even though you have your choice in mind.
20. Imagine a new method of completing an old task.
21. Wear something uncharacteristic.

Things to do every day:

- Be available without an appointment.
- Wear your wristwatch on your opposite arm.
- Answer the phone with your opposite hand.

A 21-Day Plan for Becoming Less Expressive

1. Clasp your hands behind your back when talking to another person.
2. At a meeting, wait for three people to speak before you offer your opinion.
3. All day, stifle the urge to tell a story about yourself.
4. All day, stifle the urge to tell a joke.

5. All day, focus on others instead of calling attention to yourself in any manner.
6. Stay alone for one hour with no outside interruptions—no phone, TV, e-mail, and so on. You may read and write, but without the use of electronic devices.
7. Stay alone all day with no outside interruptions—no phone, TV, e-mail, and so on. You may read and write, but without the use of electronic devices.
8. All day, answer a question only after you have spent five seconds thinking of your response.
9. Stay silent in a meeting.
10. Write your expressive thoughts in a journal instead of saying them.
11. Ask open-ended questions that cause others to talk for long periods of time.
12. When someone is talking, wait to speak until her or his thought is fully expressed.
13. Write down answers to questions instead of verbally relaying them to others.
14. Resist the urge to volunteer for any activity in a meeting.
15. Wear a muted color of clothing with no sparkly accessories.
16. Go all day without interrupting someone else's conversation.
17. Send an e-mail to someone without any smiley faces ☺ or exclamation marks!!!!
18. Go to a meeting and don't share any stories before, during, or after it.
19. No phone calls all day.
20. Limit your conversations all day to business topics.
21. Don't roll your eyes or make any faces.

Things to do every day:

- Minimize your hand gestures
- Talk less
- Wait for others to speak first

A 21-Day Plan for Becoming Less Assertive

1. Keep your plan to be less Assertive to yourself.
2. Allow everyone on the highway to pass you.
3. Drive the speed limit all day.
4. Drive courteously—no honking or rude gestures.
5. Stand at the end of the line and allow others to butt in.
6. Schedule an activity with cushion time for last-minute glitches.
7. Walk (as opposed to run) to every appointment.
8. Keep your opinion to yourself.
9. Volunteer to do an activity for others that you normally would not do.
10. When a group of people are discussing where to go for lunch, remain silent on the subject and go to whichever restaurant they decide.
11. Give in to other people's arguments.
12. Step on the escalator and stay on the same step until you reach the end.
13. Push the elevator button only once.
14. In a meeting, don't raise your hand to volunteer.
15. Schedule a task for next week or next month but not today.
16. Sit still for one hour.
17. Let others do what they think is best.
18. Let someone else choose what movie to see.
19. Let someone else make a decision that affects you.
20. Take only well-considered actions.
21. Take a long time to make a decision.

Things to do every day:

- Acquiesce to the decisions of others.
- Refrain from commenting, even if you disagree.
- Let others go first.

A 21-Day Plan for Becoming Less Flexible

1. Decide what to do on an outing before you get in the car.
2. Break tasks into smaller units.
3. Refuse to take on additional volunteer work.
4. Refuse to take on another project until you have finished the one on your desk.
5. Stick to your original plan for the day and do not deviate except in an emergency.
6. Announce the time the group is leaving and stick to it.
7. Begin and end every meeting exactly on time, as announced.
8. Announce your opinion and be prepared to justify your reasoning.
9. Schedule a trip, determine the route, and stop along the way only if it is in the itinerary.
10. Present one option as the best option, even though there are several choices.
11. Set and announce the meeting agenda for the day and adhere to the allotted time intervals.
12. Begin a project and stick with it without digressing until you are finished.
13. Read a manual from page one, page by page to the end.
14. Give strict instructions and do not deviate from them.
15. Arrive at and leave work on time.
16. Sit in the same chair all day.
17. Be focused all day.
18. If someone disagrees with you, stick to your opinion.
19. Finish your project before taking any phone calls.
20. Leave your cell phone turned off all day.
21. Put all items in your desk in a special place, and put them back immediately after using them.

Things to do every day:

- Pay every bill the minute it comes in.
- Read the newspaper at the same time every day.
- Walk the same path every day at the same time.

I NEVER SAID THIS WOULD BE EASY!

Changing your Profile takes practice and perseverance. If you are determined, you will be successful. If you discover that this isn't really what you want to do, that's OK, too.

Darlene was a Structural/Social thinker who had two Analytical/Conceptual business partners. Together they owned a financial firm. Darlene decided that she wanted to add more Conceptual thought to her Profile because she wanted to better communicate with her partners. I tried to talk her out of this, as I do with most clients who want to change. I let her know that her Structural/Social thought was a great asset for her partnership. She insisted, however, so I suggested that she come up with a 21-Day Plan to increase her Conceptual attribute. She gave me a confused look and asked, "If I don't prefer Conceptual thought, how can you expect me to come up with a 21-Day Plan?"

She had a good point, but we don't live in the world alone so I suggested that she consult with her Conceptual friends. Darlene invited seven of her most Conceptual friends to lunch and solicited their ideas for increasing her Conceptual nature. Her friends assembled a plan, and the next day Darlene began her journey.

She called me on the sixteenth day and said, "You were right. I hate being Conceptual. The experiment ends right now!"

"What is causing this to end?" I inquired.

"Today is the day I'm supposed to go to work and leave the dishes in the sink," Darlene replied. "I'm sorry, but this is far too difficult!"

There Is a Limit

Let's suppose you are in the first-third for Assertiveness, and you feel you have a tendency to get pushed around. Like Steve, you follow a 21-Day Plan for increasing your Assertiveness, and are pleased with your progress. After practicing being more ASSERTIVE, you are able to do things you formerly could not have done, like tell your older sister that you don't agree with her childrearing advice, or asking the people next to you at the movie theater to be quiet. Will you ever be as ASSERTIVE as someone who is naturally in the third-third for this attribute? Probably not.

Martin is an Analytical/Conceptual thinker who is EXPRESSIVE and AS-SERTIVE. He called me one day and began the conversation by saying, "I am faxing you the contract—Oh, Geil, how are you?"

I said, "I'm fine. Why did you stop in the middle of your sentence to ask me that?"

He responded, "I'm practicing being more Social. Aren't you happy that I'm asking you how you are feeling? In the old days, I would have told you that I'm sending the contract, and that would be the end of the conversation."

I then said, "How nice of you to ask. I'm getting ready for the holidays. My son Ryan will be home on Tuesday, Morgan will be home on Wednesday, and my other son is already here. The whole family will be gathering—"

Martin interrupted, "Okay, I got it. Now can we go back to the contract?"

Martin was doing his best to increase his Social attribute, but in the end, his Analytical/Conceptual mind won out.

Martin can strengthen his Social attribute, but it will never be as strong as someone who comes originally wired for Social thought. In time, he can learn and understand the Social decision-making process, but he will never be as comfortable using his Social mind as he is using his Analytical/Conceptual mind. Furthermore, while Martin's attempt at Social thought is appreciated, people who are innately wired for Social thought will detect his non-preference, just as they will with Stuart, who worked through his Analytical brain to systematically schedule a day to compliment his employees. The people who are naturally most comfortable in a certain Thinking or Behavioral Attribute will pick up on the subtle clues of a person who is not exuding the same energy.

Don't let this prevent you from developing your less-preferred attributes, if that is what you want to do. Just keep in mind that your strengths are indeed a gift. Cubic zirconia sparkles just like diamonds, but it isn't the same thing.

UNPLANNED CHANGES

Sometimes your Profile will change without your deliberate intervention. Whenever people tell me their Profile has changed without their conscious effort, I ask them what has occurred in their life since they last answered the Emergenetics questionnaire. Usually they have a story to tell. Sometimes they are in the middle of a life transition. Sometimes they have just experienced a significant life event. Your brain never loses its ability to change in response to your life experiences, so it makes sense that your Profile can be affected as well.

Life Stages: Why Are We Here?

Some psychologists have suggested that it is possible to divide people's lives into distinct stages. It would be simpler if they all agreed with each other, but did you really think that would happen?

Erik Erikson noted that if we looked at how people grow from birth to death, they seem to go through stages of life. He identified eight stages from birth to death, and associated each stage with a crisis or dilemma—for example, the difficulty of balancing autonomy and intimacy.

Daniel Levinson, author of *The Seasons of a Man's Life* and *The Seasons of a Woman's Life,* did the research upon which Gail Sheehy's bestselling book *Passages* was based. Levinson identified five stages (or seasons) in adult development. Each stage includes predictable periods of stability and transition. It was Levinson who first identified the transition around age forty that became the popular "midlife crisis."

> I began to notice the theme of seven-year cycles in sources as varied as the work of C. G. Jung, the Torah, the New Testament, the plays of Shakespeare, American folk wisdom, Native American tradition, Buddhist lore, the philosophy of the Greek mathematician Pythagoras, and naturally, in the phases of the moon that change every seventh day . . .
>
> Joan Borysenko, PhD,
> *A Woman's Book of Life*

Joan Borysenko, who wrote *Minding the Body, Mending the Mind,* has a different approach to life stages. In her book *A Woman's Book of Life,* Borysenko divides the life of a typical woman into seven-year cycles. I have not found any scientific data that specifically supports this approach, but it certainly works empirically.

All of these experts have something to offer. While the link between life stages and biology is still theoretical, based on my conversations with thousands of people over the last twenty-five years, I believe that neuroscientists will someday find that Borysenko's theory is correct for both women and men, and that the brain goes through cycles in a seven-year pattern. I also believe we ask ourselves different questions at different ages, and that to move from one stage to the next, we must first answer certain questions.

Your Profile may temporarily change while you are transitioning in or out of one of these seven-year life stages. However, looking at the population at large, our research shows that your Profile generally stays the same. Depending on where you are in life, it may show small, temporary differences, but over the long haul, your numbers will average out to your base Profile scores.

Questions to Be Answered

Each life stage is associated with certain questions. Using Joan Borysenko's work as a starting point, I have assembled questions for each seven-year period, starting at age twenty-one. You may need to answer the questions for one stage before you can move on to the next.

Ages 21–28
- How do I transition to adulthood?
- What do I want for a career?
- Who do I want to be my friends?
- Do I want a significant other?
- Do I want children?

Ages 28–35
- What are my values?
- How do I balance my needs with those of others?
- How do I measure success?
- What will be my legacy?

Ages 35–42
- What is the meaning of success?
- Are my values and outer life congruent?
- Am I emotionally well?

Ages 42–49
- Where am I going the next half of my life?
- What is the meaning of happiness?
- How can I empty my life to concentrate on issues I value?

Ages 49–56
- Is there a transcendent meaning to my life?
- What happens to me when I die?
- How can I use my energy and wisdom to make the world a better place?

Ages 56–63
- How can I best use my post-mid-life zest?
- How can I give myself for service, altruism?

Ages 63–70
- How can I be a grandparent of vision and wisdom?
- How can I restore balance to a troubled world?

Ages 70–77
- What life lessons can I share?

Ages 77–84
- What are my greatest accomplishments, and what are the major themes in my life?

Life Cycles: Are You Feeling Scratchy?

I have found that within each seven-year stage, three smaller cycles occur. In my seminars, I always ask people where they are. After talking to approximately ten thousand people a year for the past five years, I've observed that roughly one-third of the group will raise their hands for each of the following periods:

Comfortable Period: Life is good. You have no big highs or big lows. Your professional and personal situation is good. Things are stable. But one day you wake up and you feel uncomfortable. I call this the . . .

Scratchy Period: Life is confusing. Something doesn't feel right. Sometimes you know what this is about, and sometimes you don't. During this period you are probably asking yourself what you should be doing with your life. The answers may cause some significant changes in how you live your life and how you answer the questions on the Emergenetics Profile. However, once you make the changes you need to make, you enter the . . .

Starry-Eyed Enthusiasm Period: Life is grand. You are excited because you know how the rest of your life will go. You have a new project and you are happy about it. After a while, however, your enthusiasm settles down, and you enter the Comfortable Period . . . again.

If you are in a Scratchy period, know that you are probably also heading into a transition into a new life cycle. This alone could make you experience temporary changes in your Profile. I have also found that this transition is an ideal environment for a significant life event.

Significant Life Events

As I've said, you are who you are unless you make a deliberate effort to change, or you have a significant life event. This can be anything from getting married, having a baby, buying a new home, or getting a new job to getting divorced, having a car accident, having surgery, or getting fired. Sometimes significant life events are tied to the life stage you are in. Other times they are seemingly random events that occur out of the blue.

Everyone experiences significant life events, no matter how old or young they are. But the older you get, the easier it is to recognize a significant life event. Young people grow up so fast and change so quickly that *everything* is significant. It takes a few years to gain perspective.

Sometimes your Profile will change after you experience a significant life event, but sometimes it won't. Sometimes Profile changes are a mystery, while other times they intuitively make sense (for example, having a baby usually makes new mothers more Social, perhaps because of increased oxytocin levels). Sometimes the changes are permanent, and sometimes they aren't. This all complicates Emergenetics a little bit, but I'm glad the questionnaire is able to follow people's changes.

One woman whom I'll call Anne started out a Quadra-modal (Analytical, Structural, Social, and Conceptual) with her behaviors all in the second-third. Anne was happily married with three young children when her husband, Aaron, decided to start a new business venture. It did fabulously well—until an associate mismanaged the money and ran off. Talk about a significant life event! Left with enormous debts, the family was close to declaring bankruptcy. Each day Aaron would greet Anne by saying, "This will be OK." His Conceptual brain was able to figure out how to manage the situation and his Analytical brain was figuring out how to rid of the big debts. Unfortunately, his Expressiveness did not allow him to verbalize his plan, so Anne went to her Structural brain and started counting pennies. No one in the house could spend any money without her permission.

Seven years later, when their financial statement was once again in the black, Anne lost most of her Structural attribute, though even today she still believes her counting pennies saved them from bankruptcy. She will admit, however, that Aaron taught her "to go with the 'flow' and that everything would be fine." Aaron, in the meantime, became more EXPRESSIVE because improving communication between the two of them during this stressful period saved their marriage.

Is This the Party to Whom
I Am Speaking?

Using Emergenetics to Size Up Other People

I didn't want to write this chapter because for years I have said you can't tell how people are *thinking,* only how they are *behaving.* Without an Emergenetics questionnaire, you can never know a person's Profile for certain. However, I got talked into doing this chapter because it is so helpful to use Emergenetics principles when you are dealing with other people, and it is possible to make educated guesses about others' Attributes once you know what to look for. I agreed because in the end, when you relate to others in their preferred attribute, you get better communication.

What a huge difference it makes to be able to look at someone and think, "Oh, I get it. He isn't actually arguing with me. He just needs to verify this information because he has a Structural thinking style that is very deliberate." Or, "OK, it's obvious that the holiday party committee has gone totally over budget—again. But I'm the only one here with an Analytical preference. If I say something now, they'll just think I'm being critical again."

Whether you are building a relationship with a colleague, working with a manager, training a new employee, hiring someone, or selling to a customer, it's easier to build respect and rapport when you can match your approach to the other person's preferences. But if you don't know someone's Profile—and most of the time, you won't—how can you tell what kind of person she or he is?

> Learning is experience. Everything else is information.
>
> **Albert Einstein**

This chapter is a quick and easy guide to recognizing Emergenetics clues. When I meet people, I watch for little signs that may help me ascertain their Thinking and Behavioral Attributes. Do they push the elevator button repeatedly? This often indicates Assertiveness. Do they use a lot of hand gestures when they speak? This is almost always a sign of Expressiveness. Are they particularly accommodating when you ask for assistance? This probably indicates Flexibility. Are they especially interested in your credentials and credibility? This often is a sign of the Analytical preference at work. Are they particularly concerned about the company's standard operating procedures? This may be a sign of Structural thinking. Do they express concern about your personal life? This could be a sign of Social thinking. Are they wearing an unusually stylish watch or creative piece of jewelry? Perhaps a sign of Conceptual thinking.

While I encourage you to be alert for clues, I also caution you against making snap judgments. People are complex. Your first impression of another person may be correct, but she or he may not be consistent. Some people, particularly multimodals, will flip from one attribute to another. Furthermore, Behavioral Attributes can mask Thinking Attributes. Individuals who are in the first-third of all the behaviors are difficult to read. Others often assume such people are Analytical, but this may or may not be true. Quiet people are often considered not very Social, when in fact they may be. As you become a more experienced observer, you will learn how to assemble all the clues you gather into an insightful portrait.

APPEARANCES CAN BE DECEIVING

The secret to understanding people's preferences is not only to observe what they are doing, but also to find out why they are doing it. What is the motivation behind their actions?

What Was Andrea's Motivation?

A group of us went to a convention in Spain. Everyone at the convention had completed an Emergenetics questionnaire, and they liked to believe they could guess another person's Profile, and so we started a game.

Within this group was Andrea, who was the group dancing champion. Everyone accurately agreed she was EXPRESSIVE, especially after they saw her do the splits on the dance floor the night before. One day we were scheduled to go to the Del Prado museum in Madrid. Andrea ended up declining to go with the group, but went by herself later in the day. Later on that night we were all at dinner, and we asked her what she thought of the museum. She replied, "I was in and out of there in a few minutes. The rest of the time I was buying gifts for my office staff."

"In addition to her EXPRESSIVE nature, we now know she is Social," the group proclaimed.

I then asked Andrea, "What motivated you to buy the gifts today?"

She explained, "Well, it was on my list of things to do, and it was a higher priority than spending hours at the Del Prado. I knew that I couldn't enjoy myself until I had this item crossed off my list."

See what I mean? Andrea's primary preference is not Social, but instead Structural. Her gift-buying was motivated by practicality.

What Was Mark's Real Profile?

At a corporate Emergenetics workshop, Mark's associates were shocked when they saw his Profile. His sliver of Social was swimming in a sea of Analytical. Yet Mark appeared to be the most charming guy on earth, so when they saw his Profile, his colleagues suspected there was something wrong with Emergenetics. I heard a grumbling of dissent from Mark's corner of the room.

"Why, Mark," said Charlotte, "Just this morning you complimented me on my new haircut, which I thought was awfully sweet. No one else noticed!"

Mark realized that his first thought had not been that Charlotte looked nice, but rather that something was different about her. He had evaluated her appearance while his Analytical brain tried to figure out what was new, and then he had followed up with "you look nice" simply because he was staring at her and he needed to say something.

Is Kirsten Always So Flexible?

Kirsten is a lawyer at a large transportation company. Her Profile indicates that she is an Analytical/Conceptual thinker, and she is *Flexible*—in fact, she has just 5 percent Flexibility. However, her coworkers all think Kirsten is very FLEXIBLE and easy to work with, and her performance appraisals say the same thing. Is her Profile inaccurate?

Nearly everyone in Kirsten's department is an Analytical thinker, and the group created a culture that is completely rational and logical. They are all on the same page. It's easy to be FLEXIBLE with people who think just like you.

Kirsten once told me, "I hate it when people give me information that is irrational or stupid!" and I saw a flash of that 5 percent Flexibility. Outside her job, Kirsten came across quite differently.

Form Follows Fashion—or Function?

Several years ago, I went into the office of a CEO named Neil to discuss the benefits of Emergenetics. As he invited me in, he said, "Please come into my new office. I just decorated it with new furniture. I am the first person in my city to have this style!"

As soon as I walked into Neil's office, I was struck by how Conceptual it appeared to be. All of his furniture was contemporary in design, and it was particularly unusual because each piece was connected by an intricate series of metal rails. To me it seemed very imaginative and creative. Neil was clearly excited about it, and he conveyed his enthusiasm with EXPRESSIVE gestures. Mentally I shifted to "Conceptual/EXPRESSIVE speak" to develop rapport with Neil.

I remarked to him, "Wow, what a funky, futuristic design! Tell me about it!"

Neil's eyes lit up. "I designed this office myself. Here is my desk. I have a rail that connects the desk to the computer station. Then there is another rail from the computer station that connects to a little tray for rubber bands and paper clips. Then another rail connects to a table that has three chairs for when I meet with people. You will notice there is no other furniture in the room—no lamps, sofa, or coffee tables. I installed this design to maximize efficiency and ensure that no piece of furniture ever moves from its proper place."

Oops! This office was utilitarian, not visionary. I immediately switched to "Structural/EXPRESSIVE speech."

If I had continued to approach Neil from the Conceptual point of view, I might have said to him, "Emergenetics is an experiential awakening into your own psyche. It will help you and your teammates gain insights into how to change your company for the future." And Neil would have stared at me in disbelief.

> In the study of brain functions we rely upon a biased, poorly understood, and frequently unpredictable organ in order to study the properties of another such organ; we have to use a brain to study a brain.
>
> **William C. Corning,** *The Mind*

Instead, I said, "Emergenetics will give you guidelines to becoming a more effective leader, and will make your team more efficient. Here are the three things I would like to talk to you about this morning: (1) I would like to define Emergenetics, (2) I would like to discuss how other companies use Emergenetics concepts, and (3) I would like to ask how these concepts will work in your organization."

I got the sale.

You can look to chapter 9 for a list of phrases to gain rapport with people who have different Profiles. For now, the issue is how to determine who has what preferences.

HOW TO ASK LEADING QUESTIONS

Because our assumptions about other people are so often wrong, my clients sometimes wish everybody in the world would just wear a T-shirt with their Emergenetics Profile on it. Until that day comes, here are some questions that will help you ascertain how people think and behave. You can use them formally (for example, when hiring someone) or informally.

With each question I've included actual responses that people have given. When you ask these questions yourself, look for the thinking behind the responses you receive. Ask people what they are thinking or doing, and why they are thinking or doing it. Use open-ended questions that allow people to speak freely, and see what they say.

Leading Questions to Find Out Someone's Thinking Style

1. *When a deadline is a month away, how do you finish a project and when?*

    Analytical: "Only after I have read up on all of the latest research will I begin formulating an action plan. Most likely, I will have the project completed a couple of days before the due date, to allow myself time for revisions and any last-minute research additions."

    Structural: "I usually create a systematic schedule of mini-deadlines to keep myself on track and the project moving forward. Ideally, I prefer to have the project completed one week before the due date."

    Social: "First I talk to some colleagues in my office, and then I send out a few e-mails and make some phone calls to friends I consider somewhat knowledgeable in this area (or not, for that matter). They can point me in the right direction. Ideally, I would like this done sooner rather than later, but you know people, sometimes it takes them two weeks to get back to you."

    Conceptual: "I will initially search the Internet for various ideas. After viewing themes, I will meditate on the issue until a solution calls to me. This may happen tomorrow or it may happen three days before the project is due, but when it does, it will all come at once."

2. *What is your ideal working environment?*

    Analytical: "I prefer an office that is outfitted with the latest cutting-edge technology. I also like to have a white board, so I can diagram my thinking in flow charts."

    Structural: "All of the machines and offices must be well laid out, in a practical manner. And the equipment must be reliable."

    Social: "I prefer my office to have a couch, so that people feel comfortable dropping by whenever they want a quick chat. I also like to have a small, round table so I can have one-on-one meetings with coworkers or clients without having to go to the large conference room."

    Conceptual: "I would prefer the office to be in perfect feng shui to allow the creative energy to flow."

3. *How do you make important life decisions?*

    Analytical: "I make an informed decision based on strict logic and analysis."

    Structural: "I typically make decisions based on what I've learned from past experience."

    Social: "I seek the advice and input of friends and loved ones."

    Conceptual: "I make decisions based on intuition."

4. *If you were to assemble a piece of furniture from the directions, how would you go about it?*

    Analytical: "I would first glance at the directions to get a rough estimate of the recommended procedures. Then I would lay out all of the pieces to make sure none are missing. Then I would view the construction as a game or puzzle, to see if I can conquer the construction on my own."

    Structural: "I would review the instructions word for word before assembling any pieces, just to make sure there are no hidden surprises in step 6 that require completion in step 3. Once I have reviewed the instructions, I will then follow them step-by-step."

    Social: "Why even read the directions, when I can call my friend Claire? She is a mechanical wizard. If she comes over to help me, I will keep her company throughout the entire process, and give her a gift afterwards."

    Conceptual: "I look at the picture on the box, dump the pieces in a pile on the floor, and then begin assembling. When the project is complete, I use the directions to start a fire."

5. *You are a new manager, and you have assembled a new team. At your first meeting, how do you have people introduce themselves to one another?*

    Analytical: "Each person would be given a handout that had a short biography of everyone in the room. I would then refer everyone to the handout."

    Structural: "I would have everybody stand up and introduce themselves in alphabetical order by her or his last name."

    Social: "I would pair people in teams and ask each person to describe the person they just met."

    Conceptual: "I would have people stand up and describe the riskiest thing they have done, something most people don't know about them."

Sometimes you will hear different combinations of brain preferences in a candidate's answer. This is an indication that you are working with a multi-modal brain. When you think you are working with a multimodal, you should pay more attention to clues that you do not hear coming from their mouth.

Leading Questions to Find Out Someone's Behavioral Attributes

Here are some questions to gain clues about a person's behavioral preferences. Remember, if someone is in the second-third of the population, they are comfortable with either answer.

1. *Assume you show up ten minutes early for a meeting. What do you do while you wait for the meeting to begin?*
   Expressive: "I will typically enter the room and look around to see if there is anyone there I know. If there is, I may or may not go talk to them. If there isn't, I will sit at my seat and review the agenda, or I will go outside and check my cell phone for any messages."
   EXPRESSIVE: "I will instinctively go talk to anyone I know or may have met. If I don't know anyone, I will sit at my place and start a conversation with anyone I can make eye contact with. Once I get started talking to this person, I won't stop until the meeting begins."

2. *When you are in a meeting with a group of managers and a confrontational issue has emerged, how do you assert your ideas?*
   Assertive: "I talk only when I am called upon."
   ASSERTIVE: "I typically offer my opinion, whether solicited or not."

3. *If your manager gives you a change in your project, how do you process this?*
   Flexible: "I am usually very hesitant towards changes, and I prefer the project to stay the same."
   FLEXIBLE: "Whatever, I like to go with the flow."

As you know, the Thinking and Behavioral Attributes work together and influence one another. For example, if you ask FLEXIBLE people, "How do you deal with change?" their answers will depend on their thinking style.

- Someone with an Analytical brain would say, "I'm OK with change, as long as it is based on a logical, rational decision."
- Someone with a Structural brain would say, "I'm OK with change, as long as it improves our efficiency."
- Someone with a Social brain would say, "I'm OK with change, as long as no one is hurt or offended in the process."
- Someone with a Conceptual brain would say, "I'm OK with change, as long as it is in line with our vision."
- A multimodal will have a tendency to jump from preference to preference.

Caution: People May Say What They Think You Want to Hear

I was looking for a new assistant, and I wanted to hire someone who could cope with the demands of a growing business. I believed that the business needed a person who could work with people, add structure to my office, and handle several tasks at the same time.

A candidate came in and took the Emergenetics questionnaire, which we often ask applicants to complete because we want to illustrate the focus of our work. She ended up testing as a Structural/Social thinker and *Flexible.* During the interview, I asked her questions like, "What is your definition of teamwork?" She would always give answers that were consistent with Structural/Social thinking. Similarly, when I asked her questions involving Flexibility, her answers were consistent with a *Flexible* profile. Interestingly, when I asked her whether she liked to work with several balls in the air, she said, "Oh yes, this is my absolute favorite thing to do. Furthermore, I really want this job."

As I pondered the interview after she left, something did not seem right. A person who is *Flexible* typically does not prefer to multitask. I decided to check her references. Her former employer told me that she was great with people and that if given a project, she would always finish on time. Then I asked, "Can she handle multiple tasks at once?"

Her former supervisor told me that this candidate's gift was "getting hold of a project and completing it from beginning to end. When she started out on a project, she was myopic. If you asked her to do a job outside the realm of her current project, she became grouchy and miserable."

I learned a valuable lesson. Emergenetics theory is a great foundation for evaluating your employment diversity needs as well as for structuring interview questions. But people can still give verbal answers that do not necessarily represent how they truly prefer to think or behave. Also, the Emergenetics questionnaire does not measure a person's actual abilities. It is based on people self-reporting their own preferences. Ultimately, it is prudent to combine Emergenetics with many evaluation strategies to make wise and rational employment decisions.

Looking at Writing Styles

Each attribute enjoys writing in a different style.

Analytical
Precise
Shows logical decisions
Formal
Factual

Conceptual
Metaphorical
Inspirational
Spiritual
Playful

Structural
Process-oriented
Articulate
Clear
Detailed

Social
Personal
Compassionate
Uplifting
Shows emotion rather than
    process

Expressive
Contemplative
Reserved

EXPRESSIVE
Uses exclamation points!
Uses "I" a lot

Assertive
Uses conciliatory language
Cooperative

ASSERTIVE
Opinions stated forcefully
Enterprising and ambitious

Flexible
Stays focused
Constantly searches for the right
    way to say something

FLEXIBLE
Digresses
Says the same thing in several
    ways

THE WRITING IS ON THE WALL

You can often tell someone's Thinking and Behavioral Attributes from the style and manner in which she or he writes. Here are some thank-you letters that have been sent to me from seminar participants over the years. I realize that including them may seem self-serving—I left the nasty ones in the file cabinet.

Letter #1

Analytical, Structural, *Flexible,* **EXPRESSIVE**

> Dear Geil,
>
> What a great program. I cannot express (being Analytical) how much I enjoyed it. My wife (a true Social) and even I, an Analytical, talked all the way home about the seminar. She wants to know what she can do about my sixth percentile Flexible rating. Of course, I told her—nothing.
>
>   Thanks again for your help, and once again (here's my little bit of Social [5%] coming out) I LOVED the program!
>
> Sincerely,
> Peter W. Hjort Jr.

Letter #2

Analytical and *Expressive*

> To: Geil Browning
> Date: 6/11/2003
> Re: XYZ Company Seminar
>
> Geil—
>   Good.
> —Van

Letter #3

Structural and ASSERTIVE

Dear Dr. Browning,

I wanted to tell you my thoughts on your presentation at the USAD Conference in Colorado Springs, Colorado, on October 13, 2004.

First, the interview which you conducted with our chairman, Leonard Root, was enjoyable. This was particularly interesting because of the breadth of your questions. You covered a multitude of topics from leadership style to family issues.

Secondly, your session entitled "A Meeting of the Minds" was very stimulating and informative. Not only was the material fascinating, but your style of delivery and teaching methods were upbeat and fun. There was not enough time for questions!

Thirdly, one of the flip charts you used had some interesting comparisons regarding the methods of presentations used for the seven Emergenetics Attributes. Please recap the information and forward it to me.

Sincerely,
Rebecca Jones Hanson

Letter #4

Social and EXPRESSIVE

Dear Geil,

What a wonderful weekend at Brasstown Valley! And what a wonderful, fulfilling day of Emergenetics!

You are the most unbelievable presenter I have ever seen, heard, witnessed, observed, or imagined! I cannot believe the stamina you have in presenting!

My personal and professional life is different after a day with you, and I look forward to using what I learned for the rest of my life!

Thank you, Geil, for a great day and for your continued participation!

Warmest Regards,
Del

Letter #5

Social, Conceptual, and "It Depends"

Dear Geil,

The aura of last evening lingers softly within the depths of my memory. The muted lights, the quiet fire, the warm smiles, the easy laughter, the comfortable sharing, and the luscious food combined, makes for an exquisite picture of which I treasure to have been a part. The image lies silently within me ready to come forth upon command to bring me pleasure at any given moment. Surely, it was a perfect ending to a perfect experience.

The expansive meaning of my being in this class cannot be adequately expressed by words. It has affected me as no other thing, person, or event has in years. I feel like I was a dry sponge and the class was a steady stream of water—pure, fresh water—coming into me; into all of me, bringing me new life. I sincerely hope it will incorporate itself within what is already here to give it newness, strength, awareness, freshness, and above all, sincere and conscientious empathy.

This special experience would not have happened without your special leadership. Thank you.

Love,
Rosemary

Letter #6

Quadra-modal and FLEXIBLE

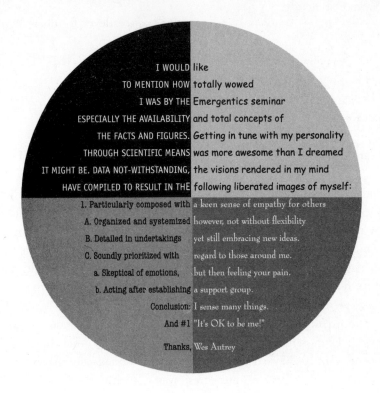

I WOULD like
TO MENTION HOW totally wowed
I WAS BY THE Emergentics seminar
ESPECIALLY THE AVAILABILITY and total concepts of
THE FACTS AND FIGURES. Getting in tune with my personality
THROUGH SCIENTIFIC MEANS was more awesome than I dreamed
IT MIGHT BE. DATA NOT-WITHSTANDING, the visions rendered in my mind
HAVE COMPILED TO RESULT IN THE following liberated images of myself:

1. Particularly composed with a keen sense of empathy for others
A. Organized and systemized however, not without flexibility
B. Detailed in undertakings yet still embracing new ideas.
C. Soundly prioritized with regard to those around me.
a. Skeptical of emotions, but then feeling your pain.
b. Acting after establishing a support group.
Conclusion: I sense many things.
And #1 "It's OK to be me!"

Thanks, Wes Autrey

MANAGERIAL STYLES: CRACKING THE CODE

People are constantly doing their best to figure out their managers. Many disagreements between employees and managers are simple miscommunications that can be avoided when people understand one another's ways of thinking and problem-solving.

Here are some clues you may observe about your manager. Keeping an open mind and appreciating your manager's uniqueness can only help you. People are who they are. If you observe these characteristics, then it would be smart to be conscious of the corresponding Emergenetics attributes and respond in a similar fashion.

Strengths of the Analytical Manager

- Favors concrete, technical information (specs, indexes, formulas, legal briefs)
- Focuses on what needs to be produced, created, or analyzed
- Is rational (not emotional)
- Prefers opinions and recommendations that are backed up with factual evidence
- Gives short directives
- Provides solid information and trusts employees to make good decisions
- Gets involved in technical/scientific discussions

If you don't have much Analytical Attribute, you might see your manager as:

- Intimidating
- Distant/cold
- Not understanding
- Too logical
- Unconditional
- Nerdy
- Boring

Strengths of the Structural Manager

- Detail oriented
- Likes safety and stability
- Maintains clear rules and lines of authority
- Is driven by the clock and productivity/efficiency
- Brings order out of chaos
- Takes care of logistics
- Leads by example

If you don't have much Structural Attribute, you might see your manager as:

- Nit-picky
- Rigid

- Controlling
- Unimaginative
- Micromanager
- Someone who can't delegate
- Bureaucratic

Strengths of the Social Manager

- Is interested in policies and programs that affect employees
- Able to communicate the difficult message
- Usually doesn't make canned decisions
- Prefers face-to-face interaction
- Sensitive to office politics
- Encouraging and collaborative
- Values relationships

If you don't have much Social Attribute, you might see your manager as:

- Emotional
- Irrational
- Not thinking
- Overly sensitive
- Soft-hearted
- Touchy-feely
- Bleeding heart

Strengths of the Conceptual Manager

- Experiments
- Pushes the envelope
- Has ideas that are global, big picture, visionary, and long term
- Is open to last-minute inspirations
- Is not structured, gives no specific directives
- Considers all impacts of potential solutions
- Expects employees to connect to the values, goals, and big picture
- Controls until competency is verified

If you don't have much Conceptual Attribute, you might see your manager as:

- Flaky
- Impractical
- Inattentive
- Scattered
- Undisciplined
- Gambler
- Not realistic

Strengths of the *Expressive* Manager

- Uses words efficiently
- Likes to blend into the crowd
- Self-contained, poised
- Allows others to start the conversation
- Selectively airs opnions
- Refrains from making faces or using hand gestures
- Listens carefully

If you aren't *Expressive,* you might see your manager as:

- Unemotional
- Uncommunicative
- Nothing to say
- Detached
- Uninterested
- Dispassionate
- Not a team player

Strengths of the EXPRESSIVE Manager

- Appears pumped up
- Talkative
- Shares information with employees
- Always participates in the discussion

- Big facial expressions and hand gestures
- Walks the halls, visits
- Uses many words for an answer

If you aren't EXPRESSIVE, you might see your manager as:

- Overacting
- Lacking self-control
- Egotistical
- Spotlight seeker
- Loud, wild, crazy
- Fake
- Excitable

Strengths of the *Assertive* Manager

- Is approachable
- Goes with the flow of the group
- Speaks quietly
- Keeps the peace
- Has a calm presence
- Takes time to listen
- Carefully phrases thoughts and opinions

If you aren't *Assertive,* you might see your manager as:

- Disconnected
- Slow, lazy
- A pushover
- Lacking drive
- Passive
- Wavering
- Halfhearted

Strengths of the ASSERTIVE Manager

- Leads by influence
- Task-oriented
- Decisive
- Ambitious
- High expectations for others
- Competitive
- Makes presence known

If you aren't ASSERTIVE, you might see your manager as:

- Overbearing
- Confrontational
- Rude
- Dictatorial
- Interruptive
- Win at all costs
- Impatient

Strengths of the *Flexible* manager

- Insists on people doing things correctly
- Sets ground rules and follows them
- Purposeful
- Keen
- Discerning
- Chooses battles carefully
- Has firm commitment to convictions

If you aren't *Flexible,* you might see your manager as:

- Stubborn
- Simple minded
- Closed minded

- Always right
- Selfish
- Control freak
- Opinionated

Strengths of the FLEXIBLE Manager

- Comfortable with equal partnership
- Open to suggestions and ideas
- Can accommodate last-minute revisions
- Can handle crises
- Keeps things open-ended
- Understands that change is part of the job
- Figures out alternative approaches

If you aren't FLEXIBLE, you might see your manager as:

- Wishy-washy
- Fickle
- Confusing
- Blowing hot and cold
- Sending mixed signals
- Indecisive
- Uncertain

TEST YOURSELF

Now let's test your recognition skills. Here are four scenarios in which someone comes into your office to interview for a job. After she or he is seated, you ask the question, "How do you prefer to work?"

Based on the descriptions that follow, try to determine each candidate's Profile. In all but one case, there is more than one Thinking preference.

Brain #1: Nicole

Nicole enters your office and you are immediately amazed at her colorful jacket with glittery sequins. She gives you a strong handshake. When you compliment her unusual jewelry, her eyes sparkle and she launches into a long story about where she found it. During the interview, she shows you a picture of her new baby. You find this picture unusual, as it only shows the baby's ear. When you ask, "How do you prefer to work?" Nicole barely allows you time to finish the question before she begins her answer.

Nicole says that she is constantly exploring the "bigger picture in this world," and that she is energized by possibilities. To guide her long-term planning, she asks, "What does success look like?" and then pursues her vision. She finds that she takes leaps in her work instead of small, careful steps, and admits that sometimes she will ask the rest of her team to work out the details involved in implementing her ideas. She likes the framework of her responsibilities to be explained, but then she wants to figure out how to do her job without a lot of rules.

When you try to interrupt Nicole to ask another question, you discover that she doesn't like to be cut short when she is explaining her philosophy. When you describe the job that is available, Nicole makes many interesting inferences.

ANSWER: Nicole has a Social/Conceptual brain with EXPRESSIVE and ASSERTIVE behaviors.

Brain #2: Nicholas

Nicholas shows up for the interview wearing a blue blazer, khaki pants, and a Save the Children tie. During the interview, he shows you a picture of his son that was taken by the school photographer. The son is also wearing a blue blazer, khaki pants, and a smaller version of the Save the Children tie. When you ask, "How do you prefer to work?" Nicholas says the keys to success are process and structure. When he is in charge of a meeting, he always prepares an agenda, then asks for input about the agenda items. He says he enjoys coaching and developing people and helping them achieve their goals. When you ask

Nicholas how he solves problems, he says he gets ideas from others, then makes a final decision using his intuition.

Nicholas has no discernable consistent pattern of behaviors. One answer is drawn out, while the other is short and to the point. You learn that he is very punctual, and enjoys going to Starbucks every day for his favorite type of coffee.

ANSWER: Nicholas has a Social/Structural brain with "it depends" behaviors.

Brain #3: Sharon

Sharon enters the office wearing a modest black suit with conservative tailoring. She is wearing understated makeup and small diamond earrings. Her watch has a black band and a face void of all numbers with a diamond where the number 12 would usually be. When you ask, "How do you prefer to work?" Sharon answers that she enjoys new challenges and experiences, and is energized when she has a variety of tasks to perform. To stay on track, she always keeps a to-do list. She says she is intuitive about ideas and likes shaping them into a workable plan. When you ask Sharon how she prefers to make decisions, she says she collects data and tries to be as logical as possible. Sharon admits she has difficulty engaging in idle chit-chat, and says, "If I could just watch behind a two-way mirror for forty-five minutes before I entered the room, then I would be OK. This would give me enough time to analyze the crowd and decide who I want to talk to before I enter."

ANSWER: Are you confused about Sharon's profile? This is because you are hearing lots of phrases that are associated with different attributes. You're seeing influences from Analytical, Structural, Conceptual, ASSERTIVE, and FLEXIBLE preferences. The important point to notice is that there are absolutely no Social concepts. If you wanted to build rapport with Sharon, you would avoid Social words.

Brain #4: Paul

Paul enters wearing a suit with a white shirt and a red and blue horizontally striped tie. He is wearing no jewelry except a digital watch. When you ask,

"How do you prefer to work?" Paul answers that quality results are of paramount importance to him. He confesses that he hates inefficiency, and is happy to work alone. Paul's answers are brief and to the point.

ANSWER: Paul has a predominantly Analytical Profile and is *Expressive*.

LOOK FOR CONSISTENT BEHAVIOR

You can tell a great deal about people by the way they manage their time, their hobbies or interests, the kind of car they drive, what books they read, how they handle their money, and so on. As you have seen from the examples in this chapter, it's a good idea to see people in different settings, if possible. As you become an experienced observer of human behavior, you'll be able to put together people's verbal and nonverbal clues into a valuable portrait of Thinking and Behavioral Attributes. When you see a consistency of energies over and over again, people's preferences become more apparent and predictable. Time will help validate or disprove your initial evaluations.

Because of the many subtle permutations of the Emergenetics attributes, it is extremely difficult to analyze how a person thinks and behaves from casual, introductory communication. While you can pick up on clues, always remember that you cannot necessarily rely on your initial impressions. Now you see why I didn't want to write this chapter! It is easy to misinterpret another person.

Don't be discouraged, however. Sizing up other people using Emergenetics attributes is absolutely worth the effort. Once you are comfortable with their preferences, you can tailor your communication to suit their Profile—which you'll learn how to do in the next chapter.

The Emergenetics Thinking and Behavioral Attributes Defined

Emergenetics is based on four Thinking Attributes and three Behavioral Attributes that can be separately identified and scientifically quantified for each individual. The attributes can be mixed and matched in different ways to express each person's uniqueness and to show her or his greatest strengths. The four Thinking Attributes are: Analytical Thinking (Blue), Structural Thinking (Green), Social Thinking (Red), and Conceptual Thinking (Yellow). The three Behavioral Attributes are: Expressiveness, Assertiveness, and Flexibility (shown in shades of Purple).

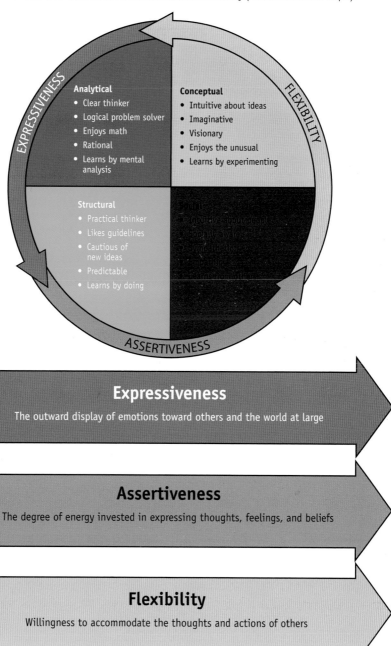

EXPRESSIVENESS

FLEXIBILITY

Analytical
- Clear thinker
- Logical problem solver
- Enjoys math
- Rational
- Learns by mental analysis

Conceptual
- Intuitive about ideas
- Imaginative
- Visionary
- Enjoys the unusual
- Learns by experimenting

Structural
- Practical thinker
- Likes guidelines
- Cautious of new ideas
- Predictable
- Learns by doing

Social
- Intuitive about people
- Socially aware
- Sympathetic
- Empathetic
- Learns from others

ASSERTIVENESS

Expressiveness
The outward display of emotions toward others and the world at large

Assertiveness
The degree of energy invested in expressing thoughts, feelings, and beliefs

Flexibility
Willingness to accommodate the thoughts and actions of others

The Emergenetics Profile

Each unique Emergenetics Profile colorfully illustrates an individual's Thinking and Behavioral Attributes. The Thinking Attributes — Analytical (Blue), Structural (Green), Social (Red), and Conceptual (Yellow) — are shown in a pie chart that indicates the relative strengths of each attribute, expressed in percentages. Wrapped around this pie chart are the Behavioral Attributes — Expressiveness, Assertiveness, and Flexibility (shown in shades of Purple) — also expressed in percentages. The Thinking and Behavioral Attributes also are pictured in bar charts that show how the individual's responses to the Emergenetics questionaire compare to the population of men as a whole or women as a whole. The bar charts are expressed in percentiles.

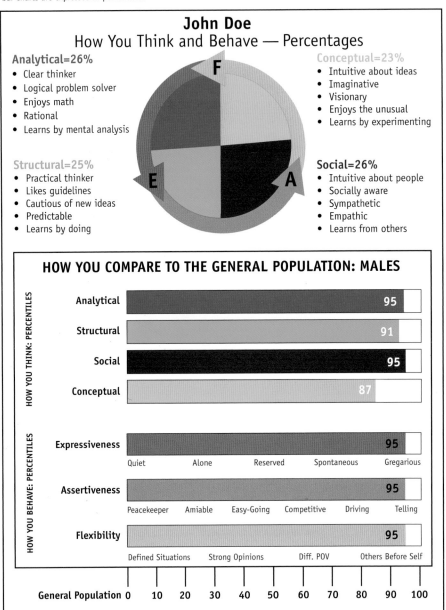

John Doe
How You Think and Behave — Percentages

Analytical=26%
- Clear thinker
- Logical problem solver
- Enjoys math
- Rational
- Learns by mental analysis

Conceptual=23%
- Intuitive about ideas
- Imaginative
- Visionary
- Enjoys the unusual
- Learns by experimenting

Structural=25%
- Practical thinker
- Likes guidelines
- Cautious of new ideas
- Predictable
- Learns by doing

Social=26%
- Intuitive about people
- Socially aware
- Sympathetic
- Empathic
- Learns from others

HOW YOU COMPARE TO THE GENERAL POPULATION: MALES

HOW YOU THINK: PERCENTILES

Attribute	Percentile
Analytical	95
Structural	91
Social	95
Conceptual	87

HOW YOU BEHAVE: PERCENTILES

Attribute		Percentile
Expressiveness	Quiet · Alone · Reserved · Spontaneous · Gregarious	95
Assertiveness	Peacekeeper · Amiable · Easy-Going · Competitive · Driving · Telling	95
Flexibility	Defined Situations · Strong Opinions · Diff. POV · Others Before Self	95

General Population 0 10 20 30 40 50 60 70 80 90 100

©Emergenetics, LLC

The Emergenetics Profile: Percentiles and Percentages

As you can see here, John Doe and John Smith have identical pie charts, yet the bar charts for their preferences are different. How is this possible? Because the ratio of their Thinking and Behavioral Attributes is the same, but the amount of energy they bring to these attributes is different.

John Smith
How You Think and Behave — Percentages

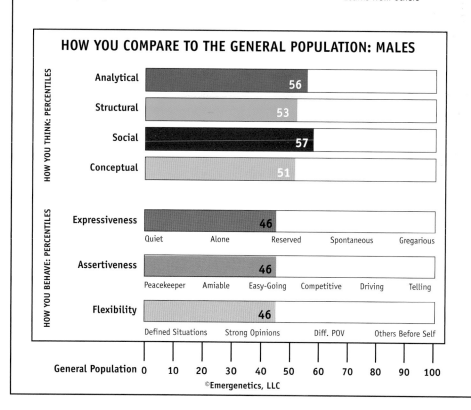

Analytical=26%
- Clear thinker
- Logical problem solver
- Enjoys math
- Rational
- Learns by mental analysis

Conceptual=23%
- Intuitive about ideas
- Imaginative
- Visionary
- Enjoys the unusual
- Learns by experimenting

Structural=25%
- Practical thinker
- Likes guidelines
- Cautious of new ideas
- Predictable
- Learns by doing

Social=26%
- Intuitive about people
- Socially aware
- Sympathetic
- Empathic
- Learns from others

HOW YOU COMPARE TO THE GENERAL POPULATION: MALES

HOW YOU THINK: PERCENTILES

- Analytical — 56
- Structural — 53
- Social — 57
- Conceptual — 51

HOW YOU BEHAVE: PERCENTILES

- Expressiveness — 46
  - Quiet | Alone | Reserved | Spontaneous | Gregarious
- Assertiveness — 46
  - Peacekeeper | Amiable | Easy-Going | Competitive | Driving | Telling
- Flexibility — 46
  - Defined Situations | Strong Opinions | Diff. POV | Others Before Self

General Population 0 10 20 30 40 50 60 70 80 90 100

©Emergenetics, LLC

WE*team* (Whole Emergentics)
All of Us Is Stronger Than One of Us

A Whole Emergenetics Team (WE*team*) includes all the Thinking and Behavioral Attributes. Each of these six people from Superior Corporation contributes something to the team. For example, Jane is great at Analytical thinking (Blue), but does not have a preference for Conceptual thought (Yellow). Fortunately, Keiko does. However, Keiko does not have a preference for Structural thinking (Green). Left to her own devices, she might forget to consider the specific steps needed for an action plan. Happily LeRoy, who has a great deal of Structural thinking (Green) in his Profile, will not let this happen! For more about WE*teams*, see chapter 10.

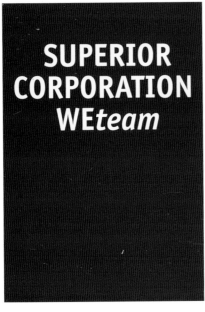

SUPERIOR CORPORATION WE*team*

Jane
How You Think and Behave — Percentages

Analytical=40%
- Clear thinker
- Logical problem solver
- Enjoys math
- Rational
- Learns by mental analysis

Conceptual=2%
- Intuitive about ideas
- Imaginative
- Visionary
- Enjoys the unusual
- Learns by experimenting

Structural=38%
- Practical thinker
- Likes guidelines
- Cautious of new ideas
- Predictable
- Learns by doing

Social=20%
- Intuitive about people
- Socially aware
- Sympathetic
- Empathic
- Learns from others

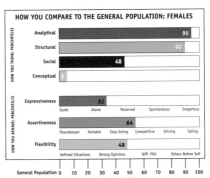

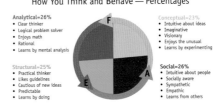

HOW YOU COMPARE TO THE GENERAL POPULATION: FEMALES

HOW YOU THINK: PERCENTILES		
Analytical	95	
Structural	90	
Social	48	
Conceptual	5	

HOW YOU BEHAVE: PERCENTILES		
Expressiveness	32	Quiet · Alone · Reserved · Spontaneous · Gregarious
Assertiveness	64	Peacekeeper · Amiable · Easy-Going · Competitive · Driving · Telling
Flexibility	48	Defined Situations · Strong Opinions · Diff. POV · Others Before Self

General Population 0 10 20 30 40 50 60 70 80 90 100
©Emergenetics, LLC

Armand
How You Think and Behave — Percentages

Analytical=26%
- Clear thinker
- Logical problem solver
- Enjoys math
- Rational
- Learns by mental analysis

Conceptual=8%
- Intuitive about ideas
- Imaginative
- Visionary
- Enjoys the unusual
- Learns by experimenting

Structural=39%
- Practical thinker
- Likes guidelines
- Cautious of new ideas
- Predictable
- Learns by doing

Social=27%
- Intuitive about people
- Socially aware
- Sympathetic
- Empathic
- Learns from others

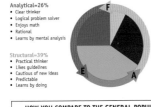

HOW YOU COMPARE TO THE GENERAL POPULATION: MALES

HOW YOU THINK: PERCENTILES		
Analytical	46	
Structural	70	
Social	49	
Conceptual	14	

HOW YOU BEHAVE: PERCENTILES		
Expressiveness	25	Quiet · Alone · Reserved · Spontaneous · Gregarious
Assertiveness	22	Peacekeeper · Amiable · Easy-Going · Competitive · Driving · Telling
Flexibility	29	Defined Situations · Strong Opinions · Diff. POV · Others Before Self

General Population 0 10 20 30 40 50 60 70 80 90 100
©Emergenetics, LLC

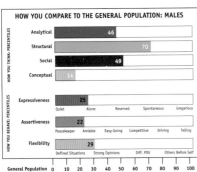

John
How You Think and Behave — Percentages

Analytical=26%
- Clear thinker
- Logical problem solver
- Enjoys math
- Rational
- Learns by mental analysis

Conceptual=23%
- Intuitive about ideas
- Imaginative
- Visionary
- Enjoys the unusual
- Learns by experimenting

Structural=25%
- Practical thinker
- Likes guidelines
- Cautious of new ideas
- Predictable
- Learns by doing

Social=26%
- Intuitive about people
- Socially aware
- Sympathetic
- Empathic
- Learns from others

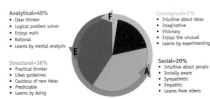

HOW YOU COMPARE TO THE GENERAL POPULATION: MALES

HOW YOU THINK: PERCENTILES		
Analytical	95	
Structural	91	
Social	95	
Conceptual	87	

HOW YOU BEHAVE: PERCENTILES		
Expressiveness	95	Quiet · Alone · Reserved · Spontaneous · Gregarious
Assertiveness	95	Peacekeeper · Amiable · Easy-Going · Competitive · Driving · Telling
Flexibility	95	Defined Situations · Strong Opinions · Diff. POV · Others Before Self

General Population 0 10 20 30 40 50 60 70 80 90 100
©Emergenetics, LLC

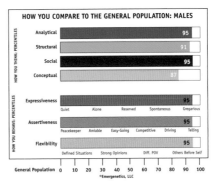

LeRoy
How You Think and Behave — Percentages

Analytical=4%
- Clear thinker
- Logical problem solver
- Enjoys math
- Rational
- Learns by mental analysis

Conceptual=3%
- Intuitive about ideas
- Imaginative
- Visionary
- Enjoys the unusual
- Learns by experimenting

Structural=50%
- Practical thinker
- Likes guidelines
- Cautious of new ideas
- Predictable
- Learns by doing

Social=44%
- Intuitive about people
- Socially aware
- Sympathetic
- Empathic
- Learns from others

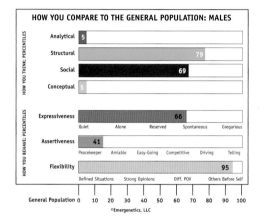

HOW YOU COMPARE TO THE GENERAL POPULATION: MALES

HOW YOU THINK: PERCENTILES

Analytical	5
Structural	79
Social	69
Conceptual	5

HOW YOU BEHAVE: PERCENTILES

Expressiveness	66
	Quiet / Alone / Reserved / Spontaneous / Gregarious
Assertiveness	41
	Peacekeeper / Amiable / Easy-Going / Competitive / Driving / Telling
Flexibility	95
	Defined Situations / Strong Opinions / Diff. POV / Others Before Self

General Population 0 10 20 30 40 50 60 70 80 90 100

©Emergenetics, LLC

Jane
Armand
John
LeRoy
Maria
Keiko

Maria
How You Think and Behave — Percentages

Analytical=37%
- Clear thinker
- Logical problem solver
- Enjoys math
- Rational
- Learns by mental analysis

Conceptual=39%
- Intuitive about ideas
- Imaginative
- Visionary
- Enjoys the unusual
- Learns by experimenting

Structural=18%
- Practical thinker
- Likes guidelines
- Cautious of new ideas
- Predictable
- Learns by doing

Social=6%
- Intuitive about people
- Socially aware
- Sympathetic
- Empathic
- Learns from others

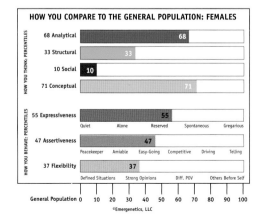

HOW YOU COMPARE TO THE GENERAL POPULATION: FEMALES

HOW YOU THINK: PERCENTILES

68 Analytical	68
33 Structural	33
10 Social	10
71 Conceptual	71

HOW YOU BEHAVE: PERCENTILES

55 Expressiveness	55
	Quiet / Alone / Reserved / Spontaneous / Gregarious
47 Assertiveness	47
	Peacekeeper / Amiable / Easy-Going / Competitive / Driving / Telling
37 Flexibility	37
	Defined Situations / Strong Opinions / Diff. POV / Others Before Self

General Population 0 10 20 30 40 50 60 70 80 90 100

©Emergenetics, LLC

Keiko
How You Think and Behave — Percentages

Analytical=4%
- Clear thinker
- Logical problem solver
- Enjoys math
- Rational
- Learns by mental analysis

Conceptual=51%
- Intuitive about ideas
- Imaginative
- Visionary
- Enjoys the unusual
- Learns by experimenting

Structural=4%
- Practical thinker
- Likes guidelines
- Cautious of new ideas
- Predictable
- Learns by doing

Social=41%
- Intuitive about people
- Socially aware
- Sympathetic
- Empathic
- Learns from others

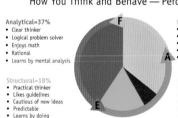

HOW YOU COMPARE TO THE GENERAL POPULATION: FEMALES

HOW YOU THINK: PERCENTILES

Analytical	5
Structural	5
Social	48
Conceptual	60

HOW YOU BEHAVE: PERCENTILES

Expressiveness	95
	Quiet / Alone / Reserved / Spontaneous / Gregarious
Assertiveness	95
	Peacekeeper / Amiable / Easy-Going / Competitive / Driving / Telling
Flexibility	66
	Defined Situations / Strong Opinions / Diff. POV / Others Before Self

General Population 0 10 20 30 40 50 60 70 80 90 100

©Emergenetics, LLC

What Percentage of the Population Each Emergenetics Profile Represents

 Quadra-modal (Blue, Green, Red, Yellow) *"Fair and balanced."* **1%**

If any one of the Thinking Attributes in an individual's Emergenetics Profile is 23% or greater, it is considered a preference. This chart shows possible preference combinations, and the percentages they represent in the population at large. For example, people who are Quadra-modal (Blue, Green, Red, and Yellow) represent only 1% of the population. (These percentages don't add up to exactly 100 because of rounding.) The Behavioral Attributes are measured in percentiles only. Thirty-three percent of the population is in the first-third, thirty-three percent is in the second-third, and thirty-three percent is in the third-third of each spectrum.

 Analytical (Blue) and Structural (Green) *"Make a plan and follow it."* **17%**

 Analytical (Blue), Conceptual (Yellow), and Social (Red) *"What do you think of this global idea?"* **13%**

 Social (Red) and Conceptual (Yellow) *"Let's create this together."* **12%**

 Conceptual (Yellow), Social (Red), and Structural (Green) *"Creative thinking with controlled emotions."* **4%**

 Analytical (Blue) and Conceptual (Yellow) *"I see the forest."* **12%**

 Analytical (Blue), Structural (Green), and Conceptual (Yellow) *"Ideas are for doing."* **5%**

 Structural (Green) and Social (Red) *"I'd love to share the experience with you, but please make an appointment first."* **11%**

 Analytical (Blue) *"In God we trust . . . all others must bring data."* **1%**

 Analytical (Blue) and Social (Red) *"An informed head with a warm heart."* **6%**

 Structural (Green) *"Of course I don't look busy, I did it right the first time."* **2%**

 Structural (Green) and Conceptual (Yellow) *"Nailing Jell-O to the wall."* **2%**

 Social (Red) *"I wear my heart on my sleeve."* **1%**

 Analytical (Blue), Structural (Green), and Social (Red) *"Efficiency with feeling."* **13%**

Conceptual (Yellow) *"I feel like I'm diagonally parked in a parallel universe."* **2%**

Expressiveness	My thoughts are my business	It depends	I can't wait to tell everyone!
Assertiveness	No need to get excited	It depends	Let's get this done now!
Flexibility	It's my way or the highway	It depends	You can do what you want
	33%	33%	33%

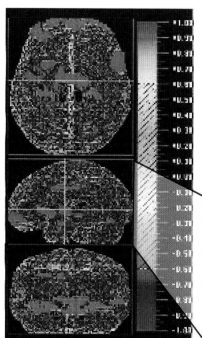

PET Scans
The Shy Brain and the
Extroverted Brain

There is evidence that people are shy or outgoing partly because of the way their brains are structured. The scans at left and below illustrate one of the ways in which our individual differences may be genetic, and may have an underlying biological base.

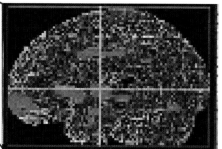

Introverts have more activity in the parts of the brain that are associated with internal processing.

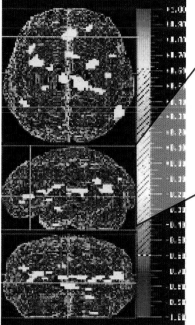

Extroverts exhibit more activity in the parts of the brain that are involved with sensory or external processing.

For more information about brain-based behavior, see chapter 2.

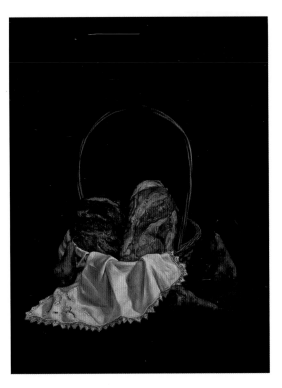

Painting with the Left Side of Your Brain

KATHRYN JACOBI

Artist Kathryn Jacobi uses her Analytical and Structural preferences to paint meticulous still lifes that are accurate to the smallest detail. For a description of her approach to painting, see chapter 11.

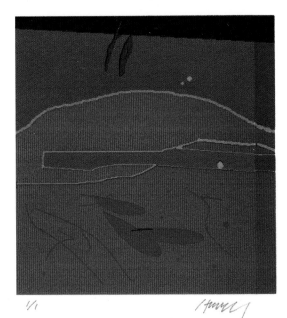

1/1   (signature)

Painting with the Right Side of Your Brain

PIERRE HENRY

Artist Pierre Henry uses his Conceptual and Social preferences to paint colorful abstract pictures that resonate with the viewer emotionally. For a description of his approach to painting, see chapter 11.

Techies versus Touchy-Feelies

Communicating with People Who Aren't Like You

In the previous chapter, you learned how to make an educated guess about another person's Profile. Now that you know what kind of person you're dealing with, you need to think about the best way to frame your approach and build rapport. Sometimes this is a challenge. For example, communication between "techies" and "touchy-feelies" requires a bit of finesse.

Suppose an extremely Analytical and *Expressive* person is sitting across the conference table from a highly Social and EXPRESSIVE person. This is the first time they have met. Guess who is doing all the talking? In all likelihood, our friend with the Social preference is speaking with great animation, possibly about something on television the night before, or something that happened on the way to work. She thinks she is establishing rapport with her Analytical colleague. Unfortunately, her attempts are having the opposite effect.

The more she talks, the more annoyed he becomes. In another two seconds, he is going to write her off as a lightweight who does not have anything valuable to say.

Can this conversation be saved? Of course it can. Ms. Social and EXPRESSIVE needs to tone down her approach and match her demeanor more closely to that of Mr. Analytical and *Expressive.* He, in turn, needs to understand that Ms. Social isn't stupid, she's just being friendly. Although being EXPRESSIVE is difficult for him, he can make an effort to acknowledge Ms. Social's affable attempts to engage his attention by extending his comments and gestures to better match her style.

An extremely Conceptual thinker once told me at dinner, "I was a Brownie Scout for forty-five minutes, and the only thing I remember was the scout leader saying, "It's not where you have been, it's where you are going." Our dinner companion, an extremely Structural thinker, said, "That's funny. I was a Brownie Scout as well, and I only remember the scout leader saying, 'Be prepared!' "

WHAT IS YOUR FILTER?

We all filter things according to our Profile. Communication is always a challenge because the same sentence can be heard and interpreted in completely different ways by completely different brains. You may think you are making yourself clear when you speak, but you run the risk of being misunderstood by other types of brains unless you make a conscious effort to appeal to each Thinking Attribute. Similarly, when you listen to other people speak, you run the risk of misunderstanding them unless you take their Profile into account.

Let's say you work for a cosmetics company that sells its products exclusively online. According to company policy, each order must ship within 48 hours. Timing is important, since impatient customers may decide to simply go the store and buy someone else's products instead.

How You Hear the Analytical Brain Speaking

It has come to the attention of Melanie, who is vice president of Direct Fulfillment, that the 48-hour limit is not always being met. Melanie, who has a highly Analytical preference, says,

> I understand efficiency is a factor, but is there a causal relationship between having fewer employees in the fulfillment department and an increase in the number of orders shipping late?

You could react to what Melanie says in one of four ways, according to your Thinking preference:

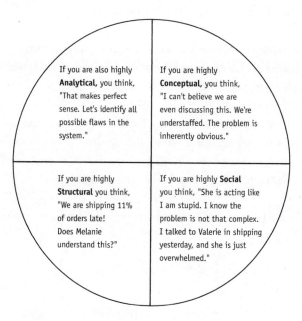

If you are also highly **Analytical,** you think, "That makes perfect sense. Let's identify all possible flaws in the system."

If you are highly **Conceptual,** you think, "I can't believe we are even discussing this. We're understaffed. The problem is inherently obvious."

If you are highly **Structural** you think, "We are shipping 11% of orders late! Does Melanie understand this?"

If you are highly **Social** you think, "She is acting like I am stupid. I know the problem is not that complex. I talked to Valerie in shipping yesterday, and she is just overwhelmed."

Now let's say you remind yourself that Melanie has an Analytical preference. This will help you to see things from her point of view:

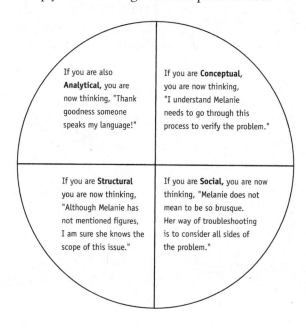

If you are also **Analytical,** you are now thinking, "Thank goodness someone speaks my language!"

If you are **Conceptual,** you are now thinking, "I understand Melanie needs to go through this process to verify the problem."

If you are **Structural** you are now thinking, "Although Melanie has not mentioned figures, I am sure she knows the scope of this issue."

If you are **Social,** you are now thinking, "Melanie does not mean to be so brusque. Her way of troubleshooting is to consider all sides of the problem."

How You Hear the Structural Brain Speaking

Continuing with this example, let's say the first person to bring up the 48-hour fulfillment problem is Chase, who is head of inventory. Chase, who has a highly Structural preference, says:

> Currently 11% of orders are shipping late. In addition, returns are up 2%. The breakdown of reasons for returns indicates that 5% of buyers are returning their items because they arrived too late. For this category of returns, this is an increase of nearly 3% over the same time last year.

You could react to what Chase says in one of four ways, according to your Thinking preference:

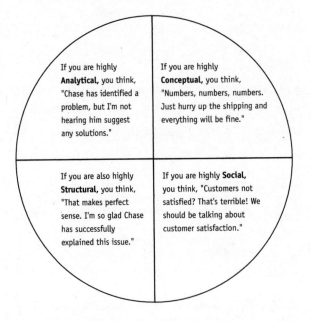

If you are highly **Analytical**, you think, "Chase has identified a problem, but I'm not hearing him suggest any solutions."

If you are highly **Conceptual**, you think, "Numbers, numbers, numbers. Just hurry up the shipping and everything will be fine."

If you are also highly **Structural**, you think, "That makes perfect sense. I'm so glad Chase has successfully explained this issue."

If you are highly **Social**, you think, "Customers not satisfied? That's terrible! We should be talking about customer satisfaction."

Now let's say you remind yourself that Chase has a Structural preference. This will help you to see things from his point of view:

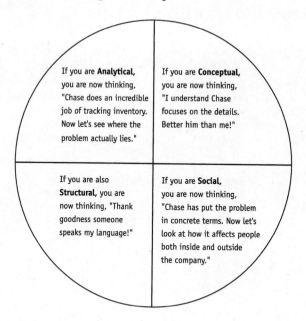

If you are **Analytical,** you are now thinking, "Chase does an incredible job of tracking inventory. Now let's see where the problem actually lies."

If you are **Conceptual,** you are now thinking, "I understand Chase focuses on the details. Better him than me!"

If you are also **Structural,** you are now thinking, "Thank goodness someone speaks my language!"

If you are **Social,** you are now thinking, "Chase has put the problem in concrete terms. Now let's look at how it affects people both inside and outside the company."

How You Hear the Social Brain Speaking

I'm sure you're getting the hang of these examples by now. This time, let's assume the first person to address the 48-hour shipping problem is Florence, who is head of human resources, and who has a very Social preference. She says,

> I just talked to Valerie in shipping again yesterday, and I have to tell you, she is just overwhelmed. She says they can hardly keep up over there, and a lot of the orders are going out late. Can we get her some help?

You could react to what Florence says in one of four ways, according to your Thinking preference:

If you are highly **Analytical,** you think, "We have just hired five new employees this month. Maybe there is another answer."

If you are highly **Conceptual,** you think, "I understand Florence focuses on people issues, but maybe we can do something creative with the environment in the shipping department."

If you are highly **Structural,** you think, "OK, so Valerie is complaining again. What are the actual figures?"

If you are also highly **Social,** you think, "That makes perfect sense. I know Valerie is a hard worker. We definitely should get her the help she needs."

Now let's say you remind yourself that Florence has a Social preference. This will help you to see things from her point of view:

If you are **Analytical,** you are now thinking, "Florence does a good job looking out for our employees. That's why turnover is so low. Let's see what the issues here really are."

If you are **Conceptual,** you are now thinking, "Maybe everybody in shipping would be less stressed if they could listen to their favorite music."

If you are **Structural,** you are now thinking, "Florence knows our people and she would not bring this up unless it was a real problem. We had better take a look at the numbers."

If you are also **Social,** you are now thinking, "Thank goodness someone speaks my language!"

How You Hear the Conceptual Brain Speaking

This time, let's say Brandon, the CEO of the company, is the person who brings up the 48-hour shipping problem. Brandon, who has a highly Conceptual preference, says:

> As you know, we are an Internet-only company. Without a bricks-and-mortar presence, there are inherent challenges we need to innovate around—or, even better, anticipate and merge into our operating systems. For example, it appears that some of our shipments are not going out on time. This has ramifications and implications we need to address sooner rather than later.

You could react to what Brandon says in one of four ways, according to your Thinking preference:

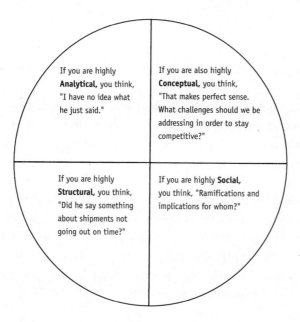

If you are highly **Analytical,** you think, "I have no idea what he just said."

If you are also highly **Conceptual,** you think, "That makes perfect sense. What challenges should we be addressing in order to stay competitive?"

If you are highly **Structural,** you think, "Did he say something about shipments not going out on time?"

If you are highly **Social,** you think, "Ramifications and implications for whom?"

Now let's say you remind yourself that Brandon has a Conceptual brain. This will help you to see things from his point of view:

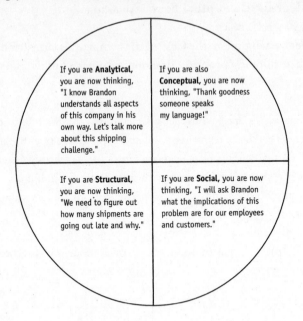

If you are **Analytical,** you are now thinking, "I know Brandon understands all aspects of this company in his own way. Let's talk more about this shipping challenge."

If you are also **Conceptual,** you are now thinking, "Thank goodness someone speaks my language!"

If you are **Structural,** you are now thinking, "We need to figure out how many shipments are going out late and why."

If you are **Social,** you are now thinking, "I will ask Brandon what the implications of this problem are for our employees and customers."

HOW TO SPEAK SO EVERYONE UNDERSTANDS YOU

Now let's say Melanie, Chase, Florence, and Brandon all have familiarized themselves with Emergenetics, and as they speak, they keep in mind that different brains have filters that cause them to focus on different kinds of information. With this is mind, they might say instead:

Right now, 11% of our orders are shipping late. We need to rectify this problem. I know the people in fulfillment are maxed out. But before we go ahead and hire more employees, we need to make sure we have not overlooked a hidden problem. For example, do we need better software to accommodate demand? Since we are an Internet-only operation, we have to be especially aware of potential problems.

Saying this could have the following effects:

• The people with an Analytical preference will appreciate the opportunity to examine all angles of the problem.

- The people with a Structural preference will like the practical point of view.
- The people with a Social preference will be relieved that the human dimension is being considered.
- The people with a Conceptual preference will be more willing to listen while big-picture approaches to the problem are discussed in the context of the company's larger mission.

When you are speaking or writing to an individual person, ask yourself what kind of brain you are communicating with. For example, if you are going to write a thank-you note to someone who is highly Analytical, should you use a lot of flowery prose and personal information? I don't think so. People with a strongly Analytical Profile would not write a thank-you note that way, and they don't want to receive it in this form, either.

Matching the language patterns of other people is one way of sharing their view of the world. It's a way of indicating, "I get it. I get *you*. I appreciate your views." Here are some key phrases and concepts to use when building rapport with people of different Profiles.

Phrases to Use When Speaking to an Analytical Brain

1. "I'll get to the point."
2. "Let's cut to the chase."
3. "What is the cost/benefit ratio?"
4. "This doesn't make rational sense to me."
5. "I have been analyzing the situation."
6. "What's the bottom line?"
7. "I'll skip the details, and just give you an executive summary."
8. "If it isn't logical, it isn't right."
9. "What does the research say?"
10. "There are many layers and intricacies to consider."
11. "Let's explore this subject in depth."
12. "I value your investigation of the facts."

Phrases to Use When Speaking to a Structural Brain

1. "We've always done it this way."
2. "If it ain't broke, don't fix it."
3. "Here are more details."
4. "Organization and order are the keys to the solution."
5. "A place for everything, and everything in its place."
6. "Slow down, let's take this one step at a time."
7. "What does the policy say?"
8. "Are we on schedule?"
9. "The results are fairly predictable."
10. "Let's take an inventory."
11. "Let's get down to business."
12. "I appreciate your efficiency."

Phrases to Use When Speaking to a Social Brain

1. "How are you feeling about this?"
2. "Respect and dignity belong above all else."
3. "I'm concerned about how others will react."
4. "I'm sure you want to be involved in the discussion."
5. "Have all the right people been included?"
6. "How will this affect your customers?"
7. "Are we administering the policies fairly to all?"
8. "Let's work through this together."
9. "How does that grab you?
10. "I am hurt. You haven't returned my phone call from yesterday."
11. "How does this appear in writing? I want to make everyone feel better."
12. "I really love your contribution to this team."

Phrases to Use When Speaking to a Conceptual Brain

1. "I had this wild idea . . ."
2. "Let's brainstorm new ways to solve this."

3. "This routine stuff is so boring."
4. "What is the bigger picture here?"
5. "Let's not rein ourselves in."
6. "How does this connect to the vision?"
7. "I'll play around with this and come up with ideas."
8. "This has the right flow."
9. "Can we be globally assigned?"
10. "We are connected, we are one."
11. "I'm looking for universal synchronicity."
12. "I treasure your ingenious ideas."

Assume Nothing

Different Profiles define and interpret words differently. For example, if you use the word "money," the Analytical brain thinks, "How to set priorities and quantify." The Structural brain thinks, "How can I save money without incurring debt?" The Social brain thinks, "Give money to others." The Conceptual brain thinks, "Money is a means to an end, not an end in itself." While you may think the meaning of the word is obvious, it resonates in each brain in a different way.

Every now and then, business books coin trendy words or phrases that everyone in business starts using. Everyone then assumes the word or phrase is uniformly understood. But assumptions usually mean trouble. For example, today it is back in style to discuss business ethics, and everybody thinks they know what this means. But to the Analytical brain, "ethics" means "we will weigh the evidence." To the Structural brain, it means "right versus wrong." To the Social brain, it means, "follow the golden rule." And to the Conceptual brain, ethics is a gray area that is constantly evolving. People with a lot of Expressive energy will talk about ethics, those with plenty of Assertive energy will push their perspective, while different degrees of Flexibility will determine whether people see ethics in black and white or shades of gray.

Another way to help ensure that everyone is on the same page is to use phrases and concepts that are stated in a positive way. For example, people will say what they do *not* want, but this doesn't build understanding about what they *do* want. They may say, "I would never buy that Rothko painting, even if I had the money—it's way too orange!" Even if everybody agrees with this speaker, all that has been achieved is consensus about what they do not like. If a client or customer says to you, "I'm interested in buying a new car because mine feels too small," you may think you know what this means. However, your next step is to ask, "What *thoughts* or *feelings* would you have if a car was the right size for you?" The Analytical brain may want a larger dashboard display that includes a tachometer and a navigational system. The Structural brain may want eight cupholders and a map compartment in both doors. The Social brain may want more room for his child's car seat, while the Conceptual brain may just want a moonroof. And you thought they were talking about leg room!

MODULATING YOUR BEHAVIORAL ATTRIBUTES
TO BUILD RAPPORT

In addition to speaking the same language, another way to build rapport is to subtly mirror another person's body language and Behavioral Attributes. You do this by using nonverbal communication that is familiar and comfortable for your audience. How others see you is influenced by how you dress, gesture, carry yourself, and so on, which is why ordinarily it is not a good idea to attend a meeting of civil engineers in a pink fluffy dress with strappy sandals and a boa.

My friend Elissa went to New York to deliver a sales pitch for her advertising agency. Elissa is in the 95th percentile for EXPRESSIVENESS, so she is by nature very lively and entertaining. On this occasion, however, she recognized through phone conversations and e-mails that Victoria, her contact in New York, was very reserved. Elissa learned right away that her jokes went nowhere, and brief conversations with Victoria were best.

I suggested that Elissa should enter the room leaving her EXPRESSIVE-NESS at the door. "Victoria will want to hear your information in a calm, understated manner," I cautioned. "If you show her your true EXPRESSIVE-NESS, you will blow her away. Try sitting on your hands."

After the meeting, Elissa called me from the airport.

"I did exactly what you said," she told me. "But there was a problem."

"What happened?"

"Well, I put my hands under my legs and spoke in a calm manner. I felt that Victoria was quite receptive to my pitch. About halfway through the meeting, however, she asked me a question and I got animated. My hands flew upwards. My new bracelet flew off my wrist, launched across the room, and *hit Victoria on the forehead.* After that there was nothing I could do to recover her attention. From now on, when I go into a meeting with an *Expressive,* I will wear no jewelry at all!"

Here are some ways to modulate your behavior to build rapport:

When You Are with People Who Are *Expressive*

1. Think before you speak.
2. Use fewer gestures and words.
3. Allow silence; feel free to leave the person alone.
4. Be understated.

When You Are with People Who Are EXPRESSIVE

1. Speak up.
2. Gesticulate.
3. Constant conversation with more than one person at a time is OK.
4. Exaggerating is OK.

When You Are with People Who Are *Assertive*

1. Keep your actions at a slow pace.
2. Be conciliatory.
3. Ask for their opinion.
4. Keep in mind that they will appear polite no matter what they are thinking.

When You Are with People Who Are ASSERTIVE

1. Fast-paced actions are OK.
2. Confrontation and lively debate are OK.
3. Promote your own opinion.
4. What you see is what you get.

When You Are with People Who Are *Flexible*

1. Do it their way.
2. Stay the course.
3. Suggest fewer changes.
4. Make a decision now.

When You Are with People Who Are FLEXIBLE

1. Do it any way.
2. Give them many options.
3. Changes and revisions are OK.
4. Punt the decision until later.

People generally experience more rapport with others who share the same model of the world that they do. When you are developing rapport with people, make every effort to communicate in what you believe to be their preference. This applies whether you are doing a performance evaluation, making a presentation, building a sale, marketing your product, or working on conflict resolution.

HOW TO COMMUNICATE MORE EFFECTIVELY
WITH YOUR DIRECT REPORTS

To build better working relationships with your people, schedule thirty minutes for coffee and conversation once a year with each individual. Use your preference-matching skills to make the other person feel comfortable. During these conversations, you are not to discuss work! The idea is to develop greater mutual understanding and better communication.

With the Analytical part of your brain, read a book on listening, interpersonal skills, or emotional intelligence before starting your conversations. If you are highly Analytical, you may wish to explain your desire to improve your communication skills. You may not feel terribly enthusiastic right now about having to schedule these conversations, so please know that the time you invest in them now will give you tremendous value down the road after you have developed greater mutual understanding.

With the Structural part of your brain, write down any relevant information after each conversation (not during it!), including items to use in future conversations.

With the Social part of your brain, ask about the person's interests outside of work.

With the Conceptual part of your brain, ask open-ended questions that will lead to further conversation. Allow digressions and tangents.

If you are EXPRESSIVE, practice listening. If you are *Expressive,* practice initiating conversations.

If you are *Assertive,* make sure the conversation is a priority for both of you. If you are ASSERTIVE, know that there is always time in your schedule for these conversations.

If you are *Flexible,* practice accepting whatever you hear. If you are FLEXIBLE, practice focusing on the conversation.

MAKING THE PERFECT PERFORMANCE EVALUATION

In my consulting work, I have surveyed hundreds of written comments from performance evaluations and 360-degree feedback appraisals. Most of the comments correlate with one of the seven Emergenetics attributes. I keep threatening to make different-color rubber stamps, each color representing a different thinking or behavioral attribute, to help streamline the performance appraisal process. I figure these stamps could fund my retirement!

Keep in mind that different Profiles have different ideas about what constitutes a performance evaluation. For example, Alicia's idea of a performance review is to spend an hour or two talking casually about work, saying, "Here are your strengths, here are some things you can do to enhance your skills; now, what would you like to talk about?" This approach just doesn't cut it with her employees who are Analytical and Structural, who don't believe this is a real appraisal and want to see everything quantified. Instead, Alicia could ask her staff to keep records of how they spent their time. Then, during the performance review, Alicia could say, "Here is a list of our clients, along with the revenue they bring into the agency. Next to the name of each client is the percentage of your time you spent with them. Does it really make sense for you to spend fifty percent of your time on the Too-Too account when it only brings in nine percent of our revenue?" This is the kind of language Alicia's Analytical/Structural employees will understand and to which they will be likely to respond.

On pages 192 and 193 you will find the strengths and developmental needs, quoted directly from performance appraisals, that speak to each Emergenetics attribute.

Their Problem—Or Yours?

The next time you fill out a performance appraisal, think about the filters of your own brain. Ask yourself, am I appraising this person based on my own preferences? Are any of these issues actually my problem? Let your appraisals show that you acknowledge their intelligence. Making them do their work your way is not the goal.

My friend Austin has a direct report, Lyle, who drives him crazy. Austin is highly Conceptual and is a big-picture thinker. Lyle, on the other hand, has a Tri-modal Profile and processes things differently.

Austin complained, "Lyle spends too much time obsessing over projects and small details!"

I had to inquire of Austin, "Is that your issue, or his?" Austin looked thoughtful, so I continued, "Lyle has to go through all the quadrants to get to the same place you go to immediately. You may overlook things that Lyle will not. In my opinion, you need to leave Lyle alone unless he isn't performing."

Performance Appraisals
Strengths of Each Emergenetics Attribute*

EXPRESSIVENESS

FLEXIBILITY

Analytical strengths
- Speaks candidly, backed by in-depth knowledge
- Makes decisions based on data
- Thinks things through before acting
- Stays focused and efficient
- Works well independently as needed

Conceptual strengths
- Creates an environment for innovation
- Provides a creative approach to problem-solving
- Keeps an eye on the big picture
- Willing to experiment with new solutions
- Has a vision for change

Quadra-modal strengths
- Able to see many sides of an issue • Looks at the total picture

Structural strengths
- Effective at organizing and planning tasks to meet an objective
- Lets others know what is expected
- Maintains organized work space
- Makes productive use of time
- Attends to all details of a project

Social strengths
- Listens with empathy
- Cares about others
- Works well in a team situation as needed
- Involves the appropriate people in decisions
- Improves morale of others

ASSERTIVENESS

Expressiveness

Expressive strengths • Easy to be around • Listens to information well	**It Depends**	**EXPRESSIVE strengths** • Influences others to be excited about work • Speaks up and represents the organization

Assertiveness

Assertive strengths • Always amiable • Keeps peace with the team	**It Depends**	**ASSERTIVE strengths** • Always prepared to deal with conflict • Is willing to ask for information and instruction when needed

Flexibility

Flexible strengths • Completes task without error • Resists temptations and distractions	**It Depends**	**FLEXIBLE strengths** • Willingly accepts input from others • Sees many points of view

* These are actual statements taken from performance appraisals.

Performance Appraisals
Developmental Needs of Each Emergenetics Attribute*

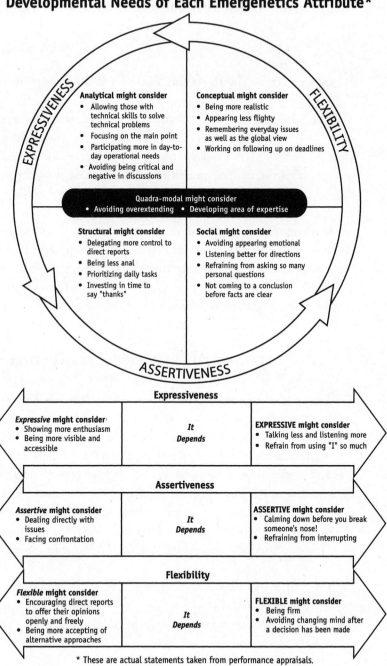

EXPRESSIVENESS

FLEXIBILITY

Analytical might consider
- Allowing those with technical skills to solve technical problems
- Focusing on the main point
- Participating more in day-to-day operational needs
- Avoiding being critical and negative in discussions

Conceptual might consider
- Being more realistic
- Appearing less flighty
- Remembering everyday issues as well as the global view
- Working on following up on deadlines

Quadra-modal might consider
- Avoiding overextending
- Developing area of expertise

Structural might consider
- Delegating more control to direct reports
- Being less anal
- Prioritizing daily tasks
- Investing in time to say "thanks"

Social might consider
- Avoiding appearing emotional
- Listening better for directions
- Refraining from asking so many personal questions
- Not coming to a conclusion before facts are clear

ASSERTIVENESS

Expressiveness

Expressive might consider
- Showing more enthusiasm
- Being more visible and accessible

It Depends

EXPRESSIVE might consider
- Talking less and listening more
- Refrain from using "I" so much

Assertiveness

Assertive might consider
- Dealing directly with issues
- Facing confrontation

It Depends

ASSERTIVE might consider
- Calming down before you break someone's nose!
- Refraining from interrupting

Flexibility

Flexible might consider
- Encouraging direct reports to offer their opinions openly and freely
- Being more accepting of alternative approaches

It Depends

FLEXIBLE might consider
- Being firm
- Avoiding changing mind after a decision has been made

* These are actual statements taken from performance appraisals.

I believe Lyle will go far in his career, as long as he doesn't fall victim to the Tri-modal curses: becoming paralyzed with indecision, or getting stuck doing needless activities. I warned Austin to be on the lookout for these issues, and he will intervene if they become a problem.

When You Are on the Receiving End of a Performance Review

The next time you receive a performance appraisal, think about your manager's most likely thinking style and how it compares to yours. This may give you clues into why you received the comments that you did. For example, let's say you are complimented for speaking candidly, backed by in-depth knowledge. Is this because your appraiser thinks similarly, or is it because she can't think this way and likes it that you can?

In addition, look at your developmental needs in light of your Emergenetics Profile. For example, if you are getting lots of comments regarding listening more or relating better to your coworkers, perhaps these correlate with the amount of Social attribute in your Profile. If you need tips on improving any attribute, go back to chapter 7 for ways to do so.

MAKING THE PERFECT PRESENTATION

The key to making a great presentation lies in being able to satisfy everyone's needs. If everyone possessed only one Thinking Attribute or Behavioral Attribute, your job would be very easy. Fortunately, humans are not that simple.

An understanding of Emergenetics principles will help you make the most effective presentation to an audience. You have an opportunity to build rapport by appealing to the Thinking and Behavioral Attributes of the people listening to you. As the saying goes, you can't please all the people all of the time—but you can at least rotate through the Attributes and hit all the bases.

The first thing to keep in mind is what you learned in speech class:

1. Begin with an opening statement that tells the audience what you are going to tell them.
2. Tell them what you want to tell them.
3. Recap what you just told them.

The abstract (Analytical and Conceptual) thinkers in your audience will appreciate an overview of what you are discussing. The concrete (Structural and Social) thinkers want you to keep things in order and tell them what to expect. If you do not have the advantage of determining the Emergenetics Profiles of your audience ahead of time, then cover all the bases by including activities that appeal to each attribute.

In addition, the best presentations tap into all of the audience's senses. Today's technology allows you to do this in a straightforward manner. Include visual aids, sounds, and writing materials for all the brains in your audience.

Here are considerations to keep in mind when making a presentation to a group of any size.

How to Present to the Analytical Brain

1. Give an overview and objectives.
2. Present the budget in numerical form.
3. Use logic, data, facts, and precise, clear language.
4. Provide written information, either ahead of time or afterward.
5. If you write any notes at the front of the room during the presentation, use color only if it enhances the presentation, and print the letters (as opposed to writing in cursive).
6. Refer to credible sources.
7. Highlight key information with graphs and charts.
8. Summarize the concepts, but be prepared to provide the details in depth if you get challenged.
9. Provide time for discussion, questions, and answers (inquiring minds want to know).
10. Begin and end on time.

Highly Analytical audiences want an instructor who is intelligent, knowledgeable, and in command of the subject. They prefer a presenter who is formal, and an environment that is bright and spare. Analytical learners like challenges and puzzles, enjoy working alone, and need quiet time for reflection.

This group wants value for time expended. The Analytical brain will not take you seriously unless you have a thorough grasp of all of the information you present. If you are giving a presentation to someone who is Analytical and

ASSERTIVE, watch out! This person likes to lead and will take over if you are not strong enough. If you are presenting to someone who is Analytical and *Flexible,* speak consistently and accurately. A simple mistake will cause this brain to discount everything you have to say. If you don't know the answer to a question, get back to the questioner as soon as possible with the correct information.

How to Present to the Structural Brain

1. Include personal experience with your biographical information to show you have "been there."
2. Prepare an agenda.
3. Speak in an orderly fashion, and avoid digressions.
4. Include all the details.
5. Keep your presentation neat, orderly, and grammatically correct.
6. Highlight key information with bulleted lists.
7. Hand out a syllabus for later review.
8. Be task-oriented, and include implementation steps or an action plan.
9. Provide time for questions and answers (to tie up any loose ends).
10. Begin and end on time.

People who are very Structural prefer a conservative presenter and an environment that is minimalist. They are hands-on learners, so provide pencils and paper and other learning tools. At the end of your session, the Structural members of your audience may want to put everything in the room back where it belongs.

The Structural brain is uncomfortable with digressions. If you do digress, reassure your listeners that you will return to the agenda. Then be sure that you do.

How to Present to the Social Brain

1. Share personal information along with your credentials.
2. Make eye contact.
3. Illustrate key information with stories, parables, and vignettes.
4. Show emotion.

5. Include pictures of people in your graphics.
6. Show how information can be applied to the self.
7. Include music.
8. Allow time for sharing.
9. Provide written directions in addition to verbal instructions.
10. Acknowledge emotional issues.

For the highly Social brain, you are their friend, interpreter, and coach. The Social attribute prefers a presenter who is casual and an environment that is informal and dimly lit. Social learners like having their senses engaged with tactile objects, aromas, music, and so on.

I usually find that as soon as I finish giving instructions for a certain activity, someone (or several people) will ask, "What did you say we are supposed to do?" It is always the Social brains who need clarification. For this reason, I also give written directions for any activities. This way the Social brains can reassure themselves without interrupting, and I don't have to keep repeating the directions.

How to Present to the Conceptual Brain

1. Move quickly to gain the attention of the Conceptual brain or you may lose it permanently.
2. Give an overview along with a reason for paying attention that includes a vision of the future.
3. Make your words flow.
4. Present the budget in pictures.
5. Highlight key information in color.
6. Change your style of presentation every ten to fifteen minutes.
7. Use metaphors.
8. Allow an opportunity to change seats or even rooms.
9. Summarize major points as you go along.
10. Leave something to the imagination.

Like Social brains, people with a Conceptual Profile prefer a presenter who can be casual and an environment that is informal. Conceptual learners enjoy pictures, metaphors, and symbols, and need time to reflect.

People who are highly Conceptual do not like being bombarded with a lot of details. They do like having an opportunity to figure things out for themselves—to connect the dots. I admit it's a challenge to give the Structural brain all the information it desires without making the Conceptual brain go to sleep. This is one reason why highly effective speakers are so rare.

Here are some suggestions for addressing the Behavioral Attributes of your audience:

To Present to the *Expressive* Profile

- Remember *Expressives* prefer safety.
- No role playing!
- Do not call on *Expressives.*
- This brain reenergizes by being alone.

To Present to the EXPRESSIVE Profile

- Remember EXPRESSIVES are willing to take risks.
- Keep things moving.
- EXPRESSIVES like to share.
- This brain reenergizes in a group setting.

To Present to the *Assertive* Profile

- Remember *Assertives* want a peaceful interaction.
- Be sensitive.
- Allow time for responses.
- *Assertives* are more comfortable following directions.

To Present to the ASSERTIVE Profile

- ASSERTIVES embrace confrontation.
- Challenge thinking with debate.
- Allow movement about the room.
- ASSERTIVES are happy to give directions to the group.

To Present to the *Flexible* Profile

- Make no errors.
- Follow the rules.
- Remember *Flexibles* prefer defined situations.
- *Flexibles* need assignments in detail.

To Present to the FLEXIBLE Profile

- Acknowledge errors and move on.
- Provide focus.
- Remember FLEXIBLES can handle ambiguous situations.
- FLEXIBLES need assignments that are focused.

Where to Begin?

Some say it's always best to begin a presentation with an activity that appeals to the left brain, such as immediately clarifying the objectives and agenda. I have found that it's best to begin with something very right-brained to capture the attention of the people who are highly Conceptual and Social, then quickly follow with information the Analytical and Structural brains will need in order to feel comfortable. You will meet with greater success if you continue in your audience's most preferred attribute and stay there until you have achieved rapport. Then you can move in any direction and they will gladly follow.

People who are very Analytical want you to provide a formal biography that lists your academic background, work history, awards, honors, and so on. Credentials are important. If the person who introduces you does not announce these things, then you must work them into the conversation yourself, as they are essential for establishing your credibility.

I once gave a speech to a group of *Expressive,* extremely Analytical scientists. There were only three Conceptual thinkers in the group, and one of them happened to be the person who introduced me to the audience. Being EXPRESSIVE, he said, "Geil needs no introduction. Two minutes after she starts, you will see how fabulous her presentation is."

I immediately dumped my planned introductory remarks and instead said, "Thank you, Tom, for your faith in me. However, ninety-two percent of the people in this room have a preference for Analytical thought, and they are now uncomfortable because they think I'm going to talk cosmic woo-woo psychobabble, and you have given them no reason to think otherwise. These brains really want to know that I have a PhD and have done postdoctoral research . . ." Providing this information was not about showing off. It was about moving quickly to secure the attention of my audience. I knew that they believed they were smarter than anybody else, and the only way to get their attention immediately was to speak their language.

SELLING AND PERSUADING

Your customers will interpret whatever you say using the filters of their Emergenetics Profile. Your success will improve if you remember the following key points:

1. Determine your customer's Profile to the best of your ability. If you are selling to more than one person, be prepared to address different Profiles.
2. Develop rapport by using words and phrases that match your customer's Thinking Attributes, and behavior that matches her or his Behavioral Attributes.
3. Address your customer's Thinking Attributes in your sales presentation. If you don't know what they are, be prepared to address all of them.
4. Answer any questions or objections. Draw out comments from people who are *Expressive.*
5. Close the sale.

A client, Amanda, is a certified financial planner who has been using Emergenetics principles in her sales calls throughout her career. She has a 97 percent closing rate. Here is her method:

I sell a non-tangible item [financial planning], Amanda says. I sell a concept. I develop a dream for people, based on where they are coming from. I sell hope that they will be able to retire, and live the life they want to. What is tangible is the reports I prepare and the materials I give out.

When clients first come in, I ask them to fill out some paperwork regarding their financial assets. As I look over their papers, I'm talking to them the whole time. I spend at least two hours with them, asking about various aspects of their information. That's how I identify where they fit in terms of Emergenetics. What is important to them? Are they concerned about their children's education? Grandchildren? I pick up on clues such as the words that they use, how they explain things to me, etc. Often one partner is very family-oriented and the other is not, so they have different ideas about what they want. I get to know them pretty well.

In my office I have a picture of two polar bears hugging. I have it there for a specific reason. People think financial planning is dry, but I tell my clients, "When I am working with you, I will know more about you than your attorney knows, than your accountant knows, and than your doctors know." I know their fears, dreams, and secrets. People call me and say, "I need this new furnace, should I buy one?" Well, heck, how should I know? I'm not a furnace person. But this says to me that they have implicit trust in me.

If I have someone come in who is an engineer or an accountant, and he has a very detailed Excel spreadsheet—which drives me nuts by the way—I let him explain it to me because he thinks I understand it the same way that he does. I do understand it, but I don't get as involved in the details. But what this conversation does, in my opinion, is develop trust because we are communicating on the same level.

After the initial interview, I prepare a proposal. I don't use a canned document. Depending on the person's Profile, I'll use different approaches. For instance, when I think someone's preference is Analytical, I'll use more data in the proposal, but I will put it in the back and refer to it in the text. I know they like to have it, but we don't necessarily have to go through the details when we review the proposal. If the person's preference seems Conceptual, I create a pictorial display. If someone has a Social preference, I use the same slide-show approach, but talk more about their family. If the person is Structural, we go through the spreadsheets.

If I have a client who says, "I'm about to retire, and I need this money while I'm traveling" I go to my Structural list of words and talk about implementation. "Here is how your income is going to go directly into your checking account, and you won't have to worry about it." The clients with a Conceptual preference don't worry about this at all, so with them I talk about the bigger picture, which is easy for me. With an Analytical client, I explain the bottom-line issues—how much money is going to come out every month, what's going to happen to it, and how much will be left over. I let the Social clients know that their family will not have to worry about money, and show them how to get others involved.

It's hard for me to control my EXPRESSIVENESS. If I'm talking to people who are very stoic, I try to mirror their level of *Expressiveness.* I try not to get too excited. I limit the big jokes and the big grins. The biggest issue is my hands. Sometimes I will wave my hands up and down like a teeter-totter to explain how interest rates work. I love to wave my hands around for emphasis, but *Expressives* do not care for this behavior, so around them I control my EXPRESSIVENESS by writing a lot of notes instead.

I just hired a new administrative assistant. She has a lot of Analytical preference, and I noticed the other day that she was really puzzled by the notes I was taking. This is because I have little pockets of information all over the place, with arrows pointing to them. There is a lot of energy on my paper. I write EXPRESSIVELY. If anyone wanted to pick this piece of paper up and read it, they would have a difficult time doing so. I know exactly what is on it, however. Although there is a shocking lack of organization, I can understand it if everything is interconnected by arrows.

I will draw pictures for people. Actually, I do that for everybody, because people are very visual. If they can see a picture, the concept seems to last longer. Everybody can relate to a graph that shows how much money they're going to have to live on for the rest of their life.

I was an art major. If I were in school today, I would be labeled learning disabled. I was not an outstanding student. I've never been able to spell, I wasn't a good reader, and I still don't do well with numbers. I have to use my calculator. But after I learned about Emergenetics, I thought, OK, I'm all right, there is nothing wrong with me. I don't have to hide who I really am. I just have to adapt a bit so others can understand me.

Can you tell what kind of brain Amanda has? In a sea of highly Analytical financial planners, Amanda has an extremely Conceptual preference. She surrounds herself with Analytical and Structural brains to do the things she doesn't prefer to do.

Amanda has a sales style that is very successful for her. Other salespeople use other successful styles based on their different attributes. Emergenetics can be utilized to make each one more successful.

MARKETING

Several years ago I was working with the management team of a national chain of department stores. All of the members of the team were highly Social, and working with them was a pleasure. To my amazement, however, I discovered that the company had no online presence. "Oh, we don't need that," the managers declared. "We know our customers, and they aren't interested in the Internet. They just want to come into our stores and shop."

I tried to persuade the team that they were making a serious oversight, but

I kept running headlong into their deeply-rooted assumptions about their market. They felt they understood their customers better than I did.

Within a couple of years it became clear that the company clearly needed an online presence, and suddenly the managers were playing catch-up, scrambling to put together a Web site. Because they had failed to look at their customers from the point of view of all the Emergenetics attributes, they had misinterpreted their market and nearly missed the boat.

We have used Emergenetics to help advertising and public relations firms with their marketing research. What better way to understand your audience than through the Thinking and Behavioral Attributes?

In seminars, we sometimes group participants by their most preferred Thinking Attribute, then ask each group, "How would you handle money?" Each group writes its answers on chart paper. When we did this with a group of bankers (what better subject for them?), here is what they said:

The Analytical group reported:

$$I = \sqrt{(F+V+D)}$$

This equation means **Income** equals the square root of **Fixed Expenses** plus **Variable Expenses** plus **Discretionary Outlays.** As one of my economics professors once stated, the meaning is inherently obvious to the most casual observer.

The Structural group wrote:

I. Life Plan
   A. Budget
       1. College Education
       2. Vacation
       3. Retirement
       4. Funeral Costs
   B. Conservative
       1. Charge on credit works for us, but always pay total bill at the end of the month—NO FINANCE CHARGES—EVER.
       2. Shop with a folder of coupons that are labeled and alphabetized by store name.
   C. Checks and Balances
II. Never spend money that is budgeted for something else.

The Social thinkers wrote:

- Call the bank to determine account balance.
- Give money to the Save the Whales Society.
- Always buy Girl Scout cookies.
- We are socially responsible investors, if we invest at all.
- Lend money to friends.
- Buy insurance in order to take care of the family.
- Always tip generously.
- Use money to buy gifts for others.

The Conceptual group stated:

- We are impulse spenders.
- We are always sure that we will win the lottery.
- Best to have someone else manage our money.
- Desire wins out over need.
- We intuitively know our bank balance, but we never actually balance anything.
- "If U buy it, it will come."
- This whole list is subject to change at a moment's notice.

The Behavioral Attributes also influence attitudes about money. Expressiveness, for example, affects how willing people are to openly discuss money. Assertiveness affects how much risk they are willing to accept in their investments. And Flexibility affects how much time they take to deliberate before making a purchase.

Giving Emergenetics information to the marketing people of their bank, this company came up with tag lines for each Thinking and Behavioral Attribute. They were as follows:

Analytical: "Online, Bottom Line, All the Time."
Structural: "Every penny in its place, your future is secure with us."
Social: "Your money is important to you, you are important to us."
Conceptual: "Dream big, we will help you get there."
Expressive: "In the quiet solitude, your money grows."
EXPRESSIVE: "Hear the roar of success! 200,000 investors can't be wrong."

Assertive: "Understated, not undervalued. No hype, just trust."
ASSERTIVE: "The line forms behind you."
Flexible: "100 years of an unchanging tradition of success."
FLEXIBLE: "Unique solutions for every customer."

Understand the ramifications of Emergenetics for directing a marketing campaign. Do you know what the Profiles of your target audience look like? Does your approach match? Or should you advertise to all the Thinking Attributes?

The overall lesson is to understand your product, know to whom it is geared, and tailor your message accordingly. A good rule of thumb is to ask different people with different Profiles to proofread an important e-mail or marketing piece. This only takes a few minutes, and it can save a lot of future grief.

CONFLICT MANAGEMENT

When techies and touchy-feelies work alongside one another, misunderstandings are bound to occur. There are going to be conflicts any time people have different Profiles. However, when you take Emergenetics principles and apply them to disagreements, each side develops a greater appreciation for the point of view of the other, making compromise more achievable.

Workplace conflicts range from simple misunderstandings to acrimonious arguments. To complicate the picture, people handle confrontation according to their Profile. People who are *Expressive* and *Assertive* may not give any outward sign that they are actually very upset. People who are EXPRESSIVE and ASSERTIVE may behave as if the world is coming to an end.

A spirited discussion of ideas doesn't have to be a conflict. In fact, the best decisions are made with input from different Profiles. In my experience, conflict gets ugly when people feel ignored or insulted. They may feel threatened or overlooked, or they may believe their point of view is being undervalued.

Here are some steps for communication during times of conflict:

Step 1—Start with your Social brain. Say something empathic. Using an "I" message (for example, "I am distressed about this situation") is an old trick, but it is effective because the other person can't disagree with what *you* are feeling.

Step 2—Move to your Analytical brain. Give an accurate, unemotional report of the situation. The goal is to have all parties agree on how things stand.

Step 3—Move on to your Conceptual brain. Allow each person an opportunity to create a solution by brainstorming options. It is impossible for someone to feel ignored when you are actively soliciting her or his opinions.

Step 4—End with your Structural brain. After brainstorming possible solutions, get organized by:

1. Selecting the best solution
2. Determining the steps to be taken to complete the goal
3. Establishing a time limit

Your Behavioral Attributes will have an effect on how you handle conflict resolution. If you are in the first-third of the Behavioral Attributes, you may need to be more Assertive, Expressive, and Flexible. If you are in the third-third of the Behavioral Attributes, you may need to be less ASSERTIVE and EXPRESSIVE so the other person does not feel you are taking up all the air in the room. Being FLEXIBLE is OK, as long as you are willing to commit to a solution.

Misunderstandings

Here is a story about e-mails gone awry involving four people: my associate Kyle, his assistant Sarah, my assistant Karen, and me.

One day Kyle called me and said, "Why won't your office staff make a Least Preferred Attribute list for me?"

I said, "They would be more then happy to make one for you. You just have to request it."

"I *did* request it," Kyle said, "and what I got back was an e-mail which rudely implied I was out of line for asking. The e-mail was written in all capital letters, saying 'KYLE IS THE ONLY ASSOCIATE WHO USES THIS REPORT!!!' "

I said, "It amazes me that Karen would communicate in this fashion. Let me check into it and get back to you."

Karen's voice is soft and well modulated. She is a Structural/Social thinker who is *Expressive* and *Assertive.* My big clue that there had been a serious misunderstanding was that it would be anathema for Karen to write an e-mail in all capital letters with several exclamation points.

Karen said, "I had a conversation with Kyle's assistant Sarah, and we were communicating just fine. I wrote the following e-mail:

Sarah,

I've attached an example of the "Least Preferred Attribute" report that you can play with. Tell Kyle that he's the ONLY one who uses this report. The other associates do a "Least Preferred Attribute" exercise and they have the participants look at their Profiles and come up with their "Least Preferred Attribute" on their own. :) Good Luck!

Karen

Karen continued, "All I meant by this was that when we had the new computer program implemented, we didn't construct an LPA [Least Preferred Attribute] program, because no other Emergenetics Associate used it. I was only pointing out this fact, and Sarah understood."

Sarah forwarded Karen's e-mail to Kyle, who was immediately offended by the wording. Because Kyle has a Social/Conceptual brain and is EXPRESSIVE, he leaped to a conclusion that was not intended. Kyle added more capital letters and exclamation points to Karen's e-mail in his head because he "heard" an implied criticism.

To resolve this conflict, I started out with a Social, empathic message in my conversation with Kyle: "I know you are unhappy about the e-mail you received, and I certainly am distressed that a communication from my office upset you."

Then I moved to the Analytical part of my brain. "My understanding is that you feel like our office is not supporting you, while Karen feels you misunderstood her e-mail."

Next I tapped into the Conceptual part of my brain. "Would you like to speak directly with Karen? Is there something you would like me to communicate to her? What should we do next?"

To wrap up my conversation with Kyle, we both used our Structural thinking. Together we:

1. Selected the best solution (Karen and Kyle would speak to each other directly to clear up any misunderstanding),
2. Determined the steps to be taken to complete the goal (Karen would call Kyle), and

3. Established a time limit (Karen would contact Kyle before the end of the day).

Kyle ended the conversation by saying, "I guess we need to mend some fences. I suggest your office and my office go out for tacos."

As I describe this misunderstanding to you, it sounds manageable. However, I assure you that at the time it was an enormous problem that caused a great deal of hurt feelings and lost time.

Many huge difficulties can be traced back to simple misinterpretations that have their basis in assumptions we make because of our Thinking and Behavioral Attributes. When we make an effort to understand the Profiles of other people, it often becomes clear that no offense was intended. The problem is not personal—it's Profile!

Emergenetics Leadership

Get Who You Need, Get Them Motivated, and Get Out of the Way

Whether you are the CEO of a large organization or the owner of a sole proprietorship who counts on the banker, lawyer, and accountant for advice, you can use Emergenetics to become a more effective leader.

WHAT MAKES AN EFFECTIVE LEADER?

Volumes upon volumes have been written about leadership, and the subject still has not been exhausted. Everyone wants to know: What qualities do the best leaders possess? What sets them apart? Is it the way they envision the future? Or the way they mobilize others? What can we learn from their successes—and mistakes? It's a discussion that has no beginning and no foreseeable end. However, Emergenetics helps leaders succeed.

People always ask me which Emergenetics Profile makes the best leaders. I answer, *"There is no such thing as a perfect Emergenetics 'leadership' Profile."* As you have seen from previous chapters, successful leaders have every type of Profile.

The best leaders I have observed are people who manage from the strengths of their Profile, but who also know how to manage using their least-preferred Attributes. Remember James, back in chapter 5? His profile is Analytical, Structural, and ASSERTIVE, but as the CEO of a 300-million-dollar company, he consciously makes the effort to communicate in a more Social and EXPRESSIVE way because it is important for his leadership.

> Power in organizations is the capacity generated by our relationships.
>
> Margaret Wheatley,
> *Leadership and the New Science*

Effective leaders understand that diversity, synergy, and energy result when ambitious folks with different preferences are allowed to perform a job together in a safe environment. If you want your team to be more creative and ultimately more productive, hire competent people, motivate and reward them appropriately, and then—stand back.

GETTING WHO YOU NEED

From the boiler room to the board room, you want the right people on board. If your company has breadth, all of your employees will reflect the corporate mission and contribute to its success. If it has depth, you'll be able to call on experienced employees when you need them, and promote loyal and knowledgeable people from within.

Everybody wants bright, competent employees with enthusiasm and integrity. This is a good start, but it's not enough. To be successful, you also need to hire all kinds of brains.

Hiring for Competence

Begin by tapping individuals who are competent in their respective fields. You can put people together and ask them to design a rocket ship to the moon, but if no one on the team has a background in engineering, science, or math, your rocket won't even make it to New Mexico.

Emergenetics does not measure competence. A preference for a certain kind of thinking does not guarantee success in that area. For example, people may have a strong preference for Analytical thought, but it doesn't necessarily mean that they will be able to build a rocket. It takes skill, effort, and often ingenuity to put preferences to productive use.

Hiring for Values

When you bring people on board, you want their values to be synonymous with those of the organization. People aren't going to tell you they are lazy, devious, or dishonest, so you'll have to ask them leading questions, find out about their reputation, and listen to what your gut tells you.

We work with MBA students who do activities in teams. Sometimes there are team members who don't contribute much to the group. A team can fall apart at the hands of one individual like this. One student was asked if she saw any correlation between specific Emergenetics Attributes and the students who were not contributing to their groups. Does one Attribute tend to be more indolent than another? "No," she observed, "slacking doesn't discriminate."

Hiring to Complement Your Profile

In addition to being able to flex all their Thinking and Behavioral Attributes, effective leaders are able to put together a team that complements their preferred Thinking style. This is important, because every organization needs representation from all the Attributes to be successful.

One of my associates once worked with a large public health group that had just converted from government-owned to private nonprofit status. The Board of Directors, who were mostly Structural/Social thinkers, remained in place. They saw their job as walking down the halls each day and talking to patients about their stay. When the company converted, the board brought in a new CEO who was an Analytical/Conceptual thinker. She would often clash with the board because she could never get them to see where the organization needed to go in the future. She was preoccupied with big ideas like, "Fifteen years down the road, we will need a bigger facility. This is Phase I and an important step for our future." Whenever she would make these comments, the board would say, "That's great, but what about Mrs. Jones who says that her Jell-O was runny?"

The communication difficulties also were a result of Behavioral differences.

The chairman of the board and a majority of the board members were *Expressive, Assertive,* and *Flexible,* while the new CEO was EXPRESSIVE, ASSERTIVE, and *Flexible.* The Board found the CEO driving and often confrontational, while she was annoyed at their glacial pace.

My associate did an Emergenetics intervention with the board of directors and the CEO. After much discussion, they all finally got it. At the conclusion of the day-long seminar, the board noted, "We must also rely on the CEO to guide us through the future. She is thinking of the long-term goals of this company, and we need to appreciate that." The CEO said, "Thankfully the board is looking after the day-to-day operations, because I don't have the time or the desire to do so."

After the seminar the board decided to amend its bylaws and double its size. With their new understanding of Emergenetics, they included more diverse members. One year later, their profits increased by 23 percent.

Hiring for Variety: Creating a WE*company*

It's essential to bring diversity and perspective to your company. Mixing it up in terms of gender and racial diversity is essential, but in this book I am only going to talk about bringing different Thinking and Behavioral styles together.

Large companies usually include a representative cross section of all kinds of Profiles. People are people, and the Emergenetics norms that are present in the population at large generally are evident across a company as well. This is a very good thing. I call an organization that encompasses all kinds of Profiles a Whole Emergenetics Company, or WE*company.*

As a leader in a particular field or industry, you may be tempted to hire people who will be specifically geared for a certain Thinking style. Don't. As much as you would like to hire people with a certain Profile, it is much more important to think of the overall landscape of the office and the multiple facets of the work you are producing. If you need convincing, here is a cautionary tale.

Brooke is a vice president of human resources for a bank that was originally a credit union. Brooke called me because she was having difficulty keeping personal bankers for any sustained length of time. She would bring in capable people, but they would not get along with their supervisors, and they would end up getting fired.

Brooke tended to hire new personal bankers whose Profiles were similar to hers: Social, Conceptual, EXPRESSIVE, and ASSERTIVE. The supervisors, on the other hand, were Analytical/Structural thinkers who were *Expressive* and *Assertive.* Because the bank was originally a credit union, they had never been trained to aggressively drum up new business, nor really concern themselves with the bottom line. Because of the huge difference in thinking styles, the supervisors regarded the incoming personal bankers as people who were not very bright and who wasted a lot of time. They told Brooke that she needed to hire a different kind of person.

While I cautioned Brooke about this, she felt it was best to appease the supervisors. We designed a questionnaire that allowed the supervisors to specify the qualities they would like to see in a perfect employee. They decided that the perfect employee was Analytical, Structural, *Expressive,* and *Assertive*—that is, just like them. For the next year, the company hired personal bankers who fit this mold. Turnover decreased, and the supervisors gave the personal bankers better evaluations than they had given the previous employees. However, after six months, the board of directors was disappointed because business revenue had decreased from the previous year.

Personal bankers are expected to drum up new business. This is a job that is well suited for a person with a Social, EXPRESSIVE, and ASSERTIVE Profile. Even though the bank trained the new personal bankers in selling techniques, they were not very effective at attracting new clients. Brooke called me and said, "We are having another problem. Our bottom line is falling."

We helped her redesign their hiring practices again. Brooke realized the company needed different brains for cross-selling purposes, and it needed personal bankers who could work well with different kinds of customers. The supervisors were going to need to learn how to be more accommodating, so Brooke sent them to a training seminar designed to improve their relationships with different types of employees.

In the end, the company achieved the best of both worlds. Brooke hired personal bankers with different Thinking and Behavioral preferences who were able to satisfy different kinds of customers, and the supervisors learned to stand back. The turnover rate was cut by 30 percent, and the bank's profits exceeded the board's expectations.

Assembling a WE*team*

A Whole Emergenetics Team, or WE*team,* is a brain trust composed of people who represent each attribute in the Emergenetics model. A WE*team* can be large or small. It may include all your managers, or it may be a special task force you assemble, or it could be a little group in one department or office. The important consideration is that the team has the proper combination of people so that all the preferences are represented, and each person understands that the others contribute in different and valuable ways. The energy that emerges from the varied Thinking and Behavioral Attributes creates an impressive combination of creative *and* productive results.

If you don't have enough people to make up a WE*team,* import the brains you need to make a brain trust. Alternatively, tell the person who comes closest to the missing preference to make a conscious choice to fill that void.

What Analytical Brains Bring to the Table

People with a strong preference for Analytical thinking can be very good at helping to define and analyze problems. They see themselves as straightforward, clear, and purposeful. They must have facts, figures, directions, and reasons to approach any task. In a team situation they say, "Let's check out our decision to see if it's feasible to implement."

If you look over the shoulder of someone with an Analytical Profile, you might see something like this:

1. Analysis
      a. Mission?
      b. Work breakdown structure
      c. Financial analysis
            i. Cost/benefit
            ii. Risk
            iii. Profitability
2. Project assignments
      a. Change management
      b. Roles and responsibilities
      c. Success metrics
3. Work the plan
      a. Communication
      b. Roadblocks/critical path
4. Review
      a. Six-month efficiency evaluation
      b. Retool

What Structural Brains Bring to the Table

People with a strong preference for Structural thinking can be excellent in defining the problem and assisting with implementation. They see themselves as the source for making systemic links to determine the scope of a problem. They organize the components of the problem and the possible solutions. In a team situation they ask, "How does this idea apply to our situation?"

If you look over the shoulder of someone with a Structural Profile, you might see something like this:

1. Define objectives
2. Develop process map
3. Identify roles/responsibilities
4. Develop timeline/schedule
5. Establish milestones and checkpoints
6. Make communication plan
7. Determine success measures
8. Identify project control mechanism

What Social Brains Bring to the Table

People with a strong preference for Social thinking can be excellent facilitators in the group process. They regard their interpersonal skills as their strongest contribution, and they keep the group working harmoniously together. They weigh all proposed solutions equally. Although they may identify the best solution, they may not know how they did so. In a team situation they ask, "What do you think of this idea?"

People with a strong Social preference can be unsurpassed at making alliances and recognizing office politics. They know, or can find out, who the players are. If you look over the shoulder of someone with a Social Profile, you might see something like this:

- Talk to Mary ASAP
- Can we do a survey?
- CALL ROBB
- What could we give out to go with this? Mugs, T-shirts?
- Meet Clark to discuss—layover at airport?

What Conceptual Brains Bring to the Table

People with a strong preference for Conceptual thinking are usually quite good at generating ideas and making the quantum leaps necessary to brainstorm and creatively solve difficult problems. They enjoy a challenge and often plunge into the problem-solving process before considering what direction to take. They focus on the importance of the outcome, not the details involved in getting there. They don't mind mistakes. In a team situation they say, "Let's look at this problem in a different way."

If you look over the shoulder of someone who is highly Conceptual, you may not even be able to understand what you are likely to see:

> >> Vision? <<
> ⟹ 5 years out?
> { possibilities for Japan? }
> ** maybe rework the master plan **

What Tri-modal or Quadra-modal Brains Bring to the Table

A multimodal thinker is needed to hold a WE*team* together. While these individuals usually are not strong in any one attribute, their gift is to recognize the unique contributions of the other team members and then act as a translator, so the Analytical understands the Social, or the Conceptual understands the Structural, and so on.

The ideal WE*team* also has a combination of different Behavioral Attributes. People with different Behavioral preferences don't just act differently, they also bring differing degrees of energy to issues involving people (Expressiveness is about communicating with others), tasks (Assertiveness is associated with getting things done), and adaptability (Flexibility has to do with accomodating other points of view).

Here is what different Behavioral Attributes bring to a team:

Why *Expressive* People Are Good on a Team	Why EXPRESSIVE People Are Good on a Team
• Know how to listen, let others talk • Will pitch in, but under the radar • Connect with others quietly	• Make sure every idea is discussed • Can take charge of meeting • Work the room
Why *Assertive* People Are Good on a Team	Why ASSERTIVE People Are Good on a Team
• Can see both sides of an issue • Make their case without creating conflict • Don't rush into things	• Embrace confrontation • Help others express their views • Concerned with getting the task done
Why *Flexible* People Are Good on a Team	Why FLEXIBLE People Are Good on a Team
• Not easily distracted • Decisive • Will make sure a decision is reached	• Easygoing • Open to many ideas • Don't mind extended discussion

THE POWER OF WE

During the last twenty minutes of an eight-hour seminar, when everyone is tired and out of energy, I will put a small group of people together who represent each Emergenetics attribute, and ask them to generate a creative and entertaining summary of the workshop.

They are given fifteen minutes to prepare. These presentations are always more ingenious than the participants imagined possible. These groups have produced songs, poems, dances (sometimes with costumes), nonverbal metaphors, and skits. Everyone is amazed that this level of imagination could be produced in such a short period of time.

Why do I end a seminar by asking seminar participants to generate something in fifteen minutes? To demonstrate the power of the WE*team*. Ask yourself:

- How long and how efficient are your meetings?
- Are you including every perspective when you ask for opinions or make important decisions?
- When you are the leader of a meeting, do you organize the meeting in such a fashion that everyone is heard?
- When you put a team together to make decisions, are you ensuring that the proper climate is in place to allow all the Thinking and Behavioral Attributes to flourish?

Assuming they are all competent, a Whole Emergenetics "brain trust" will solve problems in a creative and productive manner, and will do it in record time.

All the Pieces of the Puzzle

Once in a great while at the end of a seminar, I'll get a team that does not finish its summary. When I explore why this happens, it's always because one member had to leave the workshop early, and the team needed that brain power to accomplish the task. Whenever a team is missing an Attribute, problems arise.

In the late 1980s, I asked a vice president in a well-known technology company, "Where will your company be as we enter the new millennium?"

He was dumbfounded by my question and finally said, "We will be manufacturing what we are doing today, only bigger."

I immediately sold my stock.

Why?

I did not have any inside information about this company. It was not one of my clients, and I did not know what was going on in their boardroom. However, I was certain that the management team was not looking into the future. If there had been a WE*team* in place at the head of this company, the Conceptual minds would have made sure there was a long-term plan, the Analytical minds would have made certain it was profitable, the Structural minds would have made it possible, and the Social minds would have made sure everyone knew about it. I was expecting the vice president to give me a futuristic explanation about the technology ahead—will computers cook breakfast? will cell phones act like ATMs?—but he had nothing to say. Sure enough, the 1990s were a rough decade for this technology company, and it is still recovering.

I often do management audits during which I ask each team member to describe the mission of their company. It doesn't matter what official mission statement is posted on the wall. People will always answer the question from their own preferences. If 68 percent of the management team is highly Analytical, then roughly 68 percent of the responses will be Analytical in nature—that is, they will talk about profits, productivity, and quality. If 11 percent of the team prefers to think Structurally, then 11 percent of the responses will talk about efficiency, guidelines, and processes. People with a Social preference will refer to the needs and desires of the customer. And individuals with a strong Conceptual preference will talk about where the company is going in the future.

When I work with nonprofit organizations, where the managers are typically less Analytical, I get fewer mission statements about money and the future and more mission statements about organization and people. In for-profit organizations, the opposite is true.

Many companies hire consultants to help write their mission statements. In the best of all worlds, the consultants will create a Whole Emergenetics statement that speaks to all of the company's employees and customers. However, without a WE*team* in place, even the most wonderful Emergenetics mission statement will be ineffective because it will be overshadowed by the preferences of the management team.

I once worked with a large gourmet foods company on strategizing a plan for the coming years. Seventeen people were supposed to attend the two-day workshop, but on the first day, only sixteen showed up. The CEO was Analytical and Conceptual, and the rest of the team was a combination of Analytical, Structural, Conceptual, and ASSERTIVE. The CEO said, "We can start the meeting without Nadia. She is an executive assistant, and her presence is not crucial for this meeting." I was going to emphasize the need for Nadia's presence, but I decided to wait until the end of the day to point out her importance.

At the end of the day, the mission statement read:

XYZ Company has become the number one gourmet foods company in the nation by providing quality products at a reasonable price. We use effective and efficient administration of services, while we expand our distributorships around the world, creating profits for our shareholders.

Is there anything wrong with this statement?
If you break it down into Whole Emergenetics terms:

- The Analytical brain says "quality products at a reasonable price," and "profits."
- The Structural brain says, "Effective and efficient administration of services."
- The Conceptual brain says, "We expand our distributorships around the world."
- The ASSERTIVE attribute says, "XYZ Company has become the number one gourmet foods company in the nation."

But you will notice that there is no reference to the customer who purchases this product.

I pointed this out to the executive team, saying, "If Nadia had been here, this wouldn't have happened, because her natural Social, EXPRESSIVE, and FLEXIBLE attributes would always defer to the customers. They would be the first thing she would be thinking about."

The executive team then said, "Well, of course we are thinking about the customers. That's who we sell our products to. It's implied in the statement. Why do we need to write it down?" I acquiesced the point for the evening.

The next morning, Nadia came to the meeting, and we showed her the mission statement the team created the day before. "What are your thoughts?" I asked.

Immediately she stated, "I like it, but it seems a little cold. Why haven't you put in anything about our customers?"

The room fell silent. We spent the next hour revising the statement.

One reason I like this story is that it illustrates the importance of spelling everything out. Make no assumptions! Something that seems obvious to one Attribute may be overlooked by another. In addition, progress begins with positive words.

How to Make Life Difficult for Yourself

When I do a management audit, I also ask, "What types of challenges do you face in your job?" I can look at the Profiles of the people in the organization and predict whether the challenges are going to be Analytical, Structural, Social, Conceptual, Expressive, Assertive, or Flexible in nature. I generally see the *most* challenges associated with the Attribute that is *least* represented in the company Profile.

When a large automotive manufacturer participated in a management audit,

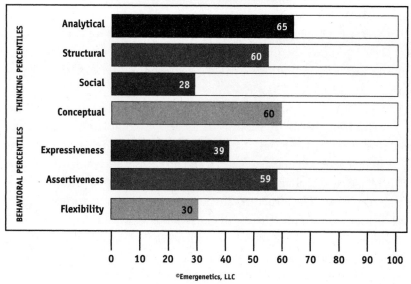

Emergenetics® Mean Scores
Automotive Executives

©Emergenetics, LLC

I profiled 175 of their executives. While Analytical, Structural, and Conceptual preferences were well represented, the Social Attribute was sadly lacking.

When I asked, "What are the challenges you are facing?" the answers reflected this imbalance: 6% of the challenges were Analytical in nature, 9% were Structural, 9% were Conceptual, 19% were Behavioral, and a whopping 57% were Social. The Social challenges included:

- How can we resolve turf wars?
- How can we develop better communication among senior management?
- How can we improve teamwork in engineering and other departments?
- How can we help top management become interested in lower-level workers?

A questionnaire that employees could answer anonymously made it clear that teamwork was a big issue for this company. The CEO, an Analytical and Structural thinker, recognized the problem, but did not have the kind of preference needed to solve it. He commissioned the human resources department to balance out the company's Thinking preferences by bringing new engineers on to the management team over the next few years who had a preference for Social thought. This was not an easy thing to do, because Social thought is not a key characteristic for engineers.

Ten years later, the company asked for another management audit. This time when I profiled the group, there was a much better balance among the Thinking preferences, and interestingly, the group's overall Flexibility score had risen as well.

I asked the same question I had ten years before, "What are your challenges today?" This time the distribution of challenges was completely proportional to each Attribute. This was a sign that all the Thinking and Behavioral Attributes were being represented in management, and no voids were being overlooked.

The Analytical challenges included "How can we increase our productivity and market share?" The Structural challenges were questions such as "How can we achieve an on-schedule delivery of parts?" and "How can we engender in the organizational culture high respect for schedules?" The Conceptual challenges were ideas like "How can we take a fresh look at old routines?" Interestingly, the Social challenges were not the same as before. Ten years previously, the questions had been negative and hostile. This time they were much more concerned with building up one another and the organization, and included "How can we ensure that all other divisions clearly understand our customers' needs, requirements, and points of view?" and "How can we better the image and self-esteem of our team?" In the interim, the group—led by the Social individuals—had received team training and had become more insightful.

Of course, you are wondering: Did this make a difference in the company's profit? Yes, it did. In the process of meeting its challenges, the company's overall market share and cost structure management improved (Analytical), its process mapping and standard work approach became more efficient (Structural), and it experienced robust new product development (Conceptual). But management believed that all the increased profit occurred because they spent more time focusing on the customer and working as a team (Social).

How to Solve Challenges

When you have a WE*team* in place, you are perfectly positioned for solving challenges. I avoid the term "problem-solving" because of the difference between a problem and a challenge. Challenges can be solved, and are seen more as lessons. By walking a challenge through the different Thinking and Behavioral Attributes, you guarantee that you are approaching it from a wide variety of angles, and you can be confident that you will generate workable solutions that appeal to all kinds of people.

Each attribute makes an important contribution to the process.

The Conceptual brain excels at throwing out ideas. People who are highly Conceptual will ask questions like:

"What is the ideal vision of success here?"
"How can we not just fix the problem, but take this to a new level?"
"What would we do if we were working with a clean slate, with no restrictions?"

The Analytical brain excels at evaluating proposed solutions. The highly Analytical members of your WE*team* will ask questions such as:

"Will this solution fully resolve the problem?"
"What are the benefits in relation to the costs?"
"What data and research do we need?"

The Structural brain also excels at evaluating proposed solutions, but from a different point of view. Highly Structural people will ask questions like:

"What rules and guidelines will apply here?"
"What is the implementation process and timeline?"
"Will this be too much of a change for us?"

The Social brain looks at ideas from the point of view of relationships. The highly Social members of your WE*team* will ask questions such as:

"How will others be affected?"
"Are enough people involved?"
"Are the right people involved?"

Expressiveness asks: "What kind of energy shall we promote to our employees and customers?"
Assertiveness asks: "How soon do we wish to get our product to market?"
Flexibility asks: "How many issues do we want to identify?"

Once you have gathered your WE*team* together, generate your Whole Emergenetics solution by using the following steps:

1. Define the challenge. What are the indicators of the challenge? Where are the signs of trouble?
2. Ask the whole team to use Conceptual thinking to generate possible solutions. (An alternative is to divide everybody into four groups according to their preferred Thinking Attribute.) Write the brainstorming ideas on a flip chart.
3. Ask the team to use Analytical thinking to apply logic and strategy to the proposed solutions. Narrow the options on your flip chart.
4. Ask the team to use Structural thinking to consider how these solutions will affect the status quo. How many workable solutions are left?
5. Ask the team to use Social thinking to further refine possible implementation guidelines. How will different people be affected?
6. To access all the Behavioral Attributes, put up three sheets of paper with a line down the middle of each one. The first sheet is for Expressiveness. Label the left half of the paper *Expressive* (or write "first-third Expressiveness"), and label the right half EXPRESSIVE! (or write "third-third Expressiveness.") Do the same for Assertiveness and Flexibility. Ask the team how different solutions will affect the behaviors.
7. By now you will have generated a solution that works for every attribute!

Here are some suggestions for producing the best ideas:

• Don't put pressure on yourself or others to be creative or to find an answer immediately. Allow everyone's natural way of thinking and behaving to flow.
• Avoid criticism.
• Withhold judgment.
• Accept all ideas, even weird ones—the more the better.
• Remember that creativity is not necessarily an explosion of something totally new.
• Celebrate one another's unique contributions to the team.

If there is a particularly thorny issue or a great deal of debate, everyone may not be equally thrilled with the proposed solution, but you should be able to achieve consensus. It's important to explicitly get everyone on board. Ask "Can you live with this solution?" until everyone is in agreement.

I once went into a meeting to sell a company on Emergenetics. There were four other people in the room, all of whom I had Profiled ahead of time. Two of the participants, including the leader of the group, were Social, Conceptual, and EXPRESSIVE. The third person was Structural, Social, and in the second-third of Expressiveness. The fourth person was an Analytical/Conceptual thinker named Megan, who was *Expressive, Assertive,* and FLEXIBLE.

People who are highly Conceptual don't want all the answers. They like to think about how to make an idea fit in a particular situation. When the presentation was over, there was a lot of positive energy in the room. I stood silent and let the two Social/Conceptual individuals brainstorm about the merits of Emergenetics and how to apply it in their organization. I knew these two would sell themselves and the others on Emergenetics. At this point, all I needed to do was be quiet.

I eventually said to the two brainstorming Social/Conceptual individuals, "These are really great ideas, but I wonder how they would work within the organization?" I turned to the Structural/Social member and asked if she had any ideas about this. She did. When this conversation ended, I knew these three were sending out buying signals.

The fourth person, Megan, gave no indication to her thoughts. Because I knew Megan's Profile, I knew this was her normal state. Before my understanding of Emergenetics, however, I would have left the room believing I had made the sale, since the majority approved my presentation and, after all, Megan wasn't the leader.

I asked everybody what they were thinking or feeling. The first three spoke in the manner in which I expected, while Megan sat quietly in her chair, looking down at her hands. It appeared she was going to bring negative energy into an otherwise positive environment. A piece of me did not want to get her opinion, but I asked, "What do you think about bringing Emergenetics into the organization?" The other three subtly leaned forward in their chairs to listen to what she was going to say.

While continuing to look at her hands, Megan replied in a muted voice, "I don't like these types of tests. They are stereotyping and too confining. However, this one seems different."

At this point, the rest of us looked at each other as if to say, "Ahhh . . . Megan approves!" It turned out that Megan *was* the decision maker—not because she had a high-level job in the corporation, but because people trusted her judgment. If I had not encouraged her to talk, she probably would not have expressed her opinion openly. Having secured her approval, however, I got the sale.

GETTING THEM MOTIVATED

Motivation is both intrinsic and extrinsic. People who connect to their jobs in a meaningful way will be intrinsically self-motivated. In addition, people are motivated by their compensation, the environment in which they work, and other extrinsic factors that contribute to their job satisfaction.

What Motivates Each Emergenetics Attribute?

When you understand how each attribute is motivated, you'll be able to maximize each employee's enthusiasm. What is inspiring to one person may leave the next one cold.

- People who are highly Analytical want to know that a project is valuable, and that the work they are being asked to complete will make a difference to its overall success. They are best motivated by a leader they believe in—someone who excels in a particular area and whose expertise they believe will benefit the group.
- People who are highly Structural like to implement projects, and want to know the time they spend doing so will add to the company's progress. They are best motivated by a leader who is organized, thoughtful, competent, and good with details.
- People who are highly Social want to feel valued and need to know that what they are doing is having an impact. They are best motivated by a leader they respect, and they will always go the extra mile for people who express trust, faith, and belief in their abilities.
- People who are highly Conceptual have to buy into the cause or they will not feel motivated. They care more about the big picture than the person leading the charge.

- *Expressive* individuals don't require a lot of fanfare, but they appreciate one-on-one encouragement.
- EXPRESSIVE people are more motivated when things are openly discussed and an open door is available.
- *Assertive* people hope everyone will move in the same direction.
- ASSERTIVE individuals are independent thinkers. They won't buy into an initiative just because someone else thinks it is the right thing to do. If they are in agreement, however, they are highly motivated.
- *Flexible* team members have to have confidence in the leader and in the project.
- FLEXIBLE individuals will go along with the team as long as a project does not contradict their morals or beliefs.

> Nobody motivates today's workers. If it doesn't come from within, it doesn't come. Fun helps remove the barriers that allow people to motivate themselves.
>
> Herman Cain,
> former CEO of Godfather's Pizza

How to Reward Each Emergenetics Attribute

Everybody wants emotional satisfaction from their job, and financial reward in any form. But if you are in the position of rallying the troops, you'll have greater success if you keep in mind that what is rewarding to one person may not be very meaningful to someone else in exactly the same position.

- People who are highly Analytical prefer some kind of compensation that is commensurate with their contribution. If they have done a tremendous amount of work on their own, don't expect them to be happy if you give an award to the whole team.
- People who are highly Structural like to be rewarded in writing, in a timely manner, in a precise way that is specific to the task. An encouraging e-mail would work for this brain—but don't use the same approach for a Social brain!
- People who are highly Social prefer to be rewarded in person with a gesture that is from the heart. If you prefer written communication, send a personal handwritten note.
- People who are highly Conceptual prefer to be rewarded with something unconventional and imaginative. Unlike other brains, they would find a whimsical token of your esteem very meaningful.
- *Expressive* individuals appreciate private encouragement.

- EXPRESSIVE people prefer pomp and ceremony, or public recognition.
- *Assertive* people will never demand recognition, so it's up to you to offer it.
- ASSERTIVE individuals will let you know what they want, and they would like it right away.
- *Flexible* team members want to know up front what kind of reward they can expect. Make sure you follow through on whatever is promised.
- FLEXIBLE individuals will be happy with any kind of recognition.

CREATING THE OPTIMAL CLIMATE

The art of leadership is to provide the right climate. The environment must be conducive so that each brain feels energized, and their self-esteem is raised to a point where they feel comfortable contributing to the group.

For this section of the book I interviewed Jim Blanchard, CEO of Synovus, a multibillion-dollar, multi-financial services company that has been ranked among the top of *Fortune*'s "100 Best Companies to Work for in America" since the magazine began publishing the list in 1998. In 1999 the company was named the "Best Company to Work for in America," and it has remained in the top ten on this list.

JIM

Jim's Profile is largely Social and Conceptual. He has fostered a culture at Synovus that emphasizes balancing work with the rest of life. The success of Synovus demonstrates that companies can achieve superior financial performance and still cultivate a positive corporate culture.

We laid the law down. We did more than just talk about it. We went out of our way to create a workplace environment that was positive and above average. We basically declared that any supervisors who were mean, manipulative, or secretive were not welcome here. We were going to guarantee that our people would work for decent, encouraging supervisors. We weeded out a lot of supervisors who did not fit that description. We basically put our reputation on the line. If we didn't fulfill that commitment, the employees of the company would have no reason to believe anything I ever said again.

You have to think of yourself in terms of being a servant, of giving yourself to your employees who have enabled your company to grow and succeed and prosper. It doesn't mean you aren't ambitious. It just means that it is not your uppermost priority. It is your desire to be a good leader that overrides.

We call it "The Culture of the Heart." It puts the primary emphasis on treating each individual with respect and admiration. We run our company this way simply because it's right, because every person who labors here has great worth and deserves to be treated so. Our company is built on these values. They define who we are.

We talk about creativity all the time. You must have great ideas coming forth. You must have an atmosphere that receives them, rather than quenches them. Creativity and ingenuity and new ideas and better ways of doing things and the spark of urgency and a passion for what you are doing are all part of the culture. Creativity is not a department, it is a trait that we encourage in everybody.

Jim
How You Think and Behave - Percentages

Analytical=3%
- Clear thinker
- Logical problem solver
- Enjoys math
- Rational
- Learns by mental analysis

Conceptual=50%
- Intuitive about ideas
- Imaginative
- Visionary
- Enjoys the unusual
- Learns by experimenting

Structural=3%
- Practical thinker
- Likes guidelines
- Cautious of new ideas
- Predictable
- Learns by doing

Social=44%
- Intuitive about people
- Socially aware
- Sympathetic
- Empathic
- Learns from others

HOW YOU COMPARE TO THE GENERAL POPULATION: MALES

HOW YOU THINK PERCENTILES		
Analytical	5	
Structural	5	
Social	83	
Conceptual	95	

HOW YOU BEHAVE PERCENTILES		
Expressiveness	82	Quiet / Alone / Reserved / Spontaneous / Gregarious
Assertiveness	87	Peacekeeper / Amiable / Easy-Going / Competitive / Driving / Telling
Flexibility	76	Defined Situations / Strong Opinions / Diff. POV / Others Before Self

General Population 0 10 20 30 40 50 60 70 80 90 100
©Emergenetics, LLC

HOW TO RUN THE PERFECT MEETING

The perfect meeting addresses each attribute and allows creativity and productivity to flourish. A WE*team* needs a leader who can develop rapport with each person in the meeting by allowing everyone to interact with each other in a safe environment. Here are some ways that the leader can address each Attribute:

- To satisfy the Analytical brains present, the leader should clearly state the objectives of the meeting.
- To make sure the Structural brains are comfortable, the leader should begin and end the meeting on time, and share an agenda. These brains appreciate attention to housekeeping details, such as stating the location of the restrooms and the time of the breaks.

- To answer the Social brain's questions, the leader should make sure that everyone understands who the other members of the team are, and why they are present. The Social brains want to be able to call everyone by name, so use name tags!
- To keep the Conceptual brains engaged, the leader should encourage brainstorming and suspend judgment of the ideas.
- The leader should allow regular moments of quiet reflection for *Expressives,* while providing lots of room for the EXPRESSIVES who are antsy to frequently move around the room.
- *Assertives* want to be gently encouraged to speak, while the ASSERTIVES must be managed so they don't dominate the discussion.
- *Flexibles* want their leader to be prepared, while the FLEXIBLES might go off on long tangents and need to be reined in.

Additional considerations:

- Begin by looking at the room where you are having the meeting. If possible, conduct your meeting in a room with windows or good lighting. If you are in a room that does not have windows, take many breaks.
- It is always a good idea, depending on the length of the meeting, to have refreshments available. All brains need fuel. Also, refreshments give the antsy people something to do with their energy.
- Start with brain activities such as the ones I outlined in chapter 1.
- Lay down your ground rules about operating in a WE*team,* such as honoring the ideas and contributions of others even though they are different than your own. State that each person was called to this meeting to bring her or his strengths. Do not let one kind of Thinking or Behavioral Attribute dominate the meeting.
- When you are in brainstorming mode, put seven pieces of paper up on the wall. Entitle each piece of paper with an Emergenetics attribute. Instruct everyone in the group to walk around and add at least one thought to each piece of paper. On the Behavioral Attributes sheets, put a line down the middle of the paper. Use the first half of the paper for first-third (i.e., *Expressive*) ideas and the second half for third-third (i.e., EXPRESSIVE) ideas. This will ensure you are acknowledging all of the attributes. Have everyone reflect on what is written.

- Have people change seats every hour. At the very least, ask everyone to change seats after every break. It's good to sit with different companions, plus people will remember what they learned before and after they moved. In addition, because information taken in the right eye and ear is processed in the left brain, and information taken in the left eye and ear is processed in the right brain, people may view their challenges in different ways when they sit in new seats.

Margy, a vice president at a technology company, decided to take my advice about changing seats. One January, the divisional vice presidents met in Chicago and brought along their teams for a strategic meeting. Each VP was supposed to work with her or his team for two days to devise a strategy for the upcoming year. Margy didn't think her team members would readily change seats, so she ordered two rooms for the meeting. Each time they took a break, approximately every two hours, they would move to the other room. This took care of the individuals who thought everyone else could simply move around them. Margy's team was the only team that finished their strategy on the first day—in ten hours. She has continued to use this technique, and her team is considered one of the most productive in the group.

GETTING OUT OF THE WAY

Inspired leadership is about letting each brain do what it is supposed to do. Emergenetics principles will help you honor the contribution of each member of your team.

Expect the Best of Your People

You are probably aware of the studies that have been done regarding the effect of teachers' expectations on student performance. When teachers are informed that unremarkable students are actually very gifted, the students excel. Similarly, when coaches are led to expect better athletic performance from certain athletes, they get it. Amazingly, the power of expectations even applies to lab rats! In one set of studies, rats that researchers believed were super-bright ran through their mazes more efficiently than rats the researchers believed were, well, ordinary. In reality, all the rats belonged to the same strain.

Expectations of success appear to be self fulfilling, so I encourage you to go forth each day as if your team is the best in the world. On some level your faith will be communicated to them, and they will live up to your expectations. Of course, the opposite is also true. If you do not believe in your people, they will live down to your expectations.

When Not to Interfere

The Behavioral Attributes of my finance manager, Karen, all fall in the first-third of the population. That, combined with her large preference for Structural thought, dictates her energy around her work. We call her "the pleasant machine." She comes to work, quietly and pleasantly says "good morning," sits at her computer, and completes whatever project is on her desk. If I need her to digress from her current task, she will appear to do so pleasantly and willingly, but I know that at the end of the day if I have requested too many digressions, she will leave the office more exhausted than if she had been allowed to work at her own pace. The best thing to do if you are responsible for the workload of someone like Karen is to give her the general idea of what needs to be done, the time in which it needs to be completed, and then LEAVE HER ALONE.

Once in the middle of a particularly stressful workday, the office was busy cranking out numerous Profiles for several seminars when the computers crashed. I frantically screamed, "Oh no, this is terrible! This is awful! What are we going to do?" Karen said, "I am going to call our technical team, then catch up on some work that doesn't require the computer." Simple. End of story. Somehow everything got taken care of, and I was the only one who wasted energy by making a huge fuss.

There is balance in the universe. Emergenetics principles will help you maintain balance in your workplace as well.

Whole-Body, Whole-Emergenetics Thinking

How to Enhance Your Intelligence

Let's begin this chapter with a new approach to intelligence.

First, I want to clarify what intelligence is not. It isn't your IQ score. It's more than your emotional intelligence, or EQ. And while Howard Gardner's theory about multiple intelligences has had an enormous impact, his seven categories—linguistic, logical-mathematical, musical, bodily-kinesthetic, spatial, interpersonal, and intrapersonal—may not be as separate as they appear, and they also seem to make an incomplete list, even to him.

There are many clever ideas about what constitutes intelligence. While the experts continue to debate, I'd like to make a suggestion. Let's use Emergenetics as an umbrella that covers all the different theories.

Emergenetics is a rational approach to the irrational: how people think and behave. It is about identifying your strengths, so you can use them to be successful. It's about working through your strengths to improve yourself. It puts mind and body back together again, through whole-body thinking. It encourages you to use Whole Emergenetics thinking to look at things from the point of view of all the Thinking and Behavioral Attributes. It helps you to be creative, gives you a structure with which to make better decisions, helps you develop your intuition, and shows you how to keep your brain sharper longer. Believe me, all these things taken together will make you more intelligent, by anyone's definition.

> **The more you learn about how your brain works, the better your chances of using it most efficiently, optimizing your intellectual capabilities, and accomplishing even more in life than many people who may score higher than you on standard intelligence tests.**
>
> Richard Restak, MD,
> *Mozart's Brain and
> the Fighter Pilot*

IQ ISN'T EVERYTHING

The original purpose of the IQ test was *not* to give people bragging rights about being a genius. The test was developed by Alfred Binet in France in 1904 to identify students who needed extra help in school. It measured such things as attention, memory, and verbal skills. Binet never intended to create a test that would be used to measure the intelligence of all students. In addition, he was quite concerned that the results of his IQ test might be used to condemn certain children as stupid. Binet did not believe that intelligence is fixed, or that the students singled out by his test were incapable of learning.

Binet died before he could see what would happen to his test. Soon it was no longer being used to eliminate the differences between children, but instead to solidify the differences between children, and between adults. In 1911 the United States began to administer the test to immigrants in order to screen out those who were "feebleminded." The IQ test became the gold standard for measuring intelligence in American schools and in the U.S. military. The idea that intelligence is a fixed, inherited, unmodifiable trait became firmly entrenched in the American psyche.

Telling children they are stupid and there is nothing they can do about it almost guarantees their failure. Interestingly, telling children they are just born smarter than everyone else also can lead to failure. Recent research shows that bright children who believe in fixed intelligence can become so invested in their super-smart status that they are unnerved by difficulty. Instead of risking failure by tackling a hard problem or signing up for a challenging course, they just don't make any effort at all. If you don't try, you can't fail—right?

Today we know that intelligence is made up of many more factors than those measured by the IQ test. It includes everything on Gardner's list plus common sense, organizational skills, social skills, motivation, perseverance, imagination, impulse control, optimism, and many other things. Ideally, intelligence is accompanied by empathy, moral guidelines, an awareness of the greater good, and perhaps some connection to spirituality as well.

WHAT MOTIVATES THE MIND TO LEARN?

Each preference is motivated to learn in different ways. This is yet another example of how different brains approach things differently, yet one approach is not inherently superior to another. When you are learning something new, you might consider how your Attributes affect how you prefer to learn:

The Analytical brain asks:

1. How can I learn all there is to know about this subject?
2. What Web sites might be useful?
3. What is the background?

The Structural brain asks:

1. Where do I start?
2. How does this information affect me?
3. When and where did events occur?

The Social brain asks:

1. Who are the leaders?
2. What is happening to the people?
3. How could I get these people to work together effectively?

The Conceptual brain asks:

1. How does this fit in with what I already know?
2. How will this information have an impact on the future?
3. Where can I take this information?

> The anachronisms in the way we measure intelligence can also be found in IQ tests, which have not changed in any major way since the 1950s. In fact, they measure a very narrow range of intelligence. You don't have to understand the effect of your behavior on others or the environment. You can be a rabid racist or a psychopath planning your next murder and still get a high score on most IQ tests. You can be "intelligent" and run your corporation in a manner that exploits instead of supports the community. You can be a Mensa member with a very high IQ and not be able to hold a job or relate to anyone.
>
> Jennifer James, PhD,
> *Thinking in the Future Tense*

Expressiveness is motivated by asking, "How much will I be speaking in this class?"

Assertiveness is motivated by asking, "At what pace will this class move?"

Flexibility is motivated by asking, "How many choices do I have?"

Today we also know that intelligence is not fixed, and that it can be cultivated. However smart you think you are, you are definitely smarter today than you used to be, unless you are not using your brain. Intelligence is an aptitude that can be affected by many environmental factors, and that is why you are reading this chapter.

WHOLE-BODY THINKING

Generally René Descartes (1596–1650) is credited with coming up with the idea of separating mind and body. As a scientist and a devout Catholic,

> A man's intelligence is the aggregate intelligence of the innumerable cells which form him—just as the intelligence of a community is the aggregate intelligence of the men and women who inhabit it.
>
> **Thomas Edison**

Descartes found himself in a difficult position. The Inquisition was busy persecuting Galileo for daring to promote the heretical idea that the planets revolved around the sun. To make it possible to be a good scientist and a good Catholic, Descartes hit on the idea of separating body and mind. Scientists could study the human body, while the church could still keep its power over men's souls. Amazingly, since Descartes we have spent hundreds of years behaving as if mind and body were separate entities, instead of two ways of remembering and expressing the same information.

The Neuropeptide Receptor System

According to Candace Pert, author of *Molecules of Emotion,* "thinking" occurs in both the brain and the body. Mind and body communicate with each other through the chemistry of emotion. Pert is fascinated by the fact that emotions exist both in the form of thought, and in the form of chemicals. Pert believes that each emotion probably has a corresponding chemical that exists in many parts of the body. These chemicals, or neuropeptides—short strings of amino acids—can be found in your brain, your muscles, your stomach, your heart, and all your major organs. They are the basis of a molecular language that allows the mind and body to communicate. They send messages back and forth in a dynamic information network, and actually run our physiology. As much as 98 percent of all communication throughout the body may be through these peptide messengers.

It used to be thought that all brain and nerve communication occurred through neurotransmitter-mediated in the brain or nervous system—or, when the target is far away, through hormones. Neurons are fixed in place and send impulses down axons and across synapses, while hormones travel through the blood. Neuropeptides, on the other hand, freely circulate through the blood, lymph, and cerebrospinal fluid and have free access to all the cells in the body. They fly through the body fluids to lock on to countless cell receptor sites and transmit their unique messages. Through neuropeptides, the brain is linked to all the systems of the body.

The neuropeptide receptor system includes at least fifty neuropeptide transmitters, each with a variety of effects on target cells. In all organ systems—the immune system, the gut, the heart, even the bones—cells can both send and receive a variety of neuropeptide messages. The message is sent as the cell releases neuropeptides into body fluids, and received when a neuropeptide locks into its specific receptor on a target cell. Unlike the synaptic system or neurotransmitter hormones, neuropeptide messages connect in both directions—brain to body, body to brain.

> Emotions are not in the head. There's a cellular consciousness. There's a wisdom in every cell. Every single cell has receptors on it. The emotional energy comes first and then peptides are released all over. . . . Just don't let the mind be in the head, because the mind is nonlocal. It's throughout the body and moves around in the body.
>
> Candace Pert, PhD,
> "Neuropeptides, AIDS, and the Science of Mind-Body Healing"

The fact that it is impossible to separate mind and body means your body must be involved in any attempt you make to enhance your intelligence. You can do this by stimulating all your senses, and of course with exercise and movement.

Stimulate Your Senses

Lawrence Katz, PhD, author of *Keep Your Brain Alive* (with Manning Rubin), says "neurobic" exercises help maintain and form new connections between nerve cells. Katz maintains that too much routine behavior contributes to brain atrophy. He bases neurobics on two principles: using all your senses during the course of each day, and experiencing the unexpected every day. He suggests combining music and smells—for example, listening to music while cooking, or writing with scented magic markers—and engaging your full at-

> But for us, the discovery of "floating" intelligence confirms the model of the body as a river. We needed a material basis for claiming that intelligence flows all through us, and now we have it.
>
> Deepak Chopra, MD,
> *Quantum Healing*

tention by shaking things up. Take a different route to work, rearrange your office furniture, or just turn your clock upside down.

Listening to Music

In 1993 researchers Gordon Shaw, PhD, and Frances Rauscher, PhD, studied the effects of listening to Mozart's Sonata for Two Pianos in D Major (K. 448) on a few dozen college students. They found a temporary enhancement of spatial-temporal reasoning, as measured by the Stanford-Binet IQ test. Perhaps because it intuitively makes sense, the so-called Mozart Effect became such a popular idea that two states, Tennessee and Georgia, began issuing Mozart CDs to new mothers in order to enhance the intelligence of their children. Unfortunately, since then the effect of Mozart on IQ has been disputed. Setting aside the issue of IQ, simply listening to music you enjoy activates your brain.

> I suggest that we are all constantly looking for patterns and relationships even when we are not conscious of this, and even when we are not sure what to do with the results. This search for relationships in patterns in space and time and their related symmetries is inherent in the mammalian cortex. We need to recognize this, understand it fully, and then exploit it properly in educating our children to think, reason, and create.
>
> Gordon Shaw, PhD,
> *Keeping Mozart in Mind*

Almost anything by Mozart is likely to bring pleasure, along with the opportunity for thoughtful reflection. Music has been shown to positively affect test performance, mood, blood pressure, heart rate, and the perception of pain. The patterns in music may prime the brain's neural pathways. Neurons are constantly firing, so what distinguishes "neural chatter" from clear thinking is the speed, sequence, and strength of the connections as they are made. Much research suggests that the brain responds not simply to raw frequencies of sound, but to pitch and tone. This means music may indeed enhance cognitive activities. And in the end, how bad is it to expose yourself or the children in your life to Mozart or Vivaldi?

A client has a forty-minute drive to work. Ten minutes before she gets to work, she puts on Vivaldi to stimulate her brain and calm down. Coming home, she puts on Vivaldi again ten minutes before she walks in the door to greet her kids.

Stimulate Your Whole Brain with Exercise

Regular aerobic exercise can improve your mental performance by counteracting stress, oxygenating your brain, promoting neurogenesis, and improving your cardiovascular fitness. Several studies reveal a direct link between exercise and intelligence, and studies of college students show that an exercise program can improve academic performance. The same was true for a study with participants over fifty years old, who improved their mental performance by 10 percent after engaging in a four-month walking program. Another study found that three key areas of the brain that are adversely affected by aging showed great benefits from exercise, which caused the rate of deterioration of the areas—the frontal, temporal, and parietal cortexes—to significantly slow down. The study also revealed that more than thirty minutes of exercise per session produces the greatest benefit to the brain. A study involving rats found that regular exercise increased the gene expression of neutrophins, a family of transmitters that support brain cell growth, function, and survival. Taken together, these studies indicate that exercise not only enhances our intelligence, but can keep us smarter longer.

Exercise that is specifically helpful to the brain includes three key parts: balance, dexterity, and strenth in the legs. You need leg strength to do exercises that involve your brain's balance and coordination centers. The ancient Chinese art of tai chi, for example, involves the whole body and combines balance, flexibility, and lower body strength. Anytime you dance, play tennis, or engage in any activity that requires smooth, coordinated responses, you activate your cerebellum.

Sports that move quickly, such as tennis or squash, require your brain to make fast decisions. It seems intuitively obvious that sports that are mentally challenging will enhance your intelligence. In fact, some experts dispute Howard Gardner's theory of multiple intelligences on the basis that kinesthetic (or bodily) intelligence cannot be separated from higher functions. Since motor control is integrated with other forms of intelligence, what is the basis for separating different types of intelligence?

Crossover Exercises

In the beginning of this book, I recommended that you do a few cross-crawls (touching each hand to the opposite ankle) to get your brain working. Any exercise is good for your brain, but activities that involve arm and leg crossovers force the left and right hemispheres of the brain to communicate better. Other crossover exercises include:

- Patting opposite knees
- Patting yourself on the opposite shoulder (alternate shoulders)
- Touching opposite elbows
- Dancing the Macarena

Imagine how much of the brain lights up when we dance! How does the brain integrate the barrage of information processed by its auditory, motor, kinesthetic, vestibular, somesthetic, and visual systems?

Mark Jude Tramo,
"Biology and Music"

WHOLE EMERGENETICS THINKING

SEE *LEARNING WITH THE BODY IN MIND* BY ERIC JENSEN, AND *SMART MOVES* AND *THE DOMINANCE FACTOR* BY CARLA HANNAFORD

As you have seen already, Whole Emergenetics companies (those with a great deal of variety) that use Whole Emergenetics teams (those with representation from all the Thinking and Behavioral Attributes) are more successful. The same principle applies inside your own head, where you can establish your own personal Emergenetics brain trust. When you approach your job and your life in a well-rounded way, looking at situations from different points of view, you are more likely to choose the best options—and you'll keep your brain sharper as well.

Whole Emergenetics Decision-Making

When making a decision, people naturally use their strongest Thinking attribute first. That's fine. But after you are finished doing your thing in your favorite mode, take a walk through the other Thinking Attributes to see what you might have overlooked. This way you will make a WE*decision.*

- Analytical decision-makers gather data and information, and consider the issue from different angles. They remember to consider financial and technical issues. They may make a list of "pros" and "cons" to organize their thinking.
- Structural decision-makers consider what rules apply to a situation, and what constraints exist. They will think about risks and consequences. They may make a timeline to make sure a solution can be implemented correctly.
- Social decision-makers question how a decision will affect other people, and excel at getting input from others. They will think about values and feelings. They may make a list of experts to contact for advice. Social brains also base their decisions on gut instinct.
- Conceptual decision-makers are good at "blue sky" thinking with no constraints. They will consider the big picture and look for creative opportunities. They will drop a question into their mental well, then walk around and do things as usual until a solution floats up. They may generate a list of ten options to ponder. They are engaged in cre-

ating new thoughts. Conceptual brains also base their decisions on WOW intuition—Wisdom withOut Words.

- The energy of the Expressiveness Attribute revolves around excitement about the decision.
- The energy of the Assertiveness Attribute focuses on driving toward the decision.
- The energy of the Flexibility Attribute is around the number of choices available.

Force yourself to approach decisions from the less-preferred parts of your brain. It's a great idea to consult friends or associates who do not think the same way you do. Over the years I have assembled a "kitchen cabinet" of remarkable minds who are willing to help me when I need it, and I am always glad I asked for their input.

There Is No Such Thing as a Logical Decision

Although consciously you may prefer logic over emotion—or vice versa—your brain actually uses both, no matter what your thinking style is. When you make a decision, your brain uses more information than you are consciously aware of, including logical reasoning and intuitive input from the brain in your head and brain in your gut.

Researchers in behavioral economics use something called the "ultimatum game" to see how people approach decisions involving money. Two people are given a one-time opportunity to split $10. One of them is designated the "proposer" while the other is the "receiver." The proposer makes an offer. If the receiver agrees, they both get to pocket the money. If the receiver disagrees, no one gets any money.

Suppose you were the receiver, and you were offered $1. You know that if you accept, the proposer will get to keep $9 to your $1. In this study, it is assumed that a purely logical decision would be to accept the $1—at least you'll walk away with something. On the other hand, $1 is not a very generous way to split the money. Would you give the proposer the satisfaction of getting more than you? Many people don't.

When researchers used functional magnetic resonance imaging (fMRI) to observe the brains of people playing the "ultimatum game," they found that two areas lit up: the anterior insula (a part of the limbic system that is associated with disgust and other negative emotions) and the dorsolateral prefrontal cortex (a cognitive area that is associated with deliberative thought). In those instances when the receiver declined an offer, there was more activity in the emotion area. So emotion won out, even though it would have been in the receiver's best interest to take whatever money was offered. Even if people thought they were making a logical decision, they were not.

This may come as a disappointment to those of you who report very Analytical and Structural preferences, but—unless your brain is damaged—it is impossible to make a decision based solely on logic. And in truth, this is a very good thing.

Antonio Damasio, author of *Descartes' Error* (among other books), tells the story of a patient named Elliot who had suffered frontal lobe damage because of a brain tumor. Elliot performed well on memory and intelligence tests, but could no longer make good decisions because he had lost his capacity to feel. Damasio and his wife, Hanna, studied hundreds of brain-damaged patients like Elliot, and determined that the missing element in their decision-making was "intuition," which they defined as the ability to know something without conscious reasoning.

Decisions are made in the presence of uncertainty, so we use past experiences to try to predict future outcomes. Intuition, sometimes described as a little voice inside, feels like a hunch, but it is partly based on the outcomes of previous experiences. The aspect of your brain called the *adaptive unconscious*—what Malcolm Gladwell, author of *Blink: The Power of Thinking Without Thinking,* calls "the big computer in your brain"—is quietly keeping track. This is a handy survival mechanism, since there isn't time to debate the relative velocity of an oncoming car when you are standing in the middle of the road. Based on previous experiences, your brain immediately comes to the conclusion that you had better jump out of the way.

One study involving the threat of receiving an electric shock (none were actually administered) showed that we are as afraid of things we have only heard about as we are of things we have actually experienced. Sometimes intuition is encouraging ("This is the job/man you should accept/marry!"), but often it is geared toward caution ("Watch out—something does not feel right."). Research shows that when we are weighing "what if—?" scenarios, we give negative concerns more weight. Potential losses worry us more than possible gains. People's flaws outweigh their good qualities. Dissatisfaction has more impact than satisfaction. We are more afraid of bad things that might happen than we are excited about good things that could happen. On the other hand, we are hopelessly optimistic when it comes to romance and, of course, buying lottery tickets.

More neural fibers project from our brain's emotional center into its rational centers than the other way around, which makes emotion a more powerful determinant of our behavior than logic. Often we respond to a situation emotionally first, because the amygdala (which evaluates threats to our well-being) works so rapidly. If someone tells you to "get a grip," they may mean, "You have more time to decide. Take a breath, so your limbic system can stop projectile vomiting onto your prefrontal cortical neurons."

> How we do think, I believe, is with two minds, experiential and rational. Our hope lies in learning to understand both of our minds and how to use them in a harmonious manner.
>
> Seymour Epstein,
> "Integration of the Cognitive and the Psychodynamic Unconscious"

CLEARING THE MIST

When other people have internal conflicts, you can use Emergenetics to help them clarify the issues and make a decision. I call this process "clearing the mist." The only person who possesses the solution to the problem is the individual to whom you are speaking, but she or he can't see the answer because the mist is too thick. Using the Emergenetics model to help them come up with the answers they need is an important part of leading and coaching.

To help others reach their answer, use the following steps:

Step 1—Start with your Social brain. Focus on how the person is feeling. Use reflective listening and your reflective voice to recognize and understand what she or he is going through. Use "I" statements to share your empathy. Rather than giving advice, speak from your own experiences.

Step 2—Use your Analytical brain to help the other person define the issue. Ask how this problem has manifested itself in the past. Ask thought-provoking questions to help her or him determine all aspects of the issue.

Step 3—Move to your Conceptual brain and ask this person open-ended questions. Connect the dots by reframing the issue in a new way.

Step 4—Finally, use your Structural brain to ask, "Where do you want to go?" If action is required, ask, "What is your next baby step?" Say, "Now that we've had this conversation, what is your action plan?"

During this conversation you will want to modulate your Behavioral Attributes to match those of the person to whom you are speaking. Be aware of your gestures and the number of words you use. The idea is not to overwhelm the other person with your brilliance, but to elicit from her or him an answer that is already present, but shrouded by confusion.

BALANCING YOUR BRAIN

I have a colleague who jokes that her family is so right-brained, they all walk around with their heads tilted to one side. To keep you from becoming too lopsided, I recommend balancing your brain by doing the opposite of what you are already doing.

My friend Sandy called me in distress the other day. Her husband was out of town, her dog was sick, and the people who were supposed to buy her house were at risk of backing out. Sandy was drowning in Social thinking. After we spoke for a while, I told her to hang up and go balance her checkbook.

"Balance my checkbook?" she asked incredulously. "Haven't you been listening?"

"I have," I answered, "and I am certain if you do something very Analytical you will feel better."

Several hours later the phone rang again. Sandy exclaimed, "I started on the checkbook, but ended up checking warranties and doing paperwork I've been putting off. I'm feeling much better—and at least I know one aspect of my life is in order!"

- When you are stuck in Social thinking (Red), try moving to Analytical (Blue), and vice versa.
- When you are stuck in Conceptual thinking (Yellow), try moving to Structural (Green), and vice versa.
- The same principle applies to the Behavioral Attributes. For example, if you are EXPRESSIVE, sit alone for awhile, and so on.

Researchers at Johns Hopkins have identified sites in the brain where worrying takes place. They found increased activity in different areas of the right hemisphere, which is typically associated with emotion. On the other hand, Richard Davidson PhD—a neuroscientist who, among other accomplishments, has collaborated with the Dalai Lama to study the brain activity of monks from

Tibet—found that greater activity in the left frontal lobe is associated with higher levels of well-being. This correlates with my belief that when you are worried, doing an activity that involves the opposite Thinking Attribute will bring you some relief.

Find a Complementary Partner

Talking to people who aren't like you is a quick way to plug into other ways of thinking and behaving. You need an opposite partner, whether at work or at home, to broaden the horizons of your Thinking and Behavioral Attributes. Look at your significant other and assess her or his way of thinking and behaving. Usually, opposites attract. If you are an Analytical and Structural thinker, you may find your partner is a Social and Conceptual thinker. If you are an *Expressive,* your partner might be EXPRESSIVE. If you have a Tri-modal Profile, you may find your partner has an attribute you don't possess. Take another look at this person's decision-making process, because it usually will give you a perspective that you have not considered.

CREATIVITY

It has been said that creativity is what makes us human. Certainly creativity enhances our productivity, efficiency, success, and happiness.

I once spoke to a mid-level manager of an Internet company on the West Coast. He had an Analytical/Structural Profile. He unhappily recalled to me that in high school he really wanted to be an artist, but after he took several career choice tests, the guidance counselor suggested he could not be an artist because he was "too left-brain." After that, he gave up the idea of being an artist. He said, "Today I make a lot of money, but there is a piece of me that has always been missing."

I hear stories like this all the time. Many people say that they "just aren't creative," probably because they think they can't draw. However, there are limitless ways to be creative, and there is no one Profile that has a monopoly on creativity! Buying the perfect gift for someone takes creativity. Figuring out how to use every inch of space in your closet is creative. Whatever your creative talents are, cherish them.

> A first-rate home-cooked soup is more creative than a second-rate painting.
>
> **Abraham Maslow**

The Analytical brain is being creative when it asks, "How could I design a system for this?"

The Structural brain is being creative when it asks, "How could I organize this?"

The Social brain is being creative when it asks "What people should I assemble?"

The Conceptual mind is being creative when it asks, "How could I paint a picture of this?"

People with different Profiles will approach the same creative task differently. For example, there are as many ways to paint a picture as there are people to paint them. For this part of the book, I interviewed two artists, one who does colorful, abstract paintings, and another who does meticulous still lifes.

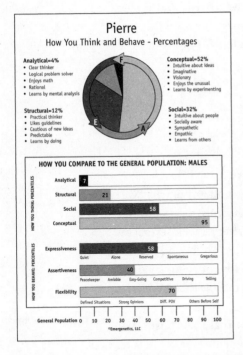

PIERRE

Pierre Henry, the abstract painter, uses his Conceptual and Social preferences the most, and says he does not have any step-by-step approach to his work.

For me, painting is always an attempt to transpose inner emotions onto a canvas, using a minimum of logical interventions. I usually say that when I start, I have no idea what I am going to do, and when I have finished, I have no idea what I have done! While this is an oversimplification, it is not that far off.

When working in abstraction, doing a painting consists of covering an area of the canvas with a first stroke of color, then—using that first stroke (or gesture) as a visual reference—doing subsequent strokes of similar, or of different, colors to eventually arrive at a composition that, in your judgment, represents an image of some significance. The process can be described as a dialogue between the painter and his canvas, since often unexpected shapes or color combinations appear, influencing your next intervention.

Now contrast this approach with that of Kathryn Jacobi, who uses the Analytical and Structural preferences in her Profile to paint meticulously elegant still lifes.

KATHRYN

You can see that Kathryn also has a preference for Conceptual thinking, which she uses in her abstract work. For her figurative paintings, however, she taps into her Analytical and Structural preferences.

I have had a box built, painted black inside, with holes that will allow me to insert lights from the direction I decide on. I put the objects to be painted in the box, with the controlled lighting, and arrange them slightly. Usually it is a fairly arbitrary choice, just things that are interesting to me, and that are difficult enough to make me stretch my skill level.

The process of painting is fairly straightforward. I draw the image onto a canvas panel with my brushes, loosely, and proceed to go over it again and again, first covering the surface with the underpainting, then refining and pushing the images until it feels real to me. A painting generally takes me about three weeks of steady work.

My task is to make the painting come to life. I get more and more specific as the painting progresses, so I try to have every seed on the bread in the right place, every detail legitimately there. It is just respecting what I'm looking at and being as faithful to my subject as I can. Inevitably there is a transaction that happens between me and the subject, which hopefully becomes something meaningful that lives and breathes in its own space.

Kathryn
How You Think and Behave - Percentages

Analytical=31%
• Clear thinker
• Logical problem solver
• Enjoys math
• Rational
• Learns by mental analysis

Conceptual=28%
• Intuitive about ideas
• Imaginative
• Visionary
• Enjoys the unusual
• Learns by experimenting

Structural=22%
• Practical thinker
• Likes guidelines
• Cautious of new ideas
• Predictable
• Learns by doing

Social=19%
• Intuitive about people
• Socially aware
• Sympathetic
• Empathic
• Learns from others

HOW YOU COMPARE TO THE GENERAL POPULATION: FEMALES

HOW YOU THINK: PERCENTILES	
Analytical	95
Structural	68
Social	58
Conceptual	88

HOW YOU BEHAVE: PERCENTILES	
Expressiveness	38
	Quiet Alone Reserved Spontaneous Gregarious
Assertiveness	30
	Peacekeeper Amiable Easy-Going Competitive Driving Telling
Flexibility	42
	Defined Situations Strong Opinions Diff. POV Others Before Self

General Population 0   10   20   30   40   50   60   70   80   90   100
©Emergenetics, LLC

BRAIN STRAIN

Brains like to be active, but can there be too much of a good thing? The evidence points to "yes."

How Does the Brain Handle Multitasking?

SEE *WHEN FASTER, HARDER, SMARTER IS NOT ENOUGH,* BY KATHRYN CRAMER, PHD.

These days we are all overwhelmed. So we have adapted by multitasking, or learning how to do several things at once.

I once had an appointment with an eye doctor who was exceptionally busy. I was somewhat confused by all her activity, so I sat quietly waiting for her attention. She took a chair at her desk, answered a phone call, started writing a prescription, and, without looking up, said, "Talk to me."

All this multitasking actually may be interfering with our getting anything done. It turns out the brain is not designed to efficiently multitask. If we really want to think creatively, we need to focus on one thing at a time.

In an unpublished study conducted at Carnegie Mellon University, a group of researchers led by Marcel Just conducted MRIs on eighteen volunteers while they were asked to do a series of language and visual tasks at the same time. The theory was that their brains should harness twice the amount of brainpower. However, this was not the case. The researchers found that if a person performed each task independently, the brain activated 37 voxels of tissue (a voxel is a unit of measurement for tissue activated in the brain). When the tasks were performed simultaneously, the brain areas activated a total of only 42 voxels. Furthermore, the amount of brain activation allocated to the visual processing task decreased by 29 percent when participants were simultaneously listening to a sentence. This suggests that when you ask the brain to focus on two activities, your performance on both tasks suffers.

When multitasking, the brain must undergo a two-stage process. First it has to decide to switch to the second task, called "goal switching," and then it has to activate the "rules" of the second task. This can take anywhere from several tenths of a second to a full second. These delays can add up over the course of a full day of multitasking.

I wish I could say that the brain can handle several mundane tasks at once, but this may not be the case. A study in the *New England Journal of Medicine* found that people who talk on a cell phone while driving are four times more likely to have an accident. Hands-free calling offered no advantage. Since the brain has to switch back and forth between paying attention to the road and paying attention to the phone call, it isn't possible to devote your full attention to both tasks at the same time.

I would be interested in seeing multitasking studies done on young people, who are able to watch TV, listen to music on headphones, talk on the telephone, paint their toenails, and do homework all at the same time. Is it possible that the human brain might slowly change in order to keep up with information overload and our obsession with multitasking? However, it's also possible that a long-term habit of multitasking could result in a loss of focusing ability, or what Richard Restak, MD, calls "cultural ADD" (attention deficit disorder).

Emotional Stress

Post-traumatic stress disorder, which can occur after a horrifying incident, is associated with significant alterations in brain function. But lower levels of stress affect the brain, too. Animal studies have shown that stress inhibits neurogenesis in the brain. The new cells that form in the hippocampus are adversely affected by stress hormones. We all know that stress is bad for our health, but it turns out stress is bad for our brain, too.

Researchers are now beginning to realize that men and women respond to stress differently. Men respond with the classic "fight or flight" reaction, but women respond with a "tend and befriend" reaction. This may seem like a blinding flash of the obvious, but now we have a scientific reason why women turn to each other. The "fight or flight" reaction in men is fueled by the release of the hormone adrenaline (epinephrine). In women, however, the stress response is also mediated by oxytocin. Women are more likely to manage their stress by nurturing their children or seeking social contact, especially with other women, with methods ranging from talking on the phone to such simple social contacts as asking for directions.

The difference between the sexes is especially apparent after a stressful workday. When the typical father comes home after a bad day at work, he wants to be left alone. When the typical mother comes home from a stressful day at work, she is more likely to focus her attention on nurturing her children.

The Sleep-Deprived Brain

If you've ever gone blank during a test after studying all night, you know how difficult it is to be intelligent and creative when your brain is sleep deprived. Even though we should know better, we tend to underestimate the seriousness of the effects of sleep deprivation. People who receive an insufficient amount of sleep in a study declare they were perfectly fit to drive, yet their performance on the road was worse than that of people who had been drinking.

Sleep researcher J. Christian Gillin noted that sleep deprivation hinders high-level thinking. His studies indicated that the sleepy brain works harder—yet accomplishes less. It's clear that the brain needs sleep to refresh itself and restore peak functioning. The subtitle for an article called "Why We Sleep" reads: "You may think it's for your body, but it's really for your brain." The article cites a German study in which subjects were given a tedious math equation that could be solved with a shortcut. A good night's sleep more than doubled the probability that participants would catch on to the trick. In other words, creative thinking—looking at the problem from another point of view—was associated with a good night's sleep.

> We think getting that first night's sleep starts the process of memory consolidation. It seems that memories normally wash out of the brain unless some process nails them down.
>
> Robert Stickgold et al., "Visual Discrimination Learning Requires Sleep After Training"

Today we know that after twenty minutes of concentrating, our thinking becomes less efficient. A brief break that allows your brain to go into a state of alpha/theta brainwaves—associated with daydreaming, relaxation, and meditating—will reset the potassium levels in your brain cells and rejuvenate your brain. Decreased effectiveness after prolonged studying may not be due to general mental fatigue, but to overuse of a specific local neural network. Refresh the network, and you can keep going.

A Harvard study reveals that both power naps and a good night's sleep can help learning. After learning a motor skill, the brain apparently consolidates its new knowledge while you sleep, resulting in 20 percent improved performance—without practice!—the following day. When subjects were deprived of sleep for thirty hours after training, then tested after returning to full alertness after two nights of recovery sleep, they showed no significant improvement. This study shows that sleep within thirty hours of learning something new is absolutely required for improved performance. The consolidation of learning and memories may be one reason babies sleep so much.

BRAIN FITNESS

How is it that some older people fade away into a vague twilight, while others stay sharp? Obviously genes play a role, but are there factors under our control?

According to researcher George Bartzokis, the brain continues to myelinate until our mid-to-late 40s, and after that it starts to deteriorate. The myelin in the brain breaks down in the reverse order of development, so complex connections that take the longest to develop are the first to go. Perhaps to compensate, older adults show activation in more areas of their brain. PET scans reveal they use both hemispheres more than their younger counterparts.

It turns out there is a great deal we can do to keep our wits with us well into old age. The neurons in our brains, and the glial cells that support them, have the capacity to stay healthy into old age, but they are dependent on oxygen and nutrients that reach them through blood vessels (if the blood vessels are compromised, the brain isn't going to be healthy). Although the brain does deteriorate somewhat as we get older, it also compensates by creating new brain cells, new dendrites, and new neural connections. What matters is not the number of brain cells you possess, but the richness and density of the connections between the brain cells you have. The aging brain has a remarkable ability to grow, adapt, and change its patterns of connections.

> If I had to live my life again I would have made a rule to read some poetry and listen to some music at least once a week; for perhaps the parts of my brain now atrophied could thus have been kept active through use.
>
> Charles Darwin, *Autobiography*

Experiences That Harm Your Brain

During my workshops, I often include information about protecting the brain. If you want to be fully yourself, and to experience the full capacity of your brain for as long as possible, there are many things you can do. Up until this point, you may have been the victim of circumstances beyond your control, or you may not have been aware of certain aspects of brain health. From now on, your brain is your responsibility. Be nice to it.

- *Smoking.* Cigarette smoke contains thousands of chemicals that are potentially harmful to the brain, and inhaling smoke interferes with the oxygen supply to your brain, which affects your reflexes and mental clarity. A study in 2000 revealed that just one cigarette can cause lasting changes in the "reward" areas of the brain, increasing the desire for more cigarettes. Nicotine's damaging effect on the brain is what keeps people addicted.

> Nicotine causes the most selective degeneration in the brain I have ever seen.
>
> Gaylord Ellison,
> "Nicotine Causes Selective Damage in the Brain"

- *Recreational Drugs.* Remember the classic advertisement that involved a hot frying pan, a couple of eggs, and the slogan "This is your brain on drugs"? The ad was not just hyperbole. Drugs really do fry your brain. If you look at a PET scan of the brain of someone who has taken cocaine, you'll see dark areas that represent a loss of normal brain activity. Cocaine causes the disruption of many brain functions. Methamphetamine, on the other hand, strongly activates certain systems of the brain, and can cause permanent damage even if the user quits. PET scans show that inhalants, which also can cause permanent neurological damage, move quickly to the brain. Both inhalants and cocaine have been shown to interfere with brain myelination. Researchers are worried that the long-term effects of Ecstasy on serotonin levels in the brain could create an entire generation of depressed adults. Marijuana interferes with normal cognitive functioning, while PCP (angel dust) interferes with multiple neurotransmitter systems in the brain. Discussing all the terrible things drugs do to your brain is beyond the scope of this chapter. If you plan on using your brain in the future, don't scramble it with drugs today.

- *Alcohol.* Everybody knows that drinking impairs brain processes. Alcohol also alters the body's testosterone levels, and interferes with the body's metabolism of fat, which can lead to the familiar "beer belly." Long-term use of alcohol damages the frontal lobes of the brain and causes an overall reduction in brain size. Even moderate drinking causes brain atrophy as early as middle age. People with a genetic predisposition to alcoholism are at greater risk of losing control of their drinking, but alcohol is an equal opportunity addiction that can affect anyone.

Happily there is a great deal you can do to enhance your intelligence and keep your cognitive skills sharp into old age. One way to protect against mental decline is to keep forming new neural connections with fresh ideas and novel experiences.

Use It or Lose It

The brain's food is oxygen and nutrients, but the brain's enrichment is education, reading, and life experiences. The brain grows denser in response to intellectual and social stimulation.

The key to keeping a mental edge is lifelong learning. Novelty—taking risks, questioning assumptions, being exposed to new ideas, and trying something new each day—keeps the brain active. For some people, going to a different restaurant is novel enough. Others may want to take up skydiving, start doing crossword puzzles, or learn about Chinese pottery. Dr. K. Warner Schaie designed a project called the Seattle Longitudinal Study that began in 1956 and is considered one of the most extensive psychological research studies of how people change through adulthood. Dr. Schaie found that the willingness to improvise and to try unorthodox ways of doing things was a major predictor of mental vivacity in later years. Conversely, the more mentally rigid people became as they aged, the more quickly their intellect deteriorated.

Socializing brings added benefits to complex and stimulating activities. Listening to someone play the guitar is good. Learning to play the guitar yourself is better. Playing the guitar with your friends is best. Of course, if guitar isn't your thing, find a different activity you enjoy and share it with someone you like.

Research has shown that cognitive activity is protective against Alzheimer's disease. A study published in the *Journal of the American Medical Association* in 2002 followed 740 members of the Catholic clergy (nuns, priests, and brothers) for an average of 4.5 years. Their activities—ranging from listening to the radio to playing cards to visiting museums—were closely monitored using a point system. Of the participants in the study, 111 developed Alzheimer's disease. However, a one-point increase in activity was associated with a 33 percent reduction in the risk of developing Alzheimer's.

> Do something that challenges and engages your mind, not because it's difficult, but because it's different from what you normally do.
>
> Lawrence Katz, PhD, and Manning Rubin, *Keep Your Brain Alive*

The Value of Education

It appears that the higher you go up the educational ladder, the more dendritic material there is in the brain. Ronald Kotulak, author of *Inside the Brain,* compares education to a mental vaccine that protects the brain against premature aging. Scientists at UCLA found in autopsy studies that the brains of university graduates who remained mentally active had up to 40 percent more dendritic connections than the brains of high school dropouts. That is a dramatic difference. However, the brains of university graduates who led mentally inactive lives had fewer connections than those of university graduates who kept learning, which shows that some of the advantages of education can be lost.

In the famous "nun study" (different from the study noted above), an ongoing study directed by David Snowdon, PhD at the

> Individuals will increasingly have to take responsibility for their own continual learning and relearning, for their own self-development and for their own careers. They can no longer assume that what they have learned as children and as youngsters will be the "foundation" for the rest of their lives. It will be the "launching pad"—the place to take off from rather than the place to build on and to rest on.
>
> Peter Drucker, *The Essential Drucker*

University of Kentucky, 678 members of the School Sisters of Notre Dame agreed to donate their brains to science when they die. From the age of twenty on, the nuns have lived in the same environment, eaten the same meals, and had the same health care. The only major differences are (1) the level of education they have when they become nuns, and (2) the types of jobs they have. It turns out that the more highly educated nuns generally live longer in better mental and physical health, while the nuns who have less than a bachelor's degree have twice the death rate at every age level.

Enhance Your Cognitive Skills

One aspect of intelligence is cognitive skills. Happily, the brain responds to cognitive challenges by becoming sharper. You can enhance your memory and mental fitness with puzzles and exercises such as those found in *Mozart's Brain and the Fighter Pilot* by Richard Restak, MD. There is also a great deal of research that supports the importance of reading in keeping your brain sharp.

> Passive observation is not enough; one must interact with the environment. One way to be certain of continued enrichment is to maintain curiosity through a lifetime. Always asking questions of yourself or others and in turn seeking out the answers provides continual challenge to nerve cells.
>
> **Marian Diamond,**
> *Enriching Heredity*

I had the good fortune to attend a lecture by neuroanatomist Marian Diamond, PhD, at the Learning and the Brain conference in Cambridge, Massachusetts. In the course of her presentation, Dr. Diamond told a disturbing story about her experience while teaching in Africa in 1988. She found that pregnant women in Kenya, in order to avoid delivering large babies, stopped eating protein. When the babies were born, the dendrites in their brains were not fully developed. Putting the babies on a protein-rich diet in a stimulating environment benefited their brains, but their dendrites never fully recovered. At the conclusion of her remarks, I asked Dr. Diamond what she considered important for the aging brain, and she listed the following five things:

1. *Diet.* What we eat unquestionably affects how our brain functions.
2. *Daily exercise.* Exercising the body helps maintain a healthy brain.
3. *Challenge.* Seek continual learning that stimulates different parts of the brain.
4. *Newness.* We need new ideas, new pursuits, and new activities in our lives.
5. *Love.* We must nurture ourselves and each other.

Did I mention love? Dr. Diamond noted that at one time her lab rats, to whom she feels quite indebted, were generally living around 600 days. When she learned that lab rats in Germany were living far longer, she wanted to find out why. It turned out that the rats in Germany were getting more human attention. Dr. Diamond and her assistants began holding the rats against their lab coats and petting them, and the rats began to live much longer—900 days! If a pat on the back every day extends the life of a rat by that much, think what a daily hug could do for people.

> TV puts pictures in your eye. Books put pictures in your mind.
>
> **Carol Powell (member of** *Influence,* **an executive leadership course)**

THE IMPORTANCE OF REFLECTION

In general, we do not take enough time to reflect. We are so busy doing that we don't take time for thinking. Some people are more likely to ponder than others, but reflection is a good idea for everyone. It taps into all aspects of your experiences, clarifies your thinking, and consolidates in your mind what matters and what you wish to achieve. It also adds neural circuitry to your brain, and expands the cerebral cortex by anchoring and deepening your learning.

Keeping a Journal

Keeping a journal is a good way to reflect. At the end of each day, take a moment to think about everything that happened. Write down your thoughts. The act of writing will consolidate your ideas better than just noodling about your day before you fall asleep:

- Use your Analytical brain to figure out what worked and what didn't.
- Use your Structural brain to decide on concrete steps to take tomorrow.
- Use your Social brain to get in touch with your own feelings, as well as to think about other people in your life.
- Use your Conceptual brain to consider the overview and long-term goals, and to get in touch with what inspires you.
- What happens with your energy around your Expressiveness, Assertiveness, and Flexibility? How do your Behavioral Attributes affect your personal energy level and your energy around other people?

I am certain that Whole Emergenetics journaling helps everybody use different parts of their brain. A WE*journal* could help us all, both men and women, keep our brains sharper longer. To get you started, I have included below some questions for you to ponder regarding your Emergenetics preferences and how they relate to your work. How you answer these questions in your journal will depend on your preferences. You may want to write an analysis, or you may want to draw pictures!

> To gain knowledge, learn something every day.
>
> To gain wisdom, forget something each day.
>
> Lao Tzu

Time for Reflection

What life cycle am I in? (See chapter 7 to refresh your memory about life cycles.)

What are my unique gifts?

How do I manage my time?

How do I make decisions?

What kind of work do I prefer?

How do I like to be assigned work?

How do I like to assign work to others?

How do I like to be rewarded?

Does my style change when I approach work overload?

What Attributes best complement my Profile?

How comfortable am I working with people whose Attributes are different from mine?

How can I capitalize on my strengths to be more effective?

Work Through Your Strengths to Succeed

Do Your Job Your Way

Harrison has an interesting Profile for someone with an engineering degree, a master's degree in mathematics, and an employment history that includes working for NASA on their Space Shuttle program. His brain is 75% Conceptual and 16% Social, and the remaining 9% is Analytical and Structural.

The board of directors of the technology company where Harrison works was considering making him CEO. However, when they saw his Profile, they wondered if they should let him have the position.

Friday morning, Harrison called me to say the board had decided not to offer him the job at this time. They were hedging a bit, because they knew bringing in someone else meant Harrison probably would go elsewhere, and they didn't want to lose him as an employee.

I sent Harrison an e-mail reminding him that Einstein had figured out the theory of relativity based on a dream that he was riding a beam of light. The board was not correct in thinking Harrison couldn't do the job. In a company like his, where a great many people were highly Analytical and Structural, he would make an excellent CEO because he would be able to take the work of the scientists and translate it for the outside world.

Harrison forwarded my e-mail to the chairman of the board. He still thought all was lost. However, I knew the chairman was a Tri-modal, and that she would probably ponder this decision all weekend. I told Harrison to try not to worry too much, since there was a strong possibility the chairman would have a different outlook after a couple of days. Tri-modals are like that.

On Monday, Harrison got the job.

As CEO, Harrison has learned to balance out his Profile:

- He hires Structural people to help him.
- He makes an effort to communicate with the Analytical thinkers in their language, rather than his natural Conceptual Speak. He understands their mathematical and scientific problems because he has the background.
- He is consciously working on being more Social. Generally "people problems" are the last thing he wants to deal with. Harrison used to put off dealing with Social issues until late in the day, but now he makes a point of addressing them first thing in the morning, when he has more energy. Operating out of his Social attribute still fatigues him, but at least he still has the rest of the day to be energized by his Conceptual work.

> More and more people in the workforce—and most knowledge workers—will have to MANAGE THEMSELVES. They will have to place themselves where they can make the greatest contribution and they will have to learn to develop themselves. They will have to learn to stay young and mentally alive during a fifty-year working life. They will have to learn how and when to change what they do, how they do it and when they do it.
>
> Peter Drucker,
> *Management Challenges*
> *for the 21st Century*

MAKING YOUR WORK SPACE WORK FOR YOU

Often management dictates guidelines for how offices should appear and the way in which they should be organized. Usually the goal is a corporate environment that appears consistent and is efficient. However, a uniform approach is not always the ideal situation for productivity. People derive energy from their surroundings in different ways, and an environment that one person finds comfortable may drive the next person to distraction.

My experience indicates that even when people are given a standard cubicle, they will still do what they can to make their office reflect who they are. Some people require a pristine and immaculate work environment. They will work on one piece of paper at a time, and keep the rest of their work out of sight. Others cannot function unless all of their important documents are in sight and accessible. Some people need lots of toys and gadgets. Others desire a space that is warm and inviting.

In a seminar we grouped individuals by their strongest Thinking Attribute, then asked each group to draw a picture of their ideal office space. Their Behavioral Attributes also influenced their decisions, but I don't want to go into too much detail here. The point is for you to see how differently people feel about the Ideal Office.

An Office for the Analytical Brain

"We prefer to have our credentials up on the wall, and a name plate at the front of our desk. There are two work spaces for this office. The first space has two in/out file folders. We only work on one file at a time. There is a trendy high-tech gadget on the desk that we love to fool around with when we are trying to solve problems. The second space is for our computer. We don't keep a traditional appointment book, because every organizing activity is done through our PDA, which is linked to the computer. The clock drawn on the wall shows 6:20 p.m. because we want people to know that we are at work past 5:00 p.m.! There is plenty of shelf space to hold all our reading materials.

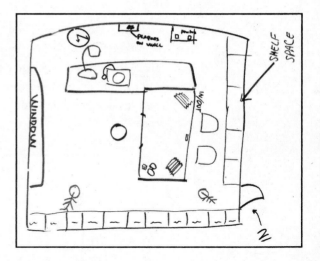

There are two pictures of our family, but they are small and placed in the corner of the book shelf. We did this to symbolize the idea that when we are in the office, we want to keep the focus on business. There are two artificial plants for decoration."

An Office for the Structural Brain

Although the Structural brains had no access to a ruler, this group managed to make all of the lines inside their drawing straight. They drew a very tidy, simple, and easy-to-clean space.

"On the desk, located in the middle of the room, is a to-do list, and a day planner, which is close by for constant checking and re-checking. There is a flat screen computer on top of our desk, in order to efficiently save space. The chair behind our desk is perfectly placed so that we can see everyone who comes in, and the proper walking and sitting areas for visitors are also readily apparent. There is a small bookshelf in the corner of our office, which holds only those books that are necessary for our job. The credenza behind the desk has nothing on it because it is a workspace! Above the credenza on the wall is our certification. On either side are two posters with words like 'Success' and 'Achieve' written on the bottom. These posters help us stay motivated."

When Social and Conceptual brains in the room saw the pictures of the two offices above, their response was the same: "BORING!" One person stated, "My firm insists that my office should look like one of these. I get my work done in this type of space, but I would be much more dynamic if I could have a different office."

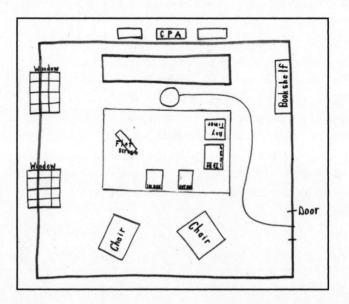

An Office for the Social Brain

The people who designed the perfect Social office did not follow the instructions. Instead of pictures, they felt a written description would be best.

"This office includes lots of windows and has an open floor plan with no walls. We keep a calendar for our regular business appointments and social events. We like to decorate with fresh plants, art, and a well-stocked bar (complete with an espresso machine) and we like to serve soft drinks in Waterford crystal glasses. There are pictures of our family generally placed throughout the room, and a suggestion box for coworkers. Music (not Muzak) wafts throughout the room, and we want a cluster of comfortable furniture. A sofa would be ideal. We also included a round table for conferencing. We prefer a video phone so that we can view the person we are talking to. Finally, we prefer the office complex has a fitness center, free child care, and a lunch room with a large socializing area."

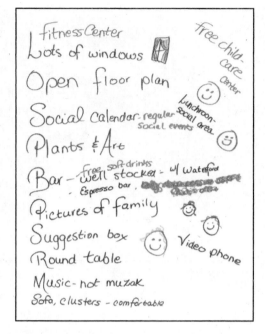

After seeing this list, the Analytical and Structural thinkers in the room remarked:

"Waterford crystal! Isn't that expensive?"

"There is a social area, chat area, and a bar. How can anyone get any work done in this office?"

I suggested that people with a lot of Social in their profile would say that they *are* working, whether they are in the gym, cafeteria, bar, or another person's office. The Social brain still considers these areas work space.

The Structural thinkers shrugged their shoulders. How could they understand this? After all, these Social brains hadn't followed the directions properly in the first place.

An Office for the Conceptual Brain

"This is not the office that we are allowed to have at our workplace, but this is what we would have if we could. Every element taps into our brain. There is a large window that brings the outside world inside. In front of the window is an aquarium. This, combined with the waterfall near the couch, helps bring life into the room. There are many toys (a dart board, a basketball hoop) scattered around the room that help us make creative connections to our brain. The room also has surround sound. We like to move around a lot, so we have included stools that are easily moved from one part of the room to another. Our desk is also very high, because sometimes we like to stand while we work. The whiteboard is important to us for capturing ideas. Our certification is in the filing cabinet. The couch in the office is for big-picture meditation. We prefer an armoire to a bookshelf, and the dog, located underneath the aquarium, is named Max."

The Analytical and Structural thinkers all agreed that this office was the most interesting to look at, but the worst place they could imagine to do work. One said, "I could work there for a while; but the 'mess' would distract me, and then I would have to reorganize the space."

Each participant in this seminar was a certified public accountant. Still thinking about stereotypes?

Do You Need Separate Work Areas?

I always tell people with a Tri-modal Analytical, Social, and Conceptual Profile that they ought to have three desks at work: one for their computer (Analytical), one for clutter (Social/Conceptual), and one that is pristine (Structural). They should take only one pile at a time from their clutter desk to their pristine desk. By keeping separate working areas, Tri-modals can bring a little bit of structure into their world.

DOING YOUR JOB YOUR WAY

A company in London invited me to give a management retreat seminar for their European partners. This retreat was held in Perugia, Italy. My assistant Karen asked the executive assistant at the London company, Valerie, to send driving directions from the airport in Rome to Perugia, which she faxed the next day.

Valerie took part in the seminar, so I had an opportunity to see her Profile and to meet her in person. She was very concerned that her Profile was Analytical, Social, and Conceptual—but lacking in Structural thinking. She said, "It seems to me that someone in my position should have a Structural preference."

I explained to Valerie that her Profile didn't measure her competence, nor determine her ability to perform her job. She still had all the capabilities she needed to effectively work as an executive assistant; she would just do it differently than others.

Valerie still did not understand, so I mentioned the directions that she sent to me before the trip.

Valerie was alarmed. "Was there something wrong with the directions? Were you not able to drive from Rome to Perugia?"

"No," I said, "the directions were perfectly fine. But they were not written in the same manner that someone with a lot of Structure in their brain would have written. They were written in narrative style, as opposed to being listed in numerical order, and they were handwritten, as opposed to typed."

"Well, I didn't know how to get from Rome to Perugia," explained Valerie, "so I asked Ferruccio, one of our Italian partners, to fax me *his* directions. He did, and I faxed that same document directly to you."

I laughed. Ferruccio also has little Structural preference in his Profile. "The point is that your brain thought it was sufficient to talk to Ferruccio, get his directions, and pass them on to me. There was nothing wrong with the directions. But an executive assistant with a Structural preference would have transposed them into sequential order and typed them into a formal document. Either one would have gotten me to Perugia. It's just a different style."

I had not succeeded in making Valerie feel better about her Profile, so I told her about two real estate agents I know who work for the same firm. Each year it is a stiff competition regarding which of them will win the salesperson of the year award. Wayne, who is Analytical, Structural, *Expressive,* ASSERTIVE, and

FLEXIBLE, will tell you he is successful because he is aggressive. Wayne promotes himself with advertising, is a constant presence in the local newspapers, and tirelessly tracks down new listings. Greg, who is Social, Conceptual, EXPRESSIVE, *Assertive,* and FLEXIBLE, says he is successful because he loves getting in a car with clients and driving them around looking at houses until they find the home of their dreams. Greg talks to everyone, empathizes with people's hopes and desires, and sends every client a basket of flowers when they move into their new home.

The truth is, both Wayne and Greg are getting a lot of listings and selling a lot of houses. They just do it in very different ways.

If you like your job, use your strengths to do it well. Reread the information on working through your strengths. Bottom line: you can do your job your way and still be true to yourself.

FINDING THE BEST JOB FOR YOU

There is a great deal of advice available about choosing a career. Books have been written and tests designed to make sure you pick a job that suits your temperament and skills. There are two problems with this. First, being inclined toward a certain kind of work doesn't mean you are actually good at it. Second, I have seen people with the most unlikely Profiles do very well at jobs in which you would not expect them to have much success. For this reason, I avoid saying that certain Profiles are best for certain jobs.

So does it even matter what kind of job you have?

Well, of course it does. You'll get weary more quickly if you have to operate out of your least-preferred preference a great deal.

I once interviewed a circus performer who had a background as a math whiz. This seemed pretty incredible, even to me. It turned out he had graduated from college summa cum laude with a degree in mathematics, and he loved solving proofs and looking at math problems from different angles. However, he couldn't stand the loneliness. He could talk only to colleagues about his work because no one else understood it. He felt very isolated, and noticed that he was the only person in his department who seemed unhappy, that day after day everyone worked in relative silence and obscurity. After two years of this, his Social brain was weeping from frustration.

I also have a young friend who had the opposite problem. When Gabe called me to tell me he had a new job, I was not sure he had made a good choice.

I knew Gabe was Analytical, Conceptual, and *Expressive,* and that his Profile included very little Social thinking, but his new position in sales basically would require talking all day. Gabe is young and energetic, and he didn't see this as a big deal.

Between his employees, customers, and management, Gabe soon found that he received an average of a hundred e-mails a day, plus at least thirty-five phone messages. Now, an EXPRESSIVE individual with a great deal of Social thinking would love all this contact with other people and find it energizing. Gabe, on the other hand, grew quickly overwhelmed. While some people can fire off fast, friendly e-mails without much effort, Gabe needed to ruminate about his correspondence. While another person might regard all those phone calls as a welcome diversion, Gabe saw them as work.

After three weeks, Gabe called to tell me he had made a mistake. He couldn't go back to his old job, and they were paying him extremely well at his new one. Today he is still there, still doing the job—and still unhappy.

ARE YOU IN THE WRONG JOB?

Sometimes it's hard to tell if you have the wrong job, or if you are just in one of those cyclical transitions that I talked about earlier. Maybe your job really isn't tapping into your strengths. On the other hand, maybe you are just in a Scratchy period. Know that you are constantly in transition. Your brain is constantly in transition. It's like a developing child. When you are in a Scratchy period, you can either ignore it or you can think of it as an opportunity to move to a new level.

If you are restless but still like your job, then tap into other strengths to make the job more enjoyable.

If you have received performance evaluations that indicate a need to build certain skills, go back to chapter 7 and build your strengths. For example, if you have a sliver of Social in your Profile and your performance appraisal indicates that you have interpersonal challenges, you know what to do. You should have a repertoire of behaviors to call upon as needed.

If you are tired out by your job, look at your Emergenetics preferences and compare them to your current career. Are they in alignment? As I've already said, you don't have to have a textbook Profile that matches your work, but it is certainly easier if you are in a position that caters to your preferences.

If you are someone like Jim Blanchard of Synovus, who has a different Profile than most of the people in his profession, but you are competent, you may reach the top of your profession more quickly. I suspect this is because you stand out from the rest of the crowd. If you are a competent multimodal, especially if your behaviors are in the second-third percentiles of the population, you may go up your career ladder quickly because you are seen as a person who can tackle many types of issues. However, you may also run the risk of getting stuck, because as your job demands more expertise, you will not appear as outstanding. If this happens to you, my advice is to pick one of your attributes and make yourself an expert in that area.

If you have persisted in your present job and things still are not working out, or if you think you are being derailed, take a look at the chart on reasons for derailment on page 267, where you'll find information that I have modified to include research from the Center for Creative Leadership. If you have gotten off track, go back to chapter 7 and see how to fix the situation by working through your strengths. If you have a work or life partner whose attributes are the opposite of yours, it would be a good idea to talk to this person about how you could do better. A complementary partner is supportive and has your best interests at heart, but will see things in a way you don't.

LOOKING FOR A NEW JOB

How do different brains go about getting a new job?

If you are highly Analytical, you will:

1. Scrutinize where you are and what your career goals are.
2. Think about what will make you happy, then consider what kind of work will bring you to that state.
3. Determine what job-search approach has the greatest likelihood of producing the kind of job you want.
4. E-mail your resume before a job interview.

If you are highly Structural, you will:

1. Update your resume, and have it reviewed and checked for errors.
2. Begin your search by scanning the newspaper and Internet.
3. Make a list of places to apply to and systematically go through it.

Primary Reasons for Derailment*

Analytical
- Appears cold and critical
- Fails to meet business objectives

Conceptual
- Appears out of step with the rest of the organization
- Lacks attention to detail

Quadra-modal
- Involved in too many things
- Has trouble making a decision

Structural
- Poor delegator
- Too narrow functional orientation

Social
- Lacks business and technical expertise
- Has difficulty with criticism

EXPRESSIVENESS

FLEXIBILITY

ASSERTIVENESS

Expressiveness
- Not a strong communicator

It Depends

- Talks over people

Assertiveness
- Fails to resolve conflicts with subordinates

It Depends

- Authoritarian, too ambitious, has to win

Flexibility
- Has trouble with new situations

It Depends

- Frequently changes mind in midstream

* Modified to include research from The Center for Creative Leadership

4. Have several copies of your resume prepared for a job interview, and confirm your references beforehand.

If you are highly Social, you will:

1. Make contact with personal friends.
2. Network with friends of friends to discuss possible career paths.
3. Set up informational interviews with people in like industries.
4. Resist the idea of preparing a formal resume.

If you are highly Conceptual, you will:

1. Ask yourself: How will changing jobs make a difference in my life ten years down the road?
2. Visualize the perfect job.
3. Be open to the new job when it shows up in your life.
4. Create an unusual resume, or maintain a Web site or blog to which you refer people.

For Expressiveness you will ask yourself: How many people will I involve in this decision?

For Assertiveness you will ask yourself: How quickly do I want to make a decision?

For Flexibility you will ask yourself: Do I take the first position that comes along or do I constantly consider all the options?

Ideally, I recommend you take a Whole Emergenetics approach to searching for a new job, to ensure that you appeal to each Attribute. However, in the end, I know that you will probably search for a job according to your brain preferences.

My friend Dave is one of the biggest Social thinkers in my database. He recently completed a successful job search. When I asked him how he goes about looking for a job, he said, "I start with relationships through people who can refer me to others. I would never search for jobs through a job fair, job boards, Internet, or newspaper. I hate the whole rigid process of the 'corporate job search.' I find it much better to go through other people. I despise the idea of informational meetings, followed by prescreening interviews, followed by set interviews, etc. Why can't we get it all done in one step? I would much rather sit down for a couple of hours and have a casual conversation.

"My girlfriend wanted me to do the exact opposite. She sends as many resumes out as possible, hoping that some of them will stick. I would rather go through people I trust, knowing they will steer me in the right direction. She would push me to actively look on the Internet for jobs, but I would always roll my eyes and resist. She was very good, however, at helping me put together a resume. If I had my way, I would never write another resume."

THE JOB INTERVIEW

You will not be surprised to hear that Emergenetics principles can successfully guide you through the process of interviewing for different positions. Here are some recommendations to help you.

What Is the Best Way to Describe Your Strengths?

Wouldn't it be easy if everyone spoke the universal language of Emergenetics? Then you could simply take your Profile with you to a job interview, and your prospective employer could see your preferences at a glance. Until that day comes, however, you need to be able to describe your strengths on paper (for example, in your resume) and in person during your job interview.

If you are highly Analytical, here are some phrases to use:

"I am results-oriented."
"I have a proven track record." (For example, "met $10,000,000 in income goal.")
"I have a solid, fact-based foundation."
"I excel at providing systems.
"I am a deep thinker."
"I do what is right for the business."
"My strategic thinking is logical and systematic."
"I lead by taking responsibility."

If you are highly Structural, here are some phrases to use:

"I follow through."
"I meet deadlines."
"I am always accountable ('the buck stops here')."
"I am dependable."
"I am organized."
"I am prompt."
"I follow the rules."
"My strategic thinking is about efficiency and completion."
"I lead by setting procedures and constantly making sure they work."

If you are highly Social, here are some phrases to use:

"I am people-oriented."
"I am empathic, nurturing, and emotionally supportive."
"I embrace diversity."
"I am a relationship builder."
"I have an open-door management style."
"I am a mentor and coach."
"I have an interest in community involvement."
"My strategic thinking is about people and how they will interact."
"I lead by networking, team-building, facilitating, and orchestrating."

If you are highly Conceptual, here are some phrases to use:

"I am an imaginative thinker."
"I have a fresh outlook."
"I am an idea person."
"Every day is a blank canvas."
"I seek solutions."
"I can take my ideas and create a cohesive concept."
"I think outside the box."
"My strategic thinking is visionary."
"I lead by moving the organization forward."

If you are a Quadra-modal, here are some phrases to use:

"I like to multitask."
"I can communicate with different kinds of people."
"I prefer to have a lot of different balls in the air."
"I can see all sides of an issue."
Note: A Quadra-modal's strategic thinking and leadership style depends on which Attribute (or Attributes) she or he chooses to emphasize.

If you are *Expressive,* here are some terms to use to describe yourself:

"I am a strong listener."
"I am calm."
"I stay on point."
"I work well independently."
"I am selective about the words I use."

If you are EXPRESSIVE, here are some terms to use to describe yourself:

"I am an enthusiastic communicator."
"I am a good motivator."
"I share ideas."
"I am comfortable presenting."
"I show high energy."

If you are *Assertive,* here are some terms to use to describe yourself:

"I have a composed manner."
"I am patient."
"I maintain the status quo."
"I quietly derive satisfaction from a job well done."
"I answer questions succinctly."

If you are ASSERTIVE, here are some terms to use to describe yourself:

"I am a driver."
"I am candid."

"I have strong opinions."

"I am competitive."

"I answer questions directly."

If you are *Flexible,* here are some terms to use to describe yourself:

"I am self-directed."

"I am consistent."

"I am focused."

"I am persistent."

"I have strong convictions."

"I prefer proven approaches."

If you are FLEXIBLE, here are some terms to use to describe yourself:

"I am open-minded."

"I am spontaneous."

"I appreciate other ideas."

"I welcome change."

"I am adaptable."

How to Conduct Yourself During a Job Interview

Of course you will want to make a good impression on your prospective employer, and a great way to do this is to match your behavior to that of the person interviewing you. Reread the information on determining the Thinking and Behavioral Attributes of another person in chapter 8, and remember to match your level of Expressiveness to that of the interviewer. If the other person is quiet as a mouse, you do not want to overwhelm her or him with the force of your personality. On the other hand, if your interviewer is bold and talkative, you do not want to seem invisible by comparison.

How to Determine If a Corporate Environment Is Right for You

Organizations have corporate cultures that, just like people, can be viewed in terms of the Emergenetics Attributes:

An Analytical corporate culture is found in long-lead time, high-stakes organizations such as research organizations or pharmaceutical companies that spend time developing products.

A Structural corporate culture is found in traditional, "slow and steady wins the race" organizations, such as railroad companies.

A Social corporate culture is found in people-centered companies, such as Mary Kay cosmetics.

A Conceptual corporate culture is found in "go-go" entrepreneurial companies, such as Google.

SEE *CORPORATE CULTURES: THE RITES AND RITUALS OF CORPORATE LIFE* BY TERRENCE E. DEAL AND ALLAN A. KENNEDY

Corporate culture is not always related to the kind of work that is being done. For example, banking is usually considered a staid and venerable business, but it is possible to approach banking with innovation and flair.

It is possible for a corporate culture to change over time, which means you could eventually end up in an environment that does not suit you. For example, you may sign on with a startup company because it is risky and visionary, but after a while the company may become stable and, well, boring. Here are some questions you can ask to determine an organization's culture:

To find out if the corporate culture is highly Analytical ask:

"What is the most critical business issue facing your company?"
"How much of your budget is devoted to research and development?"

To find out if the corporate culture is highly Structural, ask:

"What are the company's goals and priorities for the next year?"
"How stable is this organization?"

To find out if the corporate culture is highly Social, ask:

"Does your corporate environment foster teamwork?"
"What causes or charitable organizations does this company support?"

To find out if the corporate culture is highly Conceptual, ask:

"How many new products did you send to market last year?"
"Where do you expect to be in the future (at least ten years out)?"

To find out the level of Expressiveness in the organization, ask, "What would happen if I laughed out loud in the hallway?"

To find out the level of Assertiveness in the organization, ask, "What is the pace of your company?"

To find out the level of Flexibility in the organization, ask, "Do you offer job sharing, flexible hours, or the option of working from home?"

How to Determine If the the Job Is Right for You

Of course every company has different kinds of positions available. To find out if the job that is being offered matches your Thinking and Behavioral Attributes, ask the following questions.

To find out if the job would suit someone who is highly Analytical, ask:

"How does this position fit into the overall mission of the organization?"
"If I perform to your expectations, what will be my incentives?"

To find out if the job would suit someone who is highly Structural, ask:

"Can you hand me a detailed job description?"
"What are the opportunities for advancement?"

To find out if the job would suit someone who is highly Social, ask:

"Tell me about my boss—what kind of person is she or he?"
"Will you take me on a tour of your offices?" (I want to meet as many people as I can to see if it "feels right.")

To find out if the job would suit someone who is highly Conceptual, ask:

"Does this job require micromanagement?"
"Do you have performance awards for innovation?"

To find out the degree of Expressiveness that would be appropriate for the job, ask, "What is the most exciting prospect for your company this year?"

To find out the degree of Assertiveness that would be appropriate for the job, ask, "What are your pet peeves?"

To find out the degree of Flexibility that would be appropriate for the job, ask, "How much leeway will I have?"

SHOULD YOU ACCEPT THE OFFER?

Assuming that you are offered a new position that is appealing to you, now you need to make a decision. Here's how you go about it:

If you are highly Analytical, you'll do a risk/reward ratio before accepting a new job.
If you are highly Structural, you'll make a list of pros and cons.
If you are highly Social, you will contemplate any relational consequences of a new job.
If you are highly Conceptual, you will meditate about different effects of changing your position.

Now that you've done what you wanted to do anyway, it's time to take a different approach.

Take your Conceptual brain out for a metaphorical walk. Pick any item in the room—anything!—and decide how your new position is similar to the item that you pick. This will allow you to enter into a different part of your brain, and will allow your intuition to surface and play its role in your decision.

Suppose your eye catches a small propane gas grill. What do you know about a propane grill? How does it compare to your job? It's portable. It can be hot and smoky, but the end results of the cooking process are well worth the discomforts. The propane, which feeds the fire, is potentially explosive, but necessary for the grill to function correctly.

Now appease your Analytical and Structural brains by engaging in a force-field analysis. Draw a "T" on a piece of paper. On the left side of the T, write all the positives of the new position, and on the right side, write all the negatives.

Now go through each of the negatives and analyze how you can make it a positive. For example, "This job won't pay me as much money as the job I currently have" is a negative. However, perhaps you will learn skills that eventually will enable you to make more money, plus there is potential for long-term investments. You can now move this item from the negative list to the positive list. On the other hand, there may be negatives that are difficult to switch over. Your Analytical brain will enjoy assessing the pros and cons of each position, while your Structural brain will like the listing process.

Now you have to make the decision. If you still can't decide at this point, flip a coin. Before you accuse me of being ridiculous, let me explain. People can often identify the pros and cons of a decision, but still the answer is unclear to your logical mind. When you engage your gut brain, you get in touch with your values, feelings, and emotions.

When flipping the coin, it is important that you have only two options, and that you don't see the coin toss as a glib, gambling device. You must see it as a realistic way to get in touch with your inner soul. Close your eyes, take a deep breath, and flip the coin. Once the coin is flipped, you must pay attention to your initial reactions and feelings. You will instantly know whether the forced choice is right or wrong. I hope your gut reaction will not be as dramatic as Gabrielle's vomiting experience in chapter 3, but I make no guarantees!

If you are a multimodal thinker, choosing a position can be stressful. Every option sounds incredibly appealing and it can be hard to narrow down your choices. A Tri-modal is typically the jack-of-all trades but the master of none. Whenever college students can't decide on a major, I usually peg them as multimodal. When I ask them what they like, they will say things like, "I started out in English literature, then I switched to business, and now I'm thinking I want to go to med school."

This is where flexibility becomes important. If you are *Flexible,* your decisions won't be as difficult. If you are FLEXIBLE, picking a job will become a greater challenge for you. So, what's the best way to reach a decision as a multimodal?

I was in the middle of a transitional cycle shortly after I obtained my PhD. I was torn between staying in academia, becoming a public school administrator, or entering the private sector. I sent a typewritten, seven-page, single-spaced letter to the CEO of a major corporation. This man was well known for his sagacity and his long, thoughtful letters of advice. I knew he would help me.

By return mail, I received a one-paragraph letter that consisted of three sentences:

You have many options from which to choose. You have been successful in the past and you will be successful in the future. Just pick one option and move forward.

This was the best piece of advice I have ever received. The bottom line for multimodals is: pick one thing you like and go with it.

WHAT DOES IT TAKE TO BE SUCCESSFUL TODAY?

Many of us end up where we are by default, not design. Pick a job you like, one in which you feel your efforts make a difference, so you will be intrinsically motivated to do well.

> The illiterate of the future are not those who cannot read or write, but those who cannot learn, unlearn or relearn.
>
> Alvin Toffler in the Introduction to *Rethinking the Future* by Rowan Gibson
> (By the way, the future is here.)

1. Know when to learn, unlearn, and relearn.
2. Strive for perfection.
3. Take quiet moments to reflect:
    a. What are my broad goals?
    b. What are my priorities for the coming week? Month? Year?
    c. What have I learned?
    d. What work do I do well?
    e. What work needs to be done better?
    f. What things can I learn, but haven't yet?
4. When getting a new job or being reassigned to a new position ask: Based on my Profile, what do I need to be effective in this new job or position?

KEEP A POSITIVE ATTITUDE

Positive thoughts and attitudes bring about beneficial alterations in the brain. When you feel down or discouraged, adopting a positive attitude will shift your brain's activity from the right to the left prefrontal cortex. Interestingly, if you *pretend* to feel an emotion, you activate the same brain areas that would be activated if the emotion were genuine.

Psychological hardiness is characterized by:

1. A commitment to a source greater than yourself.
2. The presence of significant others (people or pets) in your life. Most psychologists agree that social support is the single greatest protection against stress.
3. Optimism.
4. Personal peace. Use your Emergenetics Profile to determine what will give you personal peace in your job and how to participate in something you find fulfilling.

> Given that so much of who we are is defined by our emotions, it is important that we uncover as much as we can about the brain mechanisms of many emotions. This task is just beginning, but the future is bright.
>
> **Joseph LeDoux, PhD,**
> *Synaptic Self*

Plan vigorous challenges for the last third of your life. You are going to live longer than your parents, and "retirement" is bad for the brain.

If each of us learns how to contribute as we are meant to, this will spread enthusiasm, creativity, and excellence throughout each workplace and have a ripple effect throughout our workplace, our industry, and the world.

PART III

The Emergenetics Toolbox

The Emergenetics Toolbox

Everyone needs the right tools to get the job done. The doctor has instruments, the plumber has wrenches, the chef has sharp knives, and you have . . . the Emergenetics Toolbox! The Toolbox contains charts that illustrate important Emergenetics concepts on one page for easy reference.

The first charts help you understand yourself and others:

- The Emergenetics Thinking and Behavioral Attributes Defined
- Determining Your Thinking and Behavioral Attributes at a Glance
- How Do You Buy a Computer?
- How Do You Complete a Project?
- How Do You Think and Behave at a Meeting?
- How Do You Think and Behave When You Receive Feedback from a Supervisor?

The next charts help you with your interactions with others:

- Communicating with Others
- How to Develop Better Communication with Your Direct Reports
- How to Make the Perfect Emergenetics Presentation
- How Each Emergenetics Attribute Listens
- How Each Emergenetics Attribute Prefers to Receive Recognition

The final charts summarize how to take a Whole Emergenetics approach to your work and personal life:

- The WE Approach to Running the Perfect Meeting

- The WE Approach to Conflict Management
- The WE Approach to Making a Decision
- The WE Approach to Writing a Mission Statement
- The WE Approach to an Implementation Plan
- The WE Approach to Change

I hope the contents of the Emergenetics Toolbox will help you use this book as a reference again and again. I think you'll find that once you are familiar with Emergenetics principles, there is no limit to the ways in which you can apply them.

The Emergenetics Thinking and Behavioral Attributes Defined

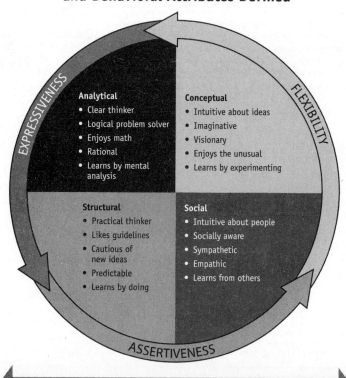

EXPRESSIVENESS

FLEXIBILITY

Analytical
- Clear thinker
- Logical problem solver
- Enjoys math
- Rational
- Learns by mental analysis

Conceptual
- Intuitive about ideas
- Imaginative
- Visionary
- Enjoys the unusual
- Learns by experimenting

Structural
- Practical thinker
- Likes guidelines
- Cautious of new ideas
- Predictable
- Learns by doing

Social
- Intuitive about people
- Socially aware
- Sympathetic
- Empathic
- Learns from others

ASSERTIVENESS

Expressiveness
The outward display of emotions toward others and the world at large

Assertiveness
The degree of energy invested in expressing thoughts, feelings, and beliefs

Flexibility
Willingness to accommodate the thoughts and actions of others

Determining Your Thinking and Behavioral Attributes at a Glance

Certain words best describe how you prefer to think and behave most of the time. Select all the words below that best describe you. You may select few or many. Select only words that identify your preferences, not your skills or how others see you. As you circle more words in a certain area, this is a clue that you have a preference in this area. If you select an equal number of words from the left (first-third) and right (third-third) ends of a Behavioral Attribute spectrum, you probably fall in the "it depends" group in the middle. Your results provide a visual representation of your Behavioral Attributes at a glance.

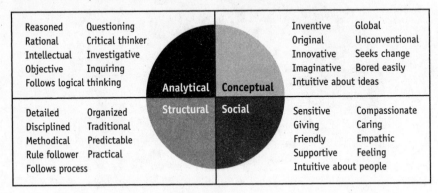

Reasoned	Questioning	Inventive	Global
Rational	Critical thinker	Original	Unconventional
Intellectual	Investigative	Innovative	Seeks change
Objective	Inquiring	Imaginative	Bored easily
Follows logical thinking		Intuitive about ideas	
Analytical	**Conceptual**		
Structural	**Social**		
Detailed	Organized	Sensitive	Compassionate
Disciplined	Traditional	Giving	Caring
Methodical	Predictable	Friendly	Empathic
Rule follower	Practical	Supportive	Feeling
Follows process		Intuitive about people	

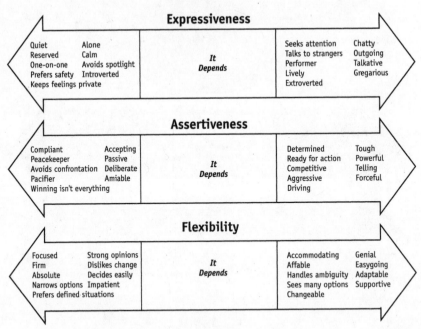

Expressiveness

Quiet Alone		Seeks attention Chatty
Reserved Calm		Talks to strangers Outgoing
One-on-one Avoids spotlight	*It Depends*	Performer Talkative
Prefers safety Introverted		Lively Gregarious
Keeps feelings private		Extroverted

Assertiveness

Compliant Accepting		Determined Tough
Peacekeeper Passive		Ready for action Powerful
Avoids confrontation Deliberate	*It Depends*	Competitive Telling
Pacifier Amiable		Aggressive Forceful
Winning isn't everything		Driving

Flexibility

Focused Strong opinions		Accommodating Genial
Firm Dislikes change		Affable Easygoing
Absolute Decides easily	*It Depends*	Handles ambiguity Adaptable
Narrows options Impatient		Sees many options Supportive
Prefers defined situations		Changeable

How Do You Buy a Computer?

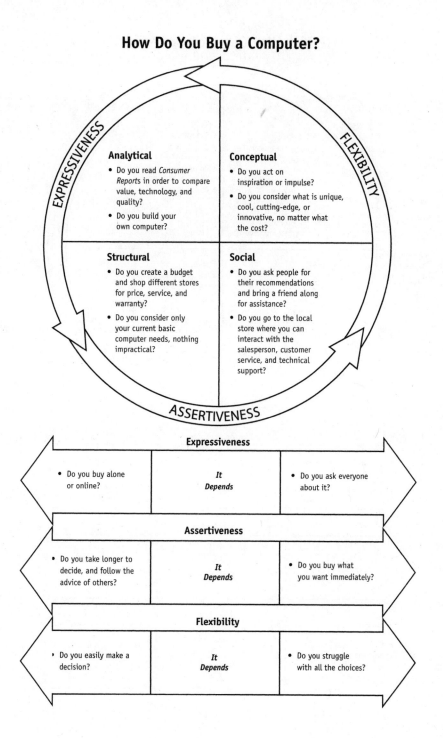

EXPRESSIVENESS

FLEXIBILITY

Analytical
- Do you read *Consumer Reports* in order to compare value, technology, and quality?
- Do you build your own computer?

Conceptual
- Do you act on inspiration or impulse?
- Do you consider what is unique, cool, cutting-edge, or innovative, no matter what the cost?

Structural
- Do you create a budget and shop different stores for price, service, and warranty?
- Do you consider only your current basic computer needs, nothing impractical?

Social
- Do you ask people for their recommendations and bring a friend along for assistance?
- Do you go to the local store where you can interact with the salesperson, customer service, and technical support?

ASSERTIVENESS

Expressiveness

• Do you buy alone or online?	*It Depends*	• Do you ask everyone about it?

Assertiveness

• Do you take longer to decide, and follow the advice of others?	*It Depends*	• Do you buy what you want immediately?

Flexibility

• Do you easily make a decision?	*It Depends*	• Do you struggle with all the choices?

How Do You Complete a Project?

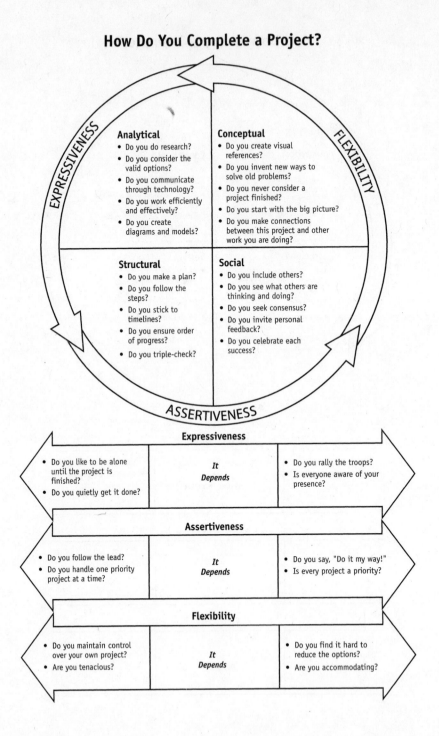

EXPRESSIVENESS

FLEXIBILITY

Analytical
- Do you do research?
- Do you consider the valid options?
- Do you communicate through technology?
- Do you work efficiently and effectively?
- Do you create diagrams and models?

Conceptual
- Do you create visual references?
- Do you invent new ways to solve old problems?
- Do you never consider a project finished?
- Do you start with the big picture?
- Do you make connections between this project and other work you are doing?

Structural
- Do you make a plan?
- Do you follow the steps?
- Do you stick to timelines?
- Do you ensure order of progress?
- Do you triple-check?

Social
- Do you include others?
- Do you see what others are thinking and doing?
- Do you seek consensus?
- Do you invite personal feedback?
- Do you celebrate each success?

ASSERTIVENESS

Expressiveness
	It Depends	
• Do you like to be alone until the project is finished? • Do you quietly get it done?		• Do you rally the troops? • Is everyone aware of your presence?

Assertiveness
	It Depends	
• Do you follow the lead? • Do you handle one priority project at a time?		• Do you say, "Do it my way!" • Is every project a priority?

Flexibility
	It Depends	
• Do you maintain control over your own project? • Are you tenacious?		• Do you find it hard to reduce the options? • Are you accommodating?

How Do You Think and Behave at a Meeting?

Analytical
- Do you want value for time spent?
- Do you focus on the data?
- Do you wonder if the meeting has value for your company?

Conceptual
- Do you see the long-term implications of ideas before anyone else?
- Do you dislike long meetings because you lose interest after the big picture has been established?
- Do you think meetings about details are a waste of your time?

Structural
- Do you always know what time it is?
- Do you arrive promptly, having budgeted time for this meeting and any necessary follow-up?
- Do you prefer to stick to the agenda, which helps prevent surprise topics and digressive discussions?

Social
- Do you prefer to have everyone's ideas honored, no matter how long it takes?
- Does time seem to drag when the meeting gets dry and boring?
- Are you happy spending time with people you don't usually get to see — but also worried about phone calls you might be missing?

EXPRESSIVENESS · FLEXIBILITY · ASSERTIVENESS

Expressiveness
- Are you hardly noticeable?
- *It Depends*
- Do you greet everyone effusively?

Assertiveness
- Do you hope others will notice your ideas?
- *It Depends*
- Do you tell everyone your ideas?

Flexibility
- Do you want the meeting to stay on topic?
- *It Depends*
- Do you go along with what everyone else is doing?

How Do You Think and Behave
When You Receive Feedback from a Supervisor?

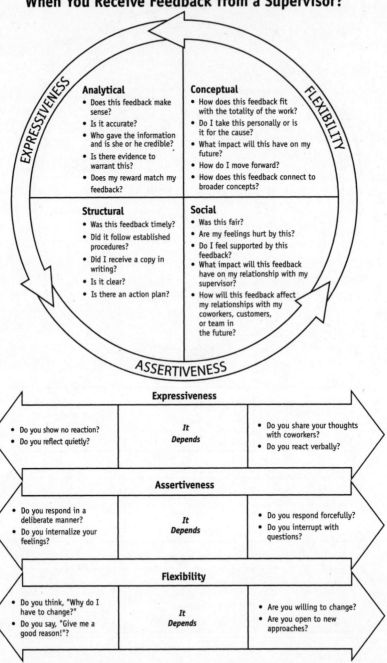

EXPRESSIVENESS

FLEXIBILITY

ASSERTIVENESS

Analytical
- Does this feedback make sense?
- Is it accurate?
- Who gave the information and is she or he credible?
- Is there evidence to warrant this?
- Does my reward match my feedback?

Conceptual
- How does this feedback fit with the totality of the work?
- Do I take this personally or is it for the cause?
- What impact will this have on my future?
- How do I move forward?
- How does this feedback connect to broader concepts?

Structural
- Was this feedback timely?
- Did it follow established procedures?
- Did I receive a copy in writing?
- Is it clear?
- Is there an action plan?

Social
- Was this fair?
- Are my feelings hurt by this?
- Do I feel supported by this feedback?
- What impact will this feedback have on my relationship with my supervisor?
- How will this feedback affect my relationships with my coworkers, customers, or team in the future?

Expressiveness

• Do you show no reaction? • Do you reflect quietly?	*It Depends*	• Do you share your thoughts with coworkers? • Do you react verbally?

Assertiveness

• Do you respond in a deliberate manner? • Do you internalize your feelings?	*It Depends*	• Do you respond forcefully? • Do you interrupt with questions?

Flexibility

• Do you think, "Why do I have to change?" • Do you say, "Give me a good reason!"?	*It Depends*	• Are you willing to change? • Are you open to new approaches?

Communicating with Others:
How to Talk or Write to Someone Who is...

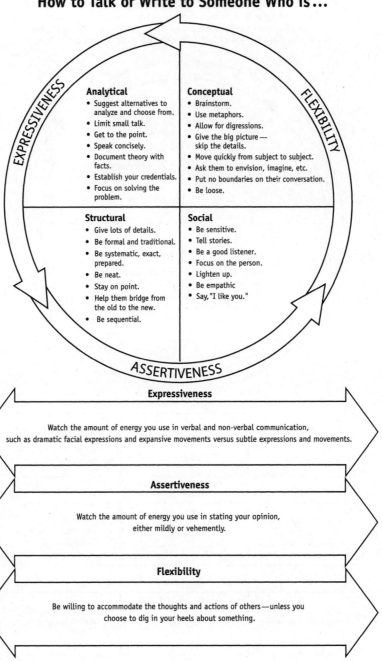

EXPRESSIVENESS

FLEXIBILITY

ASSERTIVENESS

Analytical
- Suggest alternatives to analyze and choose from.
- Limit small talk.
- Get to the point.
- Speak concisely.
- Document theory with facts.
- Establish your credentials.
- Focus on solving the problem.

Conceptual
- Brainstorm.
- Use metaphors.
- Allow for digressions.
- Give the big picture — skip the details.
- Move quickly from subject to subject.
- Ask them to envision, imagine, etc.
- Put no boundaries on their conversation.
- Be loose.

Structural
- Give lots of details.
- Be formal and traditional.
- Be systematic, exact, prepared.
- Be neat.
- Stay on point.
- Help them bridge from the old to the new.
- Be sequential.

Social
- Be sensitive.
- Tell stories.
- Be a good listener.
- Focus on the person.
- Lighten up.
- Be empathic
- Say, "I like you."

Expressiveness

Watch the amount of energy you use in verbal and non-verbal communication,
such as dramatic facial expressions and expansive movements versus subtle expressions and movements.

Assertiveness

Watch the amount of energy you use in stating your opinion,
either mildly or vehemently.

Flexibility

Be willing to accommodate the thoughts and actions of others—unless you
choose to dig in your heels about something.

How to Develop Better Communication
with Your Direct Reports

Once a year, schedule 30 minutes for coffee and conversation with each person.
Know that there is always time in your schedule to do this. Afterward, record pertinent information
to use in future communication. To get the most out of each conversation:

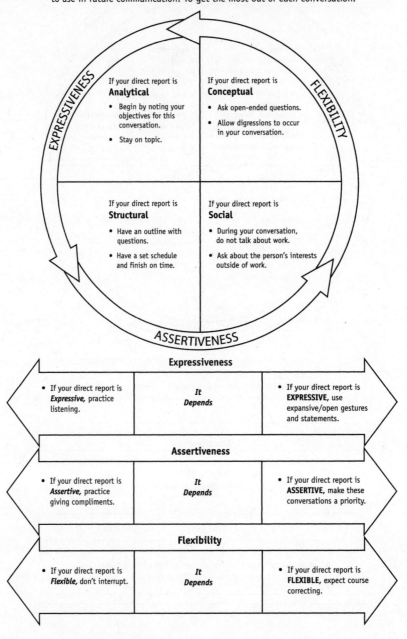

EXPRESSIVENESS

FLEXIBILITY

If your direct report is
Analytical

- Begin by noting your objectives for this conversation.
- Stay on topic.

If your direct report is
Conceptual

- Ask open-ended questions.
- Allow digressions to occur in your conversation.

If your direct report is
Structural

- Have an outline with questions.
- Have a set schedule and finish on time.

If your direct report is
Social

- During your conversation, do not talk about work.
- Ask about the person's interests outside of work.

ASSERTIVENESS

Expressiveness

• If your direct report is *Expressive,* practice listening.	*It Depends*	• If your direct report is **EXPRESSIVE,** use expansive/open gestures and statements.

Assertiveness

• If your direct report is *Assertive,* practice giving compliments.	*It Depends*	• If your direct report is **ASSERTIVE,** make these conversations a priority.

Flexibility

• If your direct report is *Flexible,* don't interrupt.	*It Depends*	• If your direct report is **FLEXIBLE,** expect course correcting.

How To Make the Perfect Emergenetics Presentation to Someone Who Is...

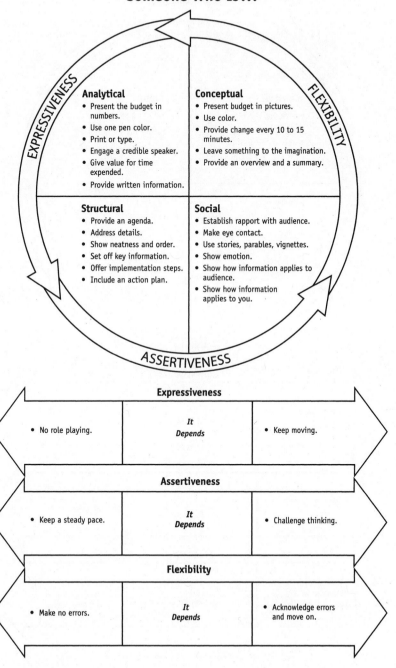

EXPRESSIVENESS

Analytical
- Present the budget in numbers.
- Use one pen color.
- Print or type.
- Engage a credible speaker.
- Give value for time expended.
- Provide written information.

Conceptual
- Present budget in pictures.
- Use color.
- Provide change every 10 to 15 minutes.
- Leave something to the imagination.
- Provide an overview and a summary.

FLEXIBILITY

Structural
- Provide an agenda.
- Address details.
- Show neatness and order.
- Set off key information.
- Offer implementation steps.
- Include an action plan.

Social
- Establish rapport with audience.
- Make eye contact.
- Use stories, parables, vignettes.
- Show emotion.
- Show how information applies to audience.
- Show how information applies to you.

ASSERTIVENESS

Expressiveness

• No role playing.	*It Depends*	• Keep moving.

Assertiveness

• Keep a steady pace.	*It Depends*	• Challenge thinking.

Flexibility

• Make no errors.	*It Depends*	• Acknowledge errors and move on.

How Each Emergenetics Attribute Listens

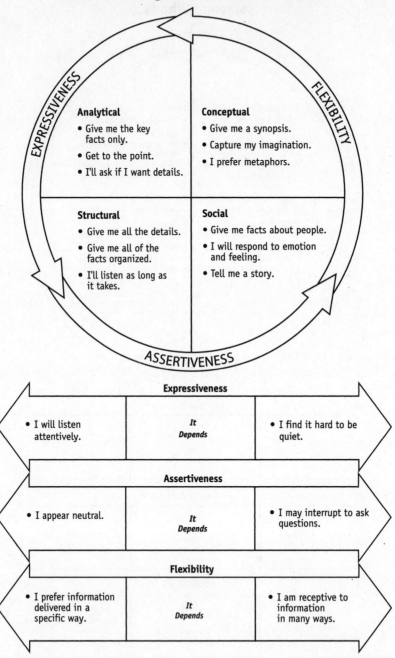

EXPRESSIVENESS

FLEXIBILITY

ASSERTIVENESS

Analytical
- Give me the key facts only.
- Get to the point.
- I'll ask if I want details.

Conceptual
- Give me a synopsis.
- Capture my imagination.
- I prefer metaphors.

Structural
- Give me all the details.
- Give me all of the facts organized.
- I'll listen as long as it takes.

Social
- Give me facts about people.
- I will respond to emotion and feeling.
- Tell me a story.

Expressiveness

	It Depends	
• I will listen attentively.		• I find it hard to be quiet.

Assertiveness

	It Depends	
• I appear neutral.		• I may interrupt to ask questions.

Flexibility

	It Depends	
• I prefer information delivered in a specific way.		• I am receptive to information in many ways.

How Each Emergenetics Attribute Prefers to Receive Recognition

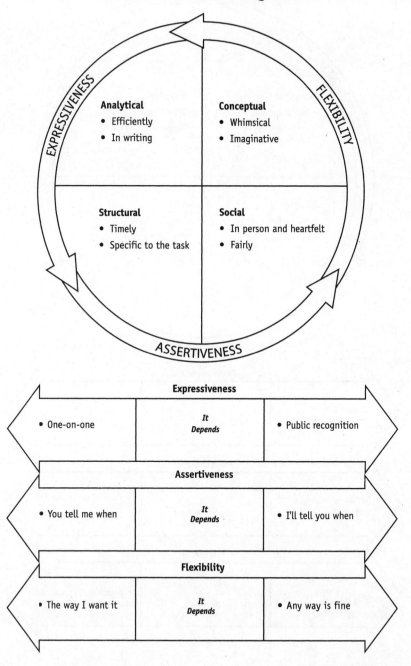

EXPRESSIVENESS

FLEXIBILITY

Analytical
- Efficiently
- In writing

Conceptual
- Whimsical
- Imaginative

Structural
- Timely
- Specific to the task

Social
- In person and heartfelt
- Fairly

ASSERTIVENESS

Expressiveness

| • One-on-one | *It Depends* | • Public recognition |

Assertiveness

| • You tell me when | *It Depends* | • I'll tell you when |

Flexibility

| • The way I want it | *It Depends* | • Any way is fine |

The WE* Approach to Running the Perfect Meeting

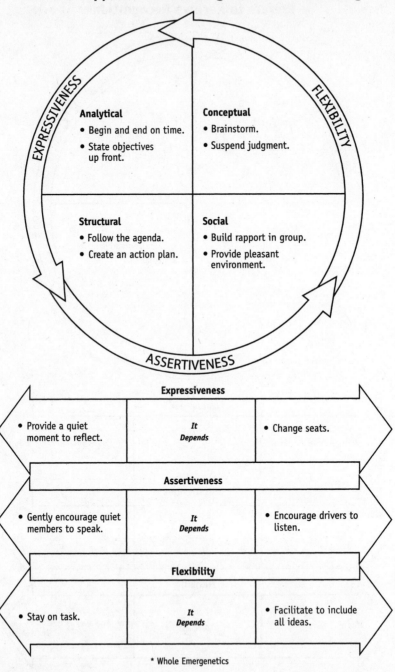

EXPRESSIVENESS

FLEXIBILITY

Analytical
- Begin and end on time.
- State objectives up front.

Conceptual
- Brainstorm.
- Suspend judgment.

Structural
- Follow the agenda.
- Create an action plan.

Social
- Build rapport in group.
- Provide pleasant environment.

ASSERTIVENESS

Expressiveness
- Provide a quiet moment to reflect.

It Depends

- Change seats.

Assertiveness
- Gently encourage quiet members to speak.

It Depends

- Encourage drivers to listen.

Flexibility
- Stay on task.

It Depends

- Facilitate to include all ideas.

* Whole Emergenetics

The WE* Approach to Conflict Management

When you are in a heated discussion, use the following steps to reach a resolution:

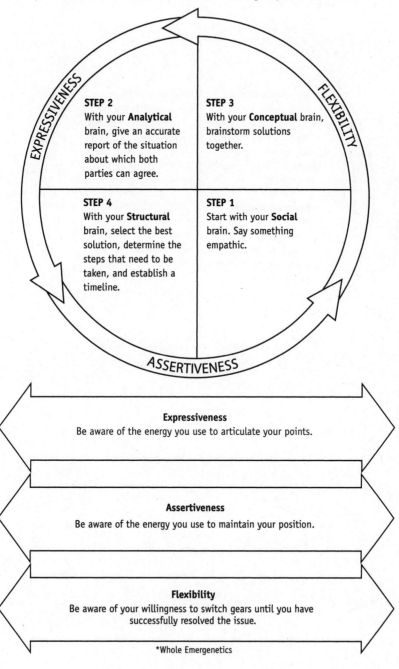

EXPRESSIVENESS

FLEXIBILITY

STEP 2
With your **Analytical** brain, give an accurate report of the situation about which both parties can agree.

STEP 3
With your **Conceptual** brain, brainstorm solutions together.

STEP 4
With your **Structural** brain, select the best solution, determine the steps that need to be taken, and establish a timeline.

STEP 1
Start with your **Social** brain. Say something empathic.

ASSERTIVENESS

Expressiveness
Be aware of the energy you use to articulate your points.

Assertiveness
Be aware of the energy you use to maintain your position.

Flexibility
Be aware of your willingness to switch gears until you have successfully resolved the issue.

*Whole Emergenetics

The WE* Approach to Making a Decision

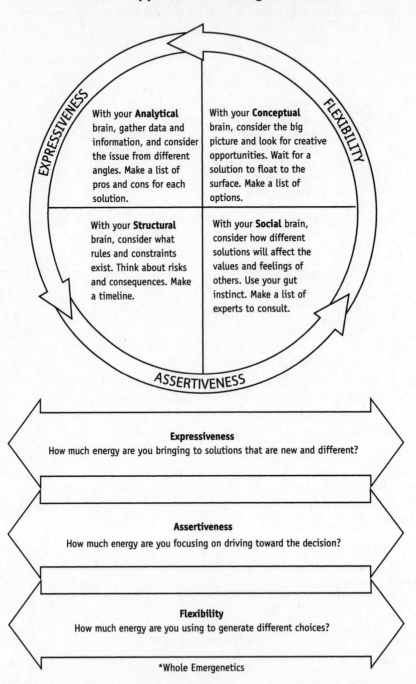

EXPRESSIVENESS

FLEXIBILITY

With your **Analytical** brain, gather data and information, and consider the issue from different angles. Make a list of pros and cons for each solution.

With your **Conceptual** brain, consider the big picture and look for creative opportunities. Wait for a solution to float to the surface. Make a list of options.

With your **Structural** brain, consider what rules and constraints exist. Think about risks and consequences. Make a timeline.

With your **Social** brain, consider how different solutions will affect the values and feelings of others. Use your gut instinct. Make a list of experts to consult.

ASSERTIVENESS

Expressiveness
How much energy are you bringing to solutions that are new and different?

Assertiveness
How much energy are you focusing on driving toward the decision?

Flexibility
How much energy are you using to generate different choices?

*Whole Emergenetics

The WE* Approach to Writing a Mission Statement

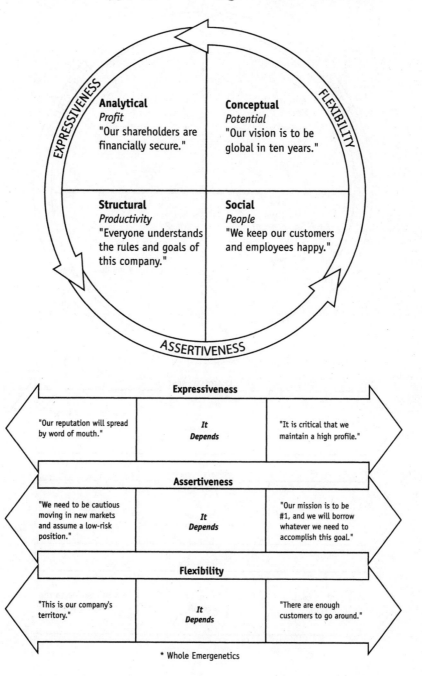

EXPRESSIVENESS

FLEXIBILITY

Analytical
Profit
"Our shareholders are financially secure."

Conceptual
Potential
"Our vision is to be global in ten years."

Structural
Productivity
"Everyone understands the rules and goals of this company."

Social
People
"We keep our customers and employees happy."

ASSERTIVENESS

Expressiveness

| "Our reputation will spread by word of mouth." | *It Depends* | "It is critical that we maintain a high profile." |

Assertiveness

| "We need to be cautious moving in new markets and assume a low-risk position." | *It Depends* | "Our mission is to be #1, and we will borrow whatever we need to accomplish this goal." |

Flexibility

| "This is our company's territory." | *It Depends* | "There are enough customers to go around." |

* Whole Emergenetics

The WE* Approach to an Implementation Plan

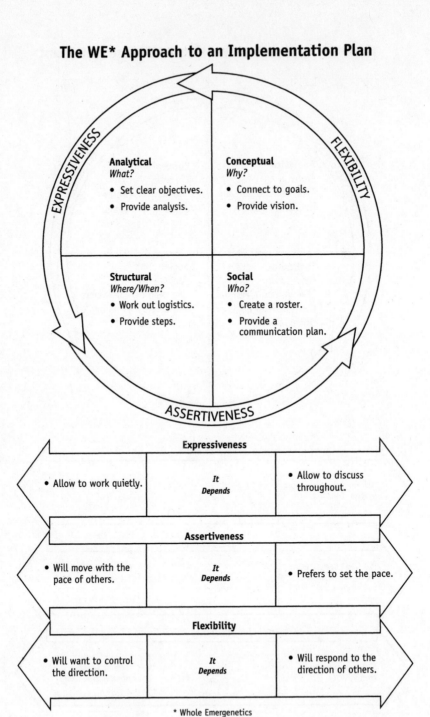

EXPRESSIVENESS

FLEXIBILITY

Analytical
What?
- Set clear objectives.
- Provide analysis.

Conceptual
Why?
- Connect to goals.
- Provide vision.

Structural
Where/When?
- Work out logistics.
- Provide steps.

Social
Who?
- Create a roster.
- Provide a communication plan.

ASSERTIVENESS

Expressiveness

| • Allow to work quietly. | *It Depends* | • Allow to discuss throughout. |

Assertiveness

| • Will move with the pace of others. | *It Depends* | • Prefers to set the pace. |

Flexibility

| • Will want to control the direction. | *It Depends* | • Will respond to the direction of others. |

* Whole Emergenetics

The WE* Approach to Change

I am (positive, motivating statement) _____ (date) _____

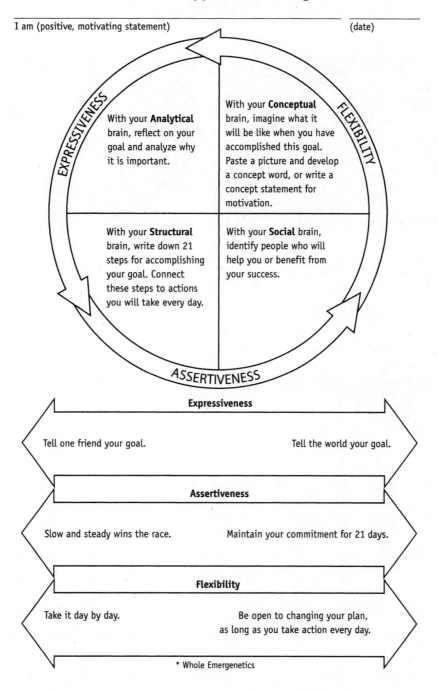

With your **Analytical** brain, reflect on your goal and analyze why it is important.

With your **Conceptual** brain, imagine what it will be like when you have accomplished this goal. Paste a picture and develop a concept word, or write a concept statement for motivation.

With your **Structural** brain, write down 21 steps for accomplishing your goal. Connect these steps to actions you will take every day.

With your **Social** brain, identify people who will help you or benefit from your success.

EXPRESSIVENESS

FLEXIBILITY

ASSERTIVENESS

Expressiveness

Tell one friend your goal.   Tell the world your goal.

Assertiveness

Slow and steady wins the race.   Maintain your commitment for 21 days.

Flexibility

Take it day by day.   Be open to changing your plan, as long as you take action every day.

* Whole Emergenetics

Appendix:
Origins and Discussion of
Emergenetics Research

This appendix gives background information that will help you understand the research and development of the Emergenetics Profile instrument.

Emergenetics Defined

1. Emergenetics is based on research that indicates: (1) individuals have inborn traits to act and think in certain ways, and (2) these traits are modified and shaped as people interact with their surroundings. The combination of experiences and genetics intertwine to form some commonly recognizable patterns of personality traits.

2. There are seven basic sets of attributes described by Emergenetics: four ways of thinking and three ways of behaving. The four Thinking Attributes are Analytical preferences (Blue), Structural preferences (Green), Social preferences (Red), and Conceptual preferences (Yellow). The three Behavioral Attributes (Purple) are Expressiveness behavior, Assertiveness behavior, and Flexibility behavior.

3. The Emergenetics instrument is a self-descriptive test. A self-descriptive test is one where people answer questions about themselves; the answers are tallied and the responses are compared with a

group norm and reported back. Several factors affect the accuracy of self-descriptive tests:

    a. They are always filtered by personal bias (i.e., our answers indicate how we choose to describe ourselves to others).

    b. Good tests are based on a sound theory and established test-developed principles, not personal opinions or ill-conceived psychobabble.

    c. Test developers are expected to follow the technical test-development guidelines published in *The Standards for Educational and Psychological Testing.*

    d. Each test factor measured should be comprised of five to seven individual test items to maximize reliability.

    e. Test results represent "patterns" and should never be considered cast in stone.

    f. As a general rule, the traits and behaviors measured by a robust test should remain consistent over time.

Development of the Emergenetics Profile

Several important factors were considered when the Emergenetics Profile instrument was developed. The underlying theory, reliability, validity, and test norms are discussed in the following sections.

The Underlying Theory

For centuries, psychologists and philosophers have been trying to understand why people behave the way they do. The arguments have drifted back and forth between theories that we are completely shaped by our environment and theories that we are completely shaped by our genetic structure.

During the first half of the 20th century, most psychologists were convinced that behaviors developed purely due to the surrounding environment. Ivan Pavlov, B. F. Skinner, and John Watson were a few of the behavioral psychologists who shared this belief. For decades, their theories provided the basis for most behavioral research.

In the late 1950s and 1960s, however, the "nature/nurture" argument began to shift back to "nature" in light of truly innovative work done with identical twins. To understand the importance of this research, we have to travel back in time to WWII. Parents in war-torn cities often sent their children to live with different families in the countryside. Many of these children happened to be identical twins.

About twenty years later, psychologists contacted many of these twin-pairs asking them to participate in a study of nature-versus-nurture effects. Their findings showed that behavior was equally influenced by *both* genetics and environment. Today, researchers know that Pavlov, Skinner, and Watson were only half right—both nature and nurture play substantial roles in determining behaviors and thinking styles.

Because it is impossible to clearly separate internal factors from behaviors, the theory of Emergenetics combines much of the early work in psychology with the most recent findings from twin research. It proposes that we have a combination of genetic tendencies to think and act in certain ways (nature), that have been modified through socialization (nurture).

The Emergenetics Profile instrument lays the groundwork for understanding this combination by measuring four common Thinking Attributes (Analytical, Structural, Social, Conceptual) and three Behavioral Attributes (Expressiveness, Assertiveness, Flexibility). Emergenetics is not a comprehensive or clinical picture of a person's total psyche, but it captures important everyday patterns that most people recognize.

Reliability

A major concern of test developers is whether each test question reliably measures the construct (i.e., deep-seated mental framework) it is supposed to measure. If a test is well designed, scores from items on one part of the test should correlate with scores from items measuring the same construct in another part of the test. Thus, test "reliability" refers to the ability of the test to produce consistent scores.

Statistical procedures used in the development of the Emergenetics Profile test include inter-item (item by item) reliability, split-half (overall) reliability, and test/re-test reliability. Inter-item reliability is an internal measure of how well each item correlates to the total score for that item. Split-half reliability is a measure of relationship between scores on the first half of the test with scores on the last half. Test/re-test reliability is a measure of how consistently a person constructs her or his Profile from one time to the next.

Inter-Item Reliability

During the development of the Emergenetics instrument, both the inter-item and construct relationships were carefully measured. For example, if the response to question 14 was supposed to measure Assertiveness, the value of this response would be expected to increase with the total score for Assertiveness. If the item score and total score were not positively correlated, question 14 would be dropped from the test.

Split-Half Reliability

The measure of split-half (overall) reliability used for the Emergenetics Profile instrument test is coefficient alpha. Coefficient alpha refers to the average of all possible inter-item and split-half correlations, both good and bad. Without relying on single indicators of reliability, which may contain large amounts of error, coefficient alpha provides an overall measure of the internal reliability of the test. The coefficient alphas for the Emergenetics Profile instrument are:

Attribute	Coefficient Alpha
Analytical	.83
Structural	.76
Social	.76
Conceptual	.76
Expressiveness	.83
Assertiveness	.83
Flexibility	.80

Test/Re-Test Reliability

Test/re-test reliability is a measure of how consistently a person answers the instrument over time. Test/re-test measures were conducted during the development of the Profile test. Results indicate that persons who completed the test after two years tended to respond in much the same manner. Here are the statistical correlations for each attribute for that study (any number .70 or greater is considered a very strong correlation):

Attribute	Correlation
Analytical	.84
Structural	.77

Social	.74
Conceptual	.82
Expressiveness	.80
Assertiveness	.78
Flexibility	.82

Further test/re-test studies were completed in 2004. This time, Emergenetics scores for 171 females and 117 males, some of whom took the test as early as 1993, were measured. This data was examined using the Analysis of Variance (ANOVA) procedure to determine whether change in test scores was due to chance. The ANOVA data showed Conceptual scores increased slightly between the first testing and second testing. This may be due to an Emergenetics "workshop effect" where participants learned that being Conceptual can be a "good thing."

Validity

The validity of a test refers to how well a test measures what it is supposed to measure. Like reliability, there are several different types of validity.

Face Validity

Face validity refers to whether a test-taker perceives the test to be credible. When measuring thinking styles and behaviors, for example, asking questions about bank deposits or religious affiliations would seriously threaten face validity. Irrelevant questions may stimulate respondents to question the validity of the entire test and thereby produce unreliable answers. Questions on the Emergenetics Profile instrument were specifically written to be relevant to everyday events and behaviors.

Content Validity

Content validity refers to the adequacy of the Emergenetics Profile instrument to measure the behavior it is supposed to measure. A typing test, for example, has a clear relationship between what the test measures and a specific skill. Content validity is more difficult to obtain for a general communication instrument. It must rely on personal feedback from people who agree or disagree that the test describes common thinking and behavioral attributes.

Participants who take the Emergenetics Profile instrument almost universally agree the test accurately measures the four Thinking Attributes and the three Behavioral Attributes.

Criterion Validity

Criterion validity is a measure correlating a person's score with performance in some other area. Using our earlier example, if a high score on the typing test could be later seen as high performance, the typing test could be considered criterion valid. Because the Emergenetics Profile instrument was not developed to predict or measure performance in specific jobs, information about criterion validity was not collected.

Construct Validity

The final form of validity is construct validity. A construct can be described as a deep-seated mental "construction" or characteristic. Construct validity refers to whether the Emergenetics Profile instrument measures the four kinds of thinking preferences and the three kinds of behaviors. No attempt was made to "peel open" participants' minds to evaluate intelligence, deep-seated emotional affects, or clinical or physiological aspects.

Construct validity is often determined using measures similar to those used in determining reliability. That is, the seven Emergenetics factors were statistically examined to see whether they were independent or covaried with one another. The table of Inter-Attributes on page 307 shows the interrelationships among the four Thinking Attributes and three Behavioral Attributes.

Relationships of the Attributes

Behavioral research is generally filled with overlapping results. How can a person, for example, not be "Assertive" when he or she is also "Expressive"? Much of this confusion comes from the fact that behavioral science is "fuzzy"—that is, one behavior often overlaps another behavior. The similarities between Attributes were recognized during our research and an Attribute was only included when it helped explain different behaviors among people with similar Thinking Attributes.

Construct Relationships

The relationships between Thinking Attributes and Behavior Attributes are the strength of Emergenetics. They also make understanding Emergenetics slightly more complex. The relationships between the Emergenetics factors are shown in the following table:

INTER-ATTRIBUTE CORRELATIONS TABLE

	Analytical	Structural	Social	Conceptual	Expressiveness	Assertiveness
Structural	.18					
Social	NS	NS				
Conceptual	.11	−.74	.26			
Expressiveness	.10	−.51	.55	.52		
Assertiveness	.25	−.50	.15	.49	.80	
Flexibility	NS	−.20	.84	.38	.66	.30

Correlations are significant at the P = <.01 level using a two-tailed test of significance; NS represents a non-significant correlation. A correlation is a measure of agreement between two numbers. It can range from −1.0 (perfect negative correlation) to 0 (no correlation) to +1.0 (perfect positive correlation).

The data from the Emergenetics research base now contains responses from tens of thousands of people. The table above shows how the relationships among behaviors and thinking styles generally vary in strength and direction. The following sections discuss some of the highlights.

Relationships Between Thinking Attributes

There is a minimal correlation between Analytical and Structural (.18, scientifically expressed as r = .18), Analytical and Conceptual (r = .11), and Social and Conceptual (r = .26). Structural showed a strong negative relationship with Conceptual (r = −.74), indicating an expected bipolarity between an expressed interest in either creativity or rule-following. Social showed no statistical relationship with either Analytical or Structural. This indicates the four Thinking Attributes tend to measure different factors, two of which move in the opposite direction.

Relationships Between Behavioral Attributes

These relationships were straightforward. Expressiveness was strongly related with Assertiveness (r = .80) and Flexibility (r = .66). While it is difficult to separate assertiveness in a social situation from assertiveness in a task situation, it is possible to be task assertive without being socially assertive. Therefore, the two Attributes, Assertiveness and Expressiveness, were chosen to determine the presence of autocratic behavior. Flexibility, on the other hand, should have a lower correlation with Assertiveness than with Expressiveness, and this was confirmed by the data (.30 compared with .66).

Relationships Between Thinking Attributes and Behavioral Attributes

The three Behaviors showed the expected relationships with each other, that is, Expressiveness and Assertiveness are highly correlated with each other, and Flexibility has a lower correlation with Assertiveness, yet it has a higher correlation with Expressiveness. The Behavioral Attributes' relationships with the Thinking Attributes were more complex. Flexibility moved independently from Analytical (r = .07, ns); negatively with Structural (r = −.20); very positively with Social (r = .84); and generally positively with Conceptual (r = .38). These relationships showed that people who rated themselves as socially or conceptually oriented thinkers also tended to rate themselves as being flexible (a beneficial trait in social and creative situations). Analytical thinking and Flexibility had no statistically significant correlations. Structural thinking was negatively related to Flexibility, which meant that people who valued rules and order were also likely to be less flexible than others.

People who rated themselves as Assertive were slightly correlated with Analytical (r = .25) and Social (r = .15); negatively related with Structural (r = −.50); and moderately correlated with Conceptual (r = .49). These relationships indicate that Assertiveness is largely associated with rule-breaking (a negative Structural characteristic) and risk-taking (a positive Conceptual characteristic).

Expressiveness is negatively associated with Structural (r = −.51) and positively associated with Analytical (r = .10), Social (r = .55), and Conceptual (r = .52). These patterns indicate that rule followers are likely to be quiet and reserved; problem solvers tend to go either way; and social and conceptual thinkers are likely to be more outgoing.

Flexibility is negatively associated with Structural (r = −.20) and positively associated with Social (r = .84) and Conceptual (r = .38). These relationships indicate that Social thinkers will almost always also be Flexible and that Conceptual thinkers are likely to be Flexible.

Putting It Together

A person's primary Thinking style does not always predict how he or she will behave. Social thinking is likely to be Expressive and Flexible, and only slightly Assertive. Conceptual thinking is probably more Expressive and Assertive and may be somewhat Flexible. Structural thinking tends to be non-Expressive, non-Assertive, and, slightly, Inflexible. Analytical thinking has little association with any of the behaviors. It correlates slightly with Expressiveness and Assertiveness and not at all with Flexibility.

Gender Differences and Normative Information

In general, the mean raw scores for males and females show interesting differences. Females scored significantly higher in Structural, Social, Expressiveness, and Flexibility attributes. Males scored higher in Analytical, Conceptual, and Assertiveness attributes. These differences are not good or bad; they are just differences. The following T-score comparisons are statistically significant at the $P = <.01$ level. They represent averages, not individual scores, and should be considered with interest, not judgment.

Analytical: Male preference is 5 points higher than female
Structural: Female preference is 2 points higher than male
Social: Female preference is 6 points higher than male
Conceptual: Male preference is 2 points higher than female
Expressiveness: Female preference is 2 points higher than male
Assertiveness: Male preference is 2 points higher than female
Flexibility: Female preference is 3 points higher than male

Because of these differences, a person's final score for each Emergenetics factor is reported in relation to others of the same sex. Gender-based norms were used to avoid sexual bias. Emergenetics norms have a standard error of less than 1.0.

Normative Updates

Emergenetics is periodically re-normed to account for test bias and to reflect changes in the culture. Through the years the norms have not shown substantive change, with two exceptions. When we compared the 1991, 1995, and 2002 data, we found there was a shift in the means and point differences in some of the Attributes, as the following chart reveals:

GENDER GAP

Attribute	Mean	1991	1995	2002
Analytical	Males higher	5 points	4 points	5 points
Structural	Females higher	2 points	2 points	2 points
Social	Females higher	7 points	6 points	6 points
Conceptual	Males higher	3 points	3 points	2 points
Expressiveness	Females higher	1 point	1 point	2 points
Assertiveness	Males higher	5 points	3 points	2 points
Flexibility	Females higher	5 points	3 points	3 points

This latest data was drawn from a base of 44,602 respondents, and all of these numbers represent statistically significant changes.

Conclusion

The Emergenetics Profile instrument meets the criteria for face validity, construct validity, content validity, split-half reliability, and inter-item reliability.

It provides valuable information about four Thinking styles and three Behavioral styles using norms generated from analyzing tens of thousands of Profiles.

The Emergenetics Profile instrument has been found to provide valuable feedback to people who wish to use the instrument for improving interpersonal effectiveness, whether in a personal or occupational setting, and it appears to reflect cultural norms over time.

Wendell Williams, PhD
Geil Browning, PhD

Sources

**CHAPTER 1   WHAT IS EMERGENETICS AND
WHY SHOULD YOU CARE?**

p. 5 *"Whatever any man does he first must do in his
mind . . ."*
See Gay Gaer Luce, and Julius Segal, *Sleep* (New
York: Coward-McCann, 1966).

p. 6 *Steven Pinker's* The Blank Slate *asserts that up to
70 percent of the variation between individuals is due to
genetics.*
See Steven Pinker, *The Blank Slate: The Modern
Denial of Human Nature* (New York: Viking Press,
2002), 374.

p. 9 *"Your brain never stops developing and changing. . . ."*
See James Trefil, *Are We Unique? A Scientist Explores
the Unparalleled Intelligence of the Human Mind* (New
York: Wiley, 1997).

p. 10 *"It's not differences that divide us . . ."*
See Margaret Wheatley, *Turning to One Another* (San
Francisco: Barrett-Koehler Publishing, 2002), 47.

p. 10 See Paul Dennison and Gail Dennison, *Brain
Gym: Simple Activities for Whole Brain Learning*
(Ventura: Edu-Kinesthetics, Inc., 1992).

p. 10 *This may help integrate both sides of your body.*
See Lynn Fishman Hellerstein, O.D., F.C.O.V.D.,
F.A.A.O., "Vision-Insights to Learning," Lecture,
Denver, CO, April 27, 2004.

CHAPTER 2   É=MB²

p. 12 *{Kagan} said that children are like a pale, gray
fabric . . .*
See Jerome Kagan, Nancy Snidman, Doreen Arcus,
and J. Steven Reznick, *Galen's Prophecy: Temperament
in Human Nature* (Boulder, CO: Westview Press,
1995), 37.

p. 12 *Studies also show that your genes affect your atti-
tudes about . . .*
See James M. Olson, Philip A. Vernon, and Julie
Aitken Harris, "The Heritability of Attitudes: A

Study of Twins," *Journal of Personality and Social Psychology* 80, no. 6 (June 2001): 845–60.

See also chapter 2, "The Genetics of Genius," by David T. Lykken, in A. Steptoe, ed., *Genes and the Mind* (New York: Oxford University Press, 1998).

See also Nancy Segal, *Entwined Lives: Twins and What They Tell Us About Human Behavior* (New York: Plume, 2000). Also see her article, "Twins' Multiple Messages for Human Behavior," *The Psychwatch Newsletter* 3, no. 24 (June 17, 2000). Available online at: http://www.psychwatch.com.

p. 13 "*. . . a greater number of marriages cannot cause a woman's D4 gene to change from four to seven repeats.*"
See Robert Plomin, John C. Defries, Ian W. Craig, and Peter McGuffin, *Behavioral Genetics in the Postgenomic Era* (Washington, DC: American Psychological Association, 2002). See chapter 5, "Assessing Genotype-Environment Interactions and Correlations in the Postegenomic Era," by David C. Rowe, 82–83.

p. 13 "*The degree of likeness {of twins}, of concordance on personality tests, holds up remarkably well, even into the eighth and ninth decades of life . . .*"
See William Clark and Michael Grunstein, *Are We Hardwired?: The Role of Genetics in Human Behavior* (New York: Oxford University Press, 2000), 19.

p. 13 *. . . Jerry Levey and Mark Newman, identical twins who did not meet until they were thirty years old.*
See John Horgan, "Eugenics Revisited," *Scientific American* 268, no. 6 (June 1993): 122–28, 130–31.

p. 13 *The story of the "twin Jims" is even more incredible.*
See: William Wright, *Born That Way: Genes, Behavior, Personality* (New York: Routledge, 1999), 27–31.

p. 14 "*The study of these reared-apart twins has led to two general and seemingly remarkable conclusions . . .*"
See Thomas Bouchard Jr., David T. Lykken, Matthew McGue, Nancy L. Segal, and Auke Tellgen, "Sources of Human Psychological Differences: The Minnesota Study of Twins Reared Apart," *Science* 250, no. 4978 (October 12, 1990): 223–26.

p. 14 "*Identical twins reared apart are highly similar . . .*"
See Steven Pinker, *The Blank Slate*, 374.

p. 15 "*For the first twenty years of my career, I wrote essays critical of the role of biology . . .*"
See William Wright, *Born That Way: Genes, Behavior, Personality*, 93. Quotation is from Jerome Kagan.

p. 15 *In a study by Debra Johnson, PhD . . .*
See D. L. Johnson, J. S. Wiebe, S. Gold, N. Andreason, R. Hichwa, L. Watkins, and L. Ponto, "Cerebral Blood Flow and Personality: A Positron Emission Tomography Study," *American Journal of Psychiatry* 156 (February 1999): 252–57.

p. 16 *Researchers Jerome Kagan, MD, and Carl Schwartz, MD, at Harvard note that some kids are bold, while others are shy . . .*
See Carl Schwart, Christopher Wright, Lisa Shin, Jerome Kagan, Paul Whalen, Katherine McMullin, and Scott Rauch, "Differential Amygdala Response to Novel versus Newly Familiar Neutral Faces: A Functional MRI Probe Developed for Studying Inhibited Temperament," *Biological Psychiatry* 53 (2003): 854–62.

p. 16 *The gene that affects serotonin re-uptake comes in two versions . . .*
See Peter D. Kramer, "Tapping the Mood Gene." *The New York Times*, July 26, 2003.

p. 16 *Sure enough, people with the short allele showed more activity in their amygdala.*
See Greg Miller, "Gene's Effect Seen in Brain's Fear Response," *Science* 297 (July 19, 2002): 319.

p. 16 "*The older one gets, however, the more most of us conclude that children come into the world with fixed personalities . . .*"
See Robert Plomin, John C. Defries, Ian W. Craig, and Peter McGuffin, *Behavioral Genetics in the Postgenomic Era* (Washington, DC: American Psychological Association, 2002). See James D. Watson's Introduction, p. xxii.

p. 16 *Dopamine mediates pleasure in the brain* . . .
See R. P. Ebstein, O. Novick, R. Umansky, B. Priel, Y. Osher, D. Blaine, E. R. Bennett, L. Nemanov, M. Katz, and R. H. Belmaker, "Dopamine D4 Receptor (D4DR) Exon III Polymorphism Associated with the Human Personality Trait of Novelty Seeking," *Nature Genetics* 12 (1996): 78–80.

p. 16 *"{Genes} switch one another on and off; they respond to the environment. . . ."*
See Matt Ridley, "What Makes You Who You Are," *Time,* June 2, 2003, 63.

p. 16 *" . . . the brains of domestic rabbits are considerably reduced in bulk, in comparison with those of the wild rabbit or hare . . ."*
See Charles Darwin, *The Descent of Man.* Available online at: http://charles-darwin.classic-literature.co.uk/the-descent-of-man/ebook-page-38.asp.

p. 17 *In a classic study, neurobiologist Marian Diamond divided rats into three different environments* . . .
See Marian Diamond, *Enriching Heredity: The Impact of the Environment on the Brain* (New York: The Free Press, 1988) 1–10. A great overview written by Dr. Diamond is available online at: http://www.newhorizons.org/neuro/diamond_aging.htm.

p. 17 *Dr. Diamond found that placing a rat in an enriched environment* . . .
See Clarence Bass, "Challenge Your Mind, as Well as Your Body." Available online at: http://www.cbass.com/Mind.htm.

p. 18 *It is made up of 80 percent water* . . .
Estimates of the water content of the brain run from 70 to 90 percent. Estimates of the amount of electricity in the brain vary, too. This estimate is taken from Carl Sagan, *The Dragons of Eden: Speculations on the Evolution of Human Intelligence* (New York: Ballantine Books, 1989), 45.

p. 18 *"The human brain is estimated to have about one hundred billion nerve cells . . ."*
See Tim Green, Stephen Heinemann, and Jim Gusella, "Molecular Neurobiology and Genetics: Investigation of Neural Function and Dysfunction," *Neuron* 20 (March 1998): 427–44.

p. 18 *We can feel the wing of a bee falling one centimeter onto our cheek . . ."*
See Robert S. Feldman, *Understanding Psychology,* 4th ed. (New York: McGraw-Hill, 1996), 98.

p. 19 *"Axons are promiscuous little things."*
See "Scientists Foresee Bridging Nerve Damage with Grafts," quoting Douglas Smith, MD. Press release dated 4/17/01 from University of Pennsylvania Health System, available online at: http://www.uphs.upenn.edu/news/News_Releases/april01/Neurons.html.

p. 21 *"Children whose neural circuits are not stimulated before kindergarten are never going to be what they could have been."*
See Sharon Begley, "Your Child's Brain," *Newsweek,* February 19, 1996, 62.

p. 21 *Research by Princeton psychologist Elizabeth Gould suggests that new neurons may even grow in the neocortex* . . .
See Etienne Benson, "Thriving on Complexity," *Monitor,* published by the American Psychological Association, vol. 33, no. 10 (November 2002). Available online at: http://www.apa.org/monitor/nov02/thriving.html.

p. 21 *"Whenever you read a book or have a conversation, the experience causes physical changes in your brain. . . ."*
See George Johnson, *In the Palaces of Memory: How We Build the World Inside Our Heads* (New York: Alfred A. Knopf, 1991), ix. Available online at http://www.santafe.edu/~johnson/palaces.preface.html.

p. 21 *In a somewhat horrifying experiment, frogs were given a transplanted third eye* . . .
See Steven R. Quartz, and Terrence J. Sejnowski, PhD, *Liars, Lovers and Heroes: What the New Brain Science Reveals About How We Become Who We Are* (New York: Quill, 2002), 57.

p. 22 *"The brain remains a dynamic structure that alters from year-to-year, day-to-day, even moment-to-moment over our lifespan."*
See Richard Restak, *The Secret Life of the Brain,* a PBS special with a book tie-in. This quote is taken from Essay 1, "The Remarkable Plasticity of the Brain," p. 1. Available online at: http://www.pbs.org/brain.

p. 22 *"The brain is a little saline pool that acts as a conductor, and it runs on electricity."*
See Judith Hooper, and Dick Teresi, *The Three-Pound Universe,* (New York: Dell, 1986).

p. 24 *"The brain is the last and grandest biological frontier . . ."*
See Foreword by James D. Watson, from Sandra Ackerman, *Discovering the Brain* (Washington, DC: National Academy Press, 1992), iii.

p. 25 *One patient tried to forcibly grab his wife with his left hand, only to be restrained by his own right hand. . . .*
For this example of split-brain thinking and others, see Sally Springer, and Georg Deutsch, *Left Brain, Right Brain: Perspectives from Cognitive Neuroscience* (New York: Worth Publishers, 1998), 40 (Citing Michael Gazzaniga, *The Bisected Brain* [New York: Appleton-Century-Crofts, 1970]).

p. 26 *"Slight hemispheric differences have been transformed by the popular press into clear-cut, all-or-nothing dichotomies . . ."*
See John Pinel, *Biopsychology* (New Jersey: Allyn & Bacon, 1990), 554.

p. 28 The information about the lobes of the brain is adapted from *Magic Trees of the Mind* by Marian Diamond, and Janet Hopson (New York: Plume Books, 1998), 41.

p. 30 *I was certain that my colleague, Wendell Williams . . .*
Wendell Williams, PhD, is managing director of SCIENTIFICSELECTION.COM, LLC. Wendell uses the core principles of industrial psychology to identify job competencies, develop and validate tests, install performance appraisal systems, and evaluate human resource systems for EEOC compliance. See his Web site at: http://www.ScientificSelection.com.

p. 31 *"The human brain is generally regarded as a complex web of adaptations . . ."*
See Michael Gazzaniga, *The Mind's Past* (Berkeley, CA: University of California Press, 2000), 14.

CHAPTER 3   GREAT MINDS DO NOT THINK ALIKE

p. 34 *"What seems astonishing is that a mere three-pound object . . ."*
See Joel Havemann, and Stephen G. Reich, MD, *A Life Shaken: My Encounter with Parkinson's Disease* (Baltimore: Johns Hopkins University Press, 2004), 45.

p. 43 *"I have come to believe over and over again . . ."*
See Audre Lorde, *Sister Outsider: Essays and Speeches* (Berkeley, CA: Crossing Press, a division of Ten Speed Press, 1984), 40.

p. 44 *However, the enteric nervous system has over 100 million neurons—more than the spinal cord.*
See Michael Gershon, MD, *The Second Brain: A Groundbreaking New Understanding of Nervous Disorders of the Stomach and Intestine* (New York: Perennial Books, 1999), 15.

p. 52 *"We are an intelligent species . . ."*
See Carl Sagan, *Broca's Brain: Reflections on the Romance of Science* (New York: Ballantine Books, 1993), 17.

CHAPTER 5   PUTTING IT ALL TOGETHER

p. 68 *"The most obvious feature of the brain is that it is not homogeneous . . ."*
Steven Rose, *From Brains to Consciousness?: Essays on the New Sciences of the Mind* (Princeton, NJ: Princeton University Press, 1998). See chapter 12, "How Might the Brain Generate Consciousness?" by Susan Greenfield, 210.

p. 81 *My associate, Chris Cox, illustrates these differences with a scenario.*

Chris is the owner and Chief Learning Officer of Amplitude, LLC. Her Web site is: http://www.amplitudetraining.com.

CHAPTER 6   WHY REAL MEN
DON'T ASK FOR DIRECTIONS

p. 107 *In his book* Executive Instinct, *author Nigel Nicholson, an expert in evolutionary psychology, compares the ways in which all-female and all-male groups tend to work.*

See Nigel Nicholson, *Executive Instinct: Managing the Human Animal in the Information Age* (New York: Crown Publishing Group, 2000), 85.

p. 112 *In women the areas of the brain associated with language, judgment, and memory are more densely packed with 18 percent more neurons.*

See S. F. Witelson, D. L. Kigar, and H. J. Stoner-Beresh, "Sex Difference in the Numerical Density of Neurons in the Pyramidal Layers of Human Prefrontal Cortex: A Stereologic Study," *Soc. Neurosci. Abstr.* vol. 27, program no. 80.18, 2001.

p. 112 *In the female brain, the corpus callosum . . .*

See Doreen Kimura, "Sex Differences in the Brain," *Scientific American,* April 2002. Available online at: http://www.sciam.com/article.cfm?articleID= 00018E9D-879D1D06-8E49809EC588EEDF.

See also: C. Davatzkikos, and S. Resnick, "Sex Differences in Anatomic Measures of Interhemispheric Connectivity: Correlations with Cognition in Women but Not Men," *Cereb Cortex* 8, no. 7 (October–November 1998): 635–40. This article can be downloaded from: http://www.cercor.oupjournals.org/cgi/reprintframed/8/7/635.

p. 112 *"If a man is shaving and you talk to him, he'll cut himself."*

See Barbara and Allen Pease, *Why Men Don't Listen and Women Can't Read Maps: How We're Different and What to Do About It* (New York: Broadway Books, 1998), 53.

p. 112 *When men and women underwent brain imaging while listening to a passage from a novel . . .*

See "Men Do Hear—But Differently Than Women, Images Show." News release from the Indiana University School of Medicine, November 28, 2000. Available online (with images of brain scans) at: http://www.medicine.indiana.edu/news_releases/ archive_00/men_hear ing00.html.

p. 113 *"There is simply more neural activity in general in the female brain at any given time."*

See Michael Gurian, *What Could He Be Thinking? How a Man's Mind Really Works* (New York: St. Martin's Press, 2003), 138. Gurian is citing the research of Ruben Gur, MD. For an interesting interview with Dr. Gur, see the following Web site: http://www.dana.org/books/radiotv/eyb_0298.cfm.

p. 114 *Men outperform women in mathematical reasoning, and boys outscore girls on the math SATs by 7 percent.*

See Anne Moir, and David Jessel, *Brain Sex* (New York: Bantam Doubleday Dell Publishing Group, 1991), 16 (Quoting C. P. Benbow, and J. C. Stanley, "Sex Differences in Mathematical Ability: Fact or Artifact," *Science* 210 (1980): 1234–36; and C. P. Benbow, and J. C. Stanley, "Sex Differences in Mathematical Ability: More facts," *Science* 222 (1983): 1029–31.

p. 114 *For example, damage to either the front or back of the left hemisphere affects speech in males, but female speech is rarely affected.*

See F. E. Bloom, and A. Lazeron, *Brain, Mind, and Behavior* (New York: W. H. Freeman, 1988), 72.

p. 114 *"A woman's face had to be really sad for men to see it," says neurologist Ruben Gur . . .*

See Deborah Blum, "Face it! Facial Expressions Are Crucial to Emotional Health," *Psychology Today,* September–October 1998.

p. 115 *"The typical teenage girl . . ."*

See Leonard Sax, MD, PhD, *Why Gender Matters* (New York: Doubleday, 2005). This quote is taken from a summary of the book available at Dr. Sax's Web site: http://www.singlesexschools.org/sax.html.

p. 115 *In a study conducted by Turhan Canli, women and men responded very differently to the same pictures.*
See T. Canli, J. Desmond, Z. Zhao, and J. Gabrieli, "Sex Differences in the Neural Basis of Emotional Memories," *Proc. Natl. Acad. Sci. USA.* 99, no. 16 (August 6, 2002): 10789–94. Available online at: http://www.pnas.org/cgi/reprint/162356599v1.pdf.

p. 115 *Some experiments done in mock offices have shown that women are 70 percent better than men at remembering the location of items found on a desktop.*
See L. Barkow, L. Cosmides, and J. Tooby, eds., *The Adapted Mind: Evolutionary Psychology and the Generation of Culture* (New York: Oxford University Press, 1992), 487–503 (specifically chapter 14, "Sex Differences in Spatial Abilities: Evolutionary Theory and Data," by Irwin Silverman and Marion Eals).

p. 116 *In an interesting study, mothers and fathers were shown ten-second video clips of babies fussing, with the sound turned down.*
See Barbara and Allan Pease, *Why Men Don't Listen and Women Can't Read Maps* (New York: Broadway, 2001), 28.

p. 116 *"What was especially interesting . . ."*
See B. A. Shaywitz, S. E. Shaywitz, K. R. Pugh, et al., "Sex Differences in the Functional Organization of the Brain for Language," *Nature* 373, no. 6515 (February 16, 1995): 607–9.

CHAPTER 7   YOU CAN CHANGE

p. 130 These drawings were adapted from "Synoptic Density," available online at: www.ala.org/ala/pla/plaissues/earlylit/workshopsparent/supet5205.doc.

p. 131 *Leslie G. Ungerleider, chief of the Laboratory of Brain and Cognition at the National Institutes of Health . . .*
See A. Karni, G. Meyer, P. Jezzard, M. M. Adams, R. Turner, and L. G. Ungerleider, "Functional MRI Evidence for Adult Motor Cortex Plasticity During Motor Skill Learning," *Nature* 377 (September 14, 1995): 155–58.

p. 132 A Web site for information about the importance of affirmations is: http://www.performance-unlimited.com/whyaffir.htm.

p. 132 *In a study at MIT, volunteers were shown photographs, then asked to recollect them.*
See K. M. O'Craven, and N. Kanwisher, "Mental Imagery of Faces and Places Activates Corresponding Stimulus-Specific Brain Regions," *Journal of Cognitive Neuroscience* 12 (2000): 1013–23. Available online at: http://web.mit.edu/bcs/nklab/publications.shtml.

p. 133 *Watch your words, because your brain is listening.*
I am indebted to Emergenetics Associate Dr. Mary Case, who drew upon her notes taken during a lecture by Herbert Bensen (author of *The Relaxation Response*) at a Harvard Mind/Body Institute seminar.

p. 133 *Dr. Marco Iacoboni at the University of California did a study that revealed a connection between facial expressions and activity in the amygdala.*
See "UCLA Imaging Study Reveals How Active Empathy Charges Emotions; Physical Mimicry of Others Jump-Starts Key Brain Activity." This news release from UCLA is available online at: http://www.newsroom.ucla.edu.

p. 149 *Daniel Levinson, author of The Seasons of a Man's Life and The Seasons of a Woman's Life . . .*
See Daniel Levinson, *The Seasons of a Woman's Life* (Ballantine Books, 1997).

p. 149 *"I began to notice the theme of seven-year cycles in sources as varied as . . ."*
See Joan Borysenko, *A Woman's Book of Life: The Biology, Psychology, and Spirituality of the Feminine Life Cycle* (New York: Riverhead Books, 1998), 4.

CHAPTER 8   IS THIS THE PARTY
TO WHOM I AM SPEAKING?

p. 157 *"In the study of brain functions we rely upon a biased, poorly understood, and frequently unpredictable organ . . ."*
See William C. Corning, *The Mind,* (New York: John Wiley & Sons, 1968).

CHAPTER 10   EMERGENETICS LEADERSHIP

p. 210 "Power in organizations . . ."
See Margaret Wheatley, *Leadership and the New Science: Discovering Order in a Chaotic World,* rev. ed. (San Francisco: Berrett-Koehler Publishing, 2001), 39.

CHAPTER 11   WHOLE-BODY, WHOLE-EMERGENETICS THINKING

p. 233 *And while Howard Gardner's theory about multiple intelligences has had an enormous impact . . .*
Howard Gardner has written several books about his theory of multiple intelligences. For an overview of his life and work, see: http://www.pz.harvard.edu/PIs/HG.htm.

p. 234 *"The more you learn about how your brain works . . ."*
See Richard Restak, *Mozart's Brain and the Fighter Pilot: Unleashing Your Brain's Potential* (New York: Three Rivers Press, 2001), 17.

p. 235 *"The anachronisms in the way we measure intelligence can also be found in IQ tests . . ."*
See Jennifer James, *Thinking in the Future Tense* (New York: Free Press, 1997), 179.

p. 237 *As much as 98 percent of all communication throughout the body may be through these peptide messengers.*
See Candace Pert, *Molecules of Emotion: Why You Feel the Way You Feel* (New York: Scribner, 1997) 139. Dr. Pert says, "Less than 2 percent of neuronal communication actually occurs at the synapse."

p. 237 *"Emotions are not in the head. There's a cellular consciousness . . ."*
See: Candace Pert, "Neuropeptides, AIDS, and the Science of Mind-Body Healing," *Alternative Therapies* v. 1, no. 3 (July 1995): 72. Available online at: http://www.alternative-therapies.com.

p. 237 *Unlike the synaptic system or neurotransmitter hormones, neuropeptide messages connect in both directions—brain to body, body to brain.*

I am again indebted to Emergenetics Associate Mary Case, MD.

p. 237 *"But for us, the discovery of 'floating' intelligence confirms the model of the body as a river . . ."*
See Deepak Chopra, *Quantum Healing: Exploring the Frontiers of Mind/Body Medicine* (New York: Bantam Books, 1990), 63.

p. 237 *Lawrence Katz, PhD, author of* Keep Your Brain Alive *(with Manning Rubin), says "neurobic" exercises help maintain and form new connections between nerve cells.*
See Lawrence Katz, and Manning Rubin, *Keep Your Brain Alive: 83 Neurobic Exercises* (New York: Workman Publishing, 1999).

p. 238 *In 1993 researchers Gordon Shaw and Frances Rauscher studied the effects of listening to Mozart's Sonata for Two Pianos in D Major (K. 448) . . .*
See Frances Rauscher, Gordon Shaw, and Katherine Ky, "Music and Spatial Task Performance" *Nature,* 365 (October 14, 1993), 611. Available online at: http://www.uvm.edu/~dhowell/lies4thedition/Clasfolder/Mozart Effect/Rauscher.html.

p. 238 *"I suggest that we are all constantly looking for patterns . . ."*
See Gordon Shaw, *Keeping Mozart in Mind* (Burlington, MA: Academic Press [Elvsevier], 2003), 109.

p. 238 For information on stimulating your whole brain with exercise, see Steven Quartz, R., and Terrence J. Sejnowski, *Liars, Lovers, and Heroes: What the New Brain Science Reveals About How We Become Who We Are* (New York: William Morrow, 2002), 248–50.

See also K. R. Isaacs, B. J. Anderson, A. A. Alcantara, J. E. Black, and W. T. Greenough, "Exercise and the Brain: Angiogenesis in the Adult Rat Cerebellum After Vigorous Physical Activity and Motor Skill Learning," *Journal of Cerebral Blood Flow and Metabolism* 12 (1992): 110–119.

p. 239 *"Imagine how much of the brain lights up when we dance!"*
See Mark Jude Tramo, "Biology and Music: En-

hanced: Music of the Hemispheres," *Science* 291 (2001): 54–56.

p. 240 See Eric Jensen, *Learning with the Brain in Mind* (San Diego, CA: Brain Store, 2000).
See also Carla Hannaford, *The Dominance Factor: How Knowing Your Dominant Eye, Ear, Brain, Hand and Foot Can Improve Your Learning* (Salt Lake City: Great River Books, 1997).

See also *Smart Moves: Why Learning Is Not All in Your Head* (Salt Lake City: Great River Books, 1995).

p. 241 *When researchers used functional magnetic resonance imaging to observe the brains of people playing the "ultimatum game" . . .*
See Alan G. Sanfey, James K. Rilling, Jessica A. Aronson, Leigh E. Nystrom, and Jonathan D. Cohen, "The Neural Basis of Economic Decision-Making in the Ultimatum Game," *Science* 300, no. 5626 (June 13, 2003): 1755–58.

p. 242 *Antonio Damasio, author of* Descartes' Error . . .
See Antonio Domasio, *Descartes' Error: Emotion, Reason, and the Human Brain* (New York: Avon Books, 1994).

p. 242 *The aspect of your brain called the adaptive unconscious—what Malcolm Gladwell, author of* Blink: The Power of Thinking Without Thinking, *calls "the big computer in your brain" . . .*
See Malcolm Gladwell, *Blink: The Power of Thinking Without Thinking* (New York: Little, Brown, 2005), 53.

p. 242 *One study involving the threat of receiving an electric shock (none were actually administered) . . .*
See Elizabeth A. Phelps, Kevin J. O'Connor, J. Christopher Getenby, John C. Gore, Christian Grillon, and Michael Davis, "Activation of the Left Amygdala to a Cognitive Representation of Fear," *Nature Neuroscience* 4, no. 4 (April 2001). Available online at: http://www.psych.nyu.edu/phelpslab/abstracts/NatureNeuro2001.pdf.

p. 242 *Research shows that when we are weighing "what if—?" scenarios, we give negative concerns more weight.*

See "Basic Behavioral Science Research for Mental Health: A National Investment: Emotion and Motivation" by the National Advisory Mental Health Council. *American Psychologist* 50, no. 10 (1995): 838–45.

p. 243 *More neural fibers project from our brain's emotional center into its rational centers than the other way around . . .*
See Eric Jensen, *Teaching with the Brain in Mind* (Danvers, MA: Association for Supervision & Curriculum Development, 1998), 74.

p. 243 *"Take a breath, so your limbic system can stop projectile vomiting onto your prefrontal cortical neurons."*
I am again indebted to Emergenetics Associate Mary Case, MD.

p. 243 *"How we do think, I believe, is with two minds, experiential and rational."*
See Seymour Epstein, "Integration of the Cognitive and the Psychodynamic Unconscious," *American Psychologist* 49, no. 8 (August 1994), 721.

p. 244 *Researchers at Johns Hopkins have identified sites in the brain where worrying takes place.*
Presentation at the Society for Neuroscience. Johns Hopkins news release is available online at: http://www.hopkinsmedicine.org/press/1997/OCTOBER/971010.HTM.

p. 244 *On the other hand, Richard Davidson PhD—a neuroscientist who, among other accomplishments, has collaborated with the Dalai Lama . . .*
See Heather L. Urry, Jack B. Nitschke, Isa Dolski, Daren C. Jackson, Kim M. Dalton, Corrina J. Mueller, Melissa A. Rosenkranz, Carol D. Ryff, Burton H. Singer, and Richard J. Davidson, "Making a Life Worth Living: Neural Correlates of Well-Being," *Psychological Science* 15, no. 6 (June 2004): 367–72.

p. 248 See Kathryn Cramer *When Faster, Harder, Smarter Is Not Enough* (New York: McGraw-Hill, 2001).

p. 248 *In an unpublished study conducted at Carnegie Mellon University, a group of researchers . . .*

See M. A. Just, P. A. Carpenter, T. A. Keller, L. Emery, H. Zajac, and K. R., Thulkorn, "Interdependence of Non-Overlapping Cortical Systems in Dual Cognitive Tasks," *NeuroImage* 14 (2001): 417–26. Available online at: http://www.ccbi.cmu.edu/reprints/reprints.htm.

See also Richard Restak, *The New Brain: How the Modern Age is Rewiring Your Mind* (Emmaus, PA: Rodale 2003), 54–59.

For a nonacademic summary of the disadvantages of doing too many things at once, see Edward Willett, "Multitasking." Available online at: http://www.edwardwillett.com/Columns/multitasking.htm.

p. 248 *A study in the* New England Journal of Medicine *found that people who talk on a cell phone while driving are four times more likely to have an accident.*
See Donald A. Redelmeier, and Robert J. Tibshirani, "Association Between Cellular-Telephone Calls and Motor Vehicle Collisions," *The New England Journal of Medicine* 336, no. 7 (February 13, 1997): 453–58.

p. 249 *Animal studies have shown that stress inhibits neurogenesis in the brain.*
See Barry L. Jacobs, Henriette van Praag, and Fred H. Gage, "Depression and the Birth and Death of Brain Cells," *American Scientist* 88, no. 4 (2000): 340. Available online at: http://www.americanscientist.org/template/AssetDetail/assetid/14738/page/2.

p. 249 *Researchers are now beginning to realize that men and women respond to stress differently.*
See S. E. Taylor, L. D. Klein, B. P. Lewis, T. L. Gruenewald, R. A. R. Gurung, and J. A. Updegraff, "Biobehavioral Responses to Stress in Females: Tend-and-Befriend, Not Fight-or-Flight," *Psychological Review* 107, no. 3 (July 2000): 411–29.

p. 250 *Sleep researcher J. Christian Gillin noted that sleep deprivation hinders high-level thinking.*
See S. P. Drummond, G. G. Brown, J. C. Gillin, J. L. Stricker, E. C. Wong, and R. B. Buxton, "Altered Brain Response to Verbal Learning Following Sleep Deprivation," *Nature* 403, no. 6770 (February 10, 2000): 655–57.

p. 250 *A Harvard study reveals that both power naps and a good night's sleep can help learning.*
See Sara C. Mednick, Ken Nakayama, Jose L. Cantero, Mercedes Atienza, Alicia A. Levin, Neha Pathak, and Robert Stickgold, "The Restorative Effect of Naps on Perceptual Deterioration," *Nature Neuroscience* (July 5, 2002): 677–81.

p. 250 *"We think getting that first night's sleep . . ."*
See R. Stickgold, L. James, and J. A. Hobson, "Visual Discrimination Learning Requires Sleep After Training," *Nature Neuroscience* 3, no. 12 (December 2000): 1237–38.

p. 250 *According to researcher George Bartzokis, the brain continues to myelinate until our mid-to-late 40s, and after that it starts to deteriorate.*
See Jeffrey Winters, "Brain Gain: Middle-Aged White Matter May Just Increase Over Time," *Psychology Today,* September–October, 2001.

p. 251 *PET scans reveal they use both hemispheres more than their younger counterparts.*
See "Language Center of Brain Shifts with Age." Press release from the American Academy of Neurology, 4/28/04. Available online at: http://www.sciencedaily.com/releases/2004/04/040428062634.htm. Details of this study were presented at the American Academy of Neurology 56th Annual Meeting in San Francisco, California, April 24–May 1, 2004.

p. 251 *"If I had to live my life again . . ."*
See Charles Darwin, *The Life and Letters of Charles Darwin, Volume 1,* 42.
Available online at: http://charles-darwin.classic-literature.co.uk/the-life-and-letters-of-charles-darwin-volume-i/ebook-page-41.asp.

p. 251 *A study in 2000 revealed that just one cigarette can cause lasting changes in the "reward" areas of the brain, increasing the desire for more cigarettes.*
See Hulbert Mansvelder, and Daniel McGehee, "Long-Term Potentiation of Excitatory Inputs to Brain Reward Areas by Nicotine," *Neuron* 27 (August 2000): 349–57.

p. 251 *"Nicotine causes the most selective degeneration in the brain I have ever seen."* Gaylord Ellison, quoted in "Nicotine Causes Selective Damage in the Brain," available online at: http://archives.cnn.com/2000/HEALTH/11/09/nicotine.brain. See also J. Carlson, B. Armstrong, R. C. Switzer 3rd, and G. Ellison, "Selective Neurotoxic Effects of Nicotine on Axons in Fasciculus Retroflexus Further Support Evidence That This Is a Weak Link in Brain Across Multiple Drugs of Abuse," *Neuropharmacology* 39, no. 13 (2000): 2792–98.

p. 252 *Long-term use of alcohol damages the frontal lobes of the brain and causes an overall reduction in brain size. Even moderate drinking causes brain atrophy as early as middle age.*
See Jingzhong Ding, Marsha L. Eigenbrodt, Thomas H. Mosley Jr., Richard G. Hutchinson, Aaron R. Folsom, Tamara B. Harris, and F. Javier Nieto, "Alcohol Intake and Cerebral Abnormalities on Magnetic Resonance Imaging in a Community-Based Population of Middle-Aged Adults," *Stroke* 35, no. 16 (2004).

p. 253 *Dr. K. Warner Schaie, who designed a project called the Seattle Longitudinal Study that began in 1956 . . .*
See Steven R. Quartz, and Terrence J. Sejnowski, *Liars, Lovers, and Heroes,* (New York: William Morrow, 2002), 245.

p. 253 *"Do something that challenges and engages your mind . . ."*
See Joe Volz, "Successful Aging: The Second 50," *Monitor on Psychology* 31, no. 1 (January 2000): 124. This quote is from Lawrence Katz, PhD, author (with Manning Rubin) of *Keep Your Brain Alive.*

p. 253 *A study published in the Journal of the American Medical Association in 2002 followed 740 members of the Catholic clergy . . .*
See R. S. Wilson, C. F. Mendes De Leon, L. L. Barnes, J. A. Schneider, J. L. Bienias, D. A. Evans, and D. A. Bennett, "Participation in Cognitively Stimulating Activities and Risk of Incident Alz-heimer's Disease" *Journal of the American Medical Association* 287, no. 6 (February 13, 2002): 742–48.

p. 253 *"Individuals will increasingly have to take responsibility for their own continual learning and re-learning . . ."*
See Peter Drucker, *The Essential Drucker* (New York: HarperBusiness, 2003), 325.

p. 253 *Scientists at UCLA recently found in autopsy studies that the brains of university graduates who remained mentally active . . .*
See Ronald Kotulak, *Inside the Brain: Revolutionary Discoveries of How the Mind Works* (New York: Andrews McMeel Publishing, 1997), 18.

p. 253 *In the famous "nun study" (different from the study noted above), an ongoing study directed by David Snowdon . . .*
See David Snowdon, *Aging with Grace: What the Nun Study Teaches Us About Leading Longer, Healthier, and More Meaningful Lives* (New York: Bantam Books, 2002).

p. 254 *"Passive observation is not enough; one must interact with the environment."*
See Marian Diamond, *Enriching Heredity: The Impact of the Environment on the Anatomy of the Brain* (New York: The Free Press, 1988).
See also "The Significance of Enrichment," available online at: http://www.newhorizons.org/neuro/diamond_enrich.htm.

p. 254 *You can enhance your memory and mental fitness with puzzles and exercises . . .*
See Richard Restak, *Mozart's Brain and the Fighter Pilot: Unleashing Your Brain's Potential* (New York: Three Rivers Press, 2001).

p. 254 More information from Dr. Marian Diamond about the aging brain is available online at: http://www.newhorizons.org/neuro/diamond_aging.htm.

CHAPTER 12   WORK THROUGH YOUR
STRENGTHS TO SUCCEED

p. 258 *"More and more people in the workforce—and most knowledge workers—will have to MANAGE THEMSELVES. . . ."*
See Peter Drucker, *Management Challenges for the 21st Century,* (New York: HarperBusiness, 2001), 163.

p. 267 Modified to include research from the *Center for Creative Leadership.*
See Craig Chappelow, and Jean Leslie, "Throwing the Right Switches: How to Keep Your Executive Career on Track." Available online at: http://www.ccl.org.
See also M. M. Lombardo, and C. D. McCauley, "The Dynamics of Management Derailment," Technical Report No. 34 (1988).

See also M. W. McCall Jr., and M. M. Lombardo, "Off the Track: Why and How Successful Executives Get Derailed," Technical Report No. 21 (1983).

p. 273 See Terrence E. Deal and Allan A. Kennedy, *Corporate Cultures: The Rites and Rituals of Corporate Life* (Reading, MA: Addison-Wesley, 1982).

p. 277 *"The illiterate of the future are not those who cannot read or write, but those who cannot learn, unlearn or relearn."*
See Rowan Gibson, *Rethinking the Future: Rethinking Business, Principles, Competition, Control & Complexity, Leadership, Markets and the World* (Nicholas Brealey Publishing, 1999). From the Introduction by Alvin Toffler.

p. 278 *"Given that so much of who we are . . ."*
See Joseph LeDoux, *Synaptic Self: How Our Brains Become Who We Are* (New York: Penguin Books, 2003), 234.

Index

brain research (*cont.*)
  "split brain," 11–12, 24–26
  on Tibetan monks, 244, 45
  "ultimatum game" in, 241–42
brainstorming, 125, 206, 216, 225, 230
brain strain, 247–50
  emotional distress in, 249
  multitasking in, 248–49
  sleep deprivation in, 249–50
brainwaves, alpha/theta, 250
Broca, Paul, 24
Broca's area, 15, 24
Broca's Brain (Sagan), 52

C

Cain, Herman, 227
Canli, Turhan, 115
Carlin, George, 60
Carnegie Mellon University, 248
Case, Mary, 111–12, 132
Cato, 48
Cavett, Dick, 32
Center for Creative Leadership, 266, 267
challenges, organizational, 220–26
  solving of, 222–26
Chopra, Deepak, 237
Clark, William, 13
clearing the mist, 243–44
cocaine, 251–52
communication, 80, 104, 152, 175, 177–208,
    211–12, 289, 290
  avoiding assumptions in, 187–88
  conflict management in, 205–8, 295
  direct reports in, 190, 290
  filters in, 178–84
  gender differences and, 116–17
  making presentations in, 194–99, 200
  marketing in, 202–5
  modulating Behavioral Attributes in, 188–89
  nonverbal, 188
  performance evaluations in, 190–94, 265
  phrases to use in, 157, 185–87, 200
  positive statements in, 187–88
  selling and persuading in, 200–202

computer purchases, 285
Conceptual/Analytical Profile, 71, 73–74, 90–91,
    103–4, 111, 114, 124–25, 147, 148, 156,
    211–12, 225
Conceptual/Analytical/Social Profile, 78–79, 93,
    262, 263
Conceptual/Analytical/Structural Profile, 78, 129
Conceptual/Social Profile, 71, 72–73, 88–89, 100,
    103–4, 173, 207, 212–13, 225, 228–29, 246,
    257–58, 264
Conceptual/Social/Structural Profile, 55, 79
Conceptual/Structural Profile, 71, 75, 76,
    100–101, 173
Conceptual Thinking, Conceptual thinkers, 4–6,
    7–8, 31, 33, 42, 46–52, 109, 113, 116, 154,
    156, 188, 225, 283–99
  as abstract thinking, 46, 52, 71, 73, 78, 195
  characteristics of, 7, 46–47
  in clearing the mist, 243
  communication filter of, 178–84
  in conflict management, 206, 207
  in corporate cultures, 273
  creativity of, 246–247
  decision-making by, 240–41
  direct reports and, 190
  drawbacks of, 48, 51
  examples of, 48–51, 200–202
  gender norms for, 105, 106, 107
  ideal office for, 262
  intuition in, 46, 47, 49, 73, 88
  job changes of, 268
  in job interviews, 270, 274, 275
  journal-keeping and, 255
  key question for, 47, 51
  knowledge base of, 50
  leading questions for, 158–61
  learning approach of, 48, 51, 235
  making presentations to, 197–98, 199
  managerial strengths of, 168–69
  money and, 204
  motivation of, 226
  at perfect meeting, 230
  performance evaluations and, 191–94
  phrases for communicating with, 186–87

managerial strengths of, 169–70
modulation of, 188–89
money and, 204
motivation of, 227
at perfect meeting, 230
performance evaluations and, 192–93
Profile changes and, 123, 124, 126, 127, 135, 148, 152
reasons for derailment of, 267
rewards preferred by, 227–28
third-third, 56, 58
21-Day Plan for decrease in, 143–44
21-Day Plan for increase in, 142
in WE*teams,* 216–17, 223
writing styles of, 162, 163, 164–65
extroversion, 15–16, 30

F

facial expressions, 114, 116
positive, 133
fat, metabolism of, 252
Faulk, Miss, 39–41
"fight or flight" reaction, 249
5-HTTLPR, 15
Flexibility, Flexibles, 4–5, 7–8, 31, 62–65, 85, 109, 111, 113, 116, 117, 154, 161, 187, 211–12, 263–64, 283–99
challenge-solving by, 223, 224
characteristics of, 7, 55, 62–63, 216
conflict management and, 206
in corporate cultures, 274
decision-making of, 63–65, 241
direct reports and, 190
drawbacks of, 63, 65
in Emergenetics Profile, 80–84
examples of, 64–65, 174
first-third, 63
gender norms for, 105, 106, 107
job changes of, 268
in job interviews, 272, 275, 276
key question for, 65
leading questions for, 160
learning approach of, 65, 236
making presentations to, 196, 198

managerial strengths of, 171–72
modulation of, 189
money and, 204, 205
motivation of, 156, 227
at perfect meeting, 230
performance evaluations and, 192–93
Profile changes and, 123, 126, 128, 134–35
reasons for derailment of, 267
rewards preferred by, 228
in teams, 63
third-third, 63–64
21-Day Plan for decrease in, 146
21-Day Plan for increase in, 142–43
in WE*teams,* 216–17, 223
writing styles of, 162, 163, 166
flipping a coin, 44, 276
fMRI (functional magnetic resonance imaging) scans, 23, 131, 241–42
Focus executive development program, 104–5, 106–7, 108, 109
Fortune, 228
From Brains to Consciousness (Rose), 68

G

Gage, Phineas, 22–23, 24
Galileo, 236
Gardner, Howard, 233, 235, 239
Gazzaniga, Michael, 24–26
gender differences, 103–17, 309–10
in brain, 104, 111–15
communication and, 116–17
evolution of, 111, 115–16
in gender-based executive development programs, 104–5, 106–7, 108, 109, 110
in hearing, 112–13, 114, 115
hormones in, 111–12
in identification of facial expressions, 114, 116
in mathematical ability, 114
in perceptual sensitivity, 114
in response to stress, 249
in spatial abilities, 103–4, 113, *113,* 114, *114,* 115–16
stereotypes of, 104–5, 107–11, 116–17

job interviews, 269–77
    accepting offers in, 275–77
    and corporate cultures, 272–74
    describing strengths in, 269–72
    optimal behavior in, 272
Johns Hopkins, 244
Johnson, Debra, 15
Johnson, George, 21
journal-keeping, 255–56
Journal of the American Medical Association, 253
Judice, Ross, 6, 23
Just, Marcel, 248

K

Kagan, Jerome, 12, 15, 16
Katz, Lawrence, 237–38, 253
Keeping Mozart in Mind (Shaw), 238
Keep Your Brain Alive (Katz and Rubin), 237, 253
Kennedy, Allan A., 273
Kenya, 254
Kenyan Children Foundation, 45–46, 54–55
King, Martin Luther, Jr., 33
Kotulak, Ronald, 253

L

Lao Tzu, 256
leadership, 12, 31, 52, 209–32, 271
    challenges defined by, 220–22
    and competent employees, 210
    complementing one's Profile in, 211–12
    diversity and, 212–13; *see also* Whole
        Emergenetics Teams
    effective, 209–10
    expectations of success in, 231–32
    hiring guidelines for, 210–17
    motivation by, 226–28
    noninterference by, 232
    optimal climate created by, 228–29
    organizational values and, 211
    rewards bestowed by, 227–28
Leadership and the New Science (Wheatley), 210
leading questions, 157–62
Learning with the Body in Mind (Jensen), 240
Lebowitz, Fran, 57

LeDoux, Joseph, 278
left brain, 11–12, 24–26, 28–29, 30, 71, 199,
        211, 277–78
    balancing of, 244–45
    Tri-modal Profiles and, 77–78
Left Brain, Right Brain (Spring and Deutsch), 25
Levey, Jerry, 13
Levinson, Daniel, 149
Lewis, Jim, 13–14
life cycles, 150–51, 265, 276–77
life events, 6, 122, 148, 151–52
life experience, 16–22, 148, 252–53
    brain altered by, 17–22
Life Shaken, A (Havemann and Reich), 34
life stages, 149–50
listening styles, 291
Lorde, Audre, 43
Luce, Gay Gaer, 5
Lykken, David, 13, 31

M

MacLean, Paul, 26–27, 29
Management Challenges for the 21st Century
        (Drucker), 258
managerial styles, 166–72, 210
Manning, Sherry, 44
marijuana, 252
Mark (Profile example), 91–93
marketing, 202–5
Mary Kay cosmetics, 273
Maslow, Abraham, 245
McLaughlin, Peter, 68
MEG (magnetoencephalography) scans, 23
Mendel, Gregor, 33
methamphetamine, 252
Midler, Bette, 55
Mind, The (Corning), 157
mind/body relationship, 236–39
Minding the Body Medning the Mind (Borysenko),
        149
mind mirror machine, 49–50
Mind's Past, The (Gazzaniga), 31
mirror twins, 14
mission statements, 219–20, 297

MIT (Massachusetts Institute of technology), 132

"Molecular Neurobiology and Genetics: Investigation of Neural Function and Dysfunction" (Green, Heinmann and Gusella), 18

Molecules of Emotion (Pert), 236

money, handling of, 203–5
   behavioral economics and, 241–42

monks, Tibetan, 244–45

motivation, 154–57
   by leadership, 226–28
   for learning, 235–36

Mozart Effect, 238

Mozart's Brain and the Fighter Pilot (Restak), 234, 254

MRI (magnetic resonance imaging) scans, 23, 248

MRS (magnetic resonance spectroscopy) scans, 23

multiple intelligences, theory of, 233, 235, 239

multitasking, 112, 161, 271
   in brain strain, 248–49

music, listening to, 237, 238

myenteric plexus, 44

Myers-Briggs Type Indicator test, 30

N

nature vs. nurture, 12–198, 30, 302–3 *see also* genetics; life experience

neurobic exercises, 237–38

neuropeptide receptor system, 236–37

"Neuropeptides, AIDS and the Science of Mind-Body Healing" (Pert), 237

neutrophins, 239

New England Journal of Medicine, 248

Newman, Mark, 13

Nicholson, Nigel, 107–9

nicotine, 251

nonverbal communication, 188

"nun study," 253–54

O

office spaces, ideal, 258–62

oxytocin, 152, 249

P

Passages (Sheehy), 149

Pavlov, Ivan, 17, 30, 302, 303

PCP (angel dust), 252

PDA (Personal Digital Assistant), 9, 65, 124, 259

peace, personal, 278

Pease, Barbara and Allan, 112

performance evaluations, 190–94, 265

personality traits, 6, 23
   genetics and, 14, 15–16

persuading, 200–202

Pert, Candace, 21, 236, 237

PET (positron emission tomography) scans, 23, 251, 252

phenotypes, 14–15

Pinel, John, 26

Pinker, Steven, 6, 14

placebo effect, 131

Plomin, Robert, 13, 16

positive attitude, 277–78

positive facial expressions, 133

positive statements, 187–88

positive thinking, 131–33

post-traumatic stress disorder, 249

Powell, Carol, 255

presentations, 194–99, 200, 217–18, 225–26

progesterone, 111–12

projects, completion of, 286

psychological hardiness, 278

psychological tests, 30

Q

Quadra-modal Profiles, 34, 70, 79–80, 96–97, 152, 166, 216, 271

Quantum Healing (Chopra), 237

R

rabbit brains, 17

Rainwater Jane, 46

Rauscher, Frances, 238

recognition, reception of, 293

recreational drugs, 251–52

reflection, 255–56
  topics for, 256
  in workplace, 277
Reich, Stephen, 26
Restak, Richard, 22, 234, 249, 254
Rethinking the Future (Gibson), 277
rewards, preferred, 228–28
Ride, Sally, 117
Ridley, Matt, 16
right brain, 11–12, 24–26, 28–29, 30, 50, 71,
    199, 231, 277–78
  balancing of, 244–45
  Tri-modal Profiles and, 77, 78–79
Rose, Stephen, 68
Rouse, Tim, 104–5
Rowe, David C., 13
Rubin, Manning, 237, 253

S

Sagan, Carl, 52
Sax, Leonard, 115
Schaie, K. Warner, 253
School Sister of Notre Dame, 253–54
Schwartz, Carl, 16
"Scientists Foresee Bridging Nerve Damage with
    Grafts" (Smith), 19
scratchy periods, 151, 265
Seattle Longitudinal Study, 253
Second Brain, The (Gershon), 44
Secret Life of the Brain, The (Restak), 22
Segal, Julius, 5
Seinfeld, Jerry, 32
self-talk, 15, 132, 133
Seligman, Martin, 132
selling, 200–202
senses, stimulation of, 237–38
serotonin, 15–16, 252
"Sex Differences in the Functional Organization of
    the Brain for Language" (Shaywitz et al.), 116
sex hormones, 111–12
Shaw, Gordon, 238
Shaywitz, Bennett A., 116
Sheehy, Gail, 149
Sister Outsider (Lorde), 43

Skinner, B. F., 30, 302, 303
Sleep (Luce and Segal), 5
sleep deprivation, 249–50
Smart Moves and the Dominance Factor (Hannaford),
    240
Smith, Douglas, 19
smoking, 251
Snowdon, David, 253–54
Social/Analytical/Conceptual Profile, 78–79, 93,
    262, 263
Social/Analytical Profile, 71, 75–76, 100
Social/Analytical/Structural Profile, 68–70, 77,
    129
Social/Conceptual Profile, 71, 72–73, 88–89, 100,
    103–4, 173, 207, 212–13, 225, 228–29,
    246, 257–58, 264
Social/Conceptual/Structural Profile, 55, 79
Social/Structural Profile, 71, 74, 91–93, 111, 147,
    161, 173–74, 206–8, 211–12, 225
Social Styles test, 30
social support, 278
Social Thinking, Social thinkers, 4–6, 7–8, 31, 34,
    42–46, 50, 85, 109, 113, 115, 116, 117,
    154, 177–78, 187, 188, 195, 244, 268–69,
    283–99
  challenge-solving by, 223, 224
  characteristics of, 7, 42–43
  in clearing the mist, 243
  communication filter of, 178–84
  conceptual thinking vs., 52
  conflict management and, 205, 207
  in corporate cultures, 273
  creativity of, 246–47
  decision-making of, 240
  direct reports and, 190
  drawbacks of, 45, 46
  examples of, 43, 45–46
  gender norms for, 105, 106, 107
  gut brain and, 44
  ideal office for, 26
  intuition in, 42, 43, 44, 45, 73, 88
  job changes of, 268–69
  in job interviews, 270, 274, 275
  journal-keeping of, 255

Social Thinking, Social thinkers (*cont.*)
key question for, 43, 46
knowledge base of, 50
leading questions for, 158–61
learning approach of, 45, 46, 235
making presentations to, 196–97, 199
managerial strengths of, 168
money and, 204
motivation of, 226
at perfect meeting, 230
performance evaluations and, 192–93
phrases for communicating with, 186
problem-solving of, 45
Profile changes and, 124, 125, 126, 127, 148, 152
reasons for derailment of, 267
rewards preferred by, 227
strengths of, 43
21-Day Plan for increase in, 140–41
in WE*teams,* 215, 218, 223, 224
writing styles of, 162, 164–65
"Sources of Human Psychological Difference: The Minnesota Study of Twins Reared Apart" (Bouchard et al.), 14
Sperry, Roger, 11, 24–26, 29
"split brain" research, 11–12, 24–26
sports, 239
Springer, Jim, 13–14
Springer, Sally, 25
Stanford-Binet IQ test, 234–35, 238
Stanley, Julian, 114
Stickgold, Robert, 250
Stranger in a Strange Land, (Heinlein), 50
stress, 60–61, 249, 278
stress hormones, 249
Structural/Analytical/Conceptual Profile, 78, 129
Structural/Analytical Profile, 71–72, 73, 87–88, 99–100, 191, 213, 245, 247, 258
Structural/Analytical/Social Profile, 68–70, 77, 129
Structural/Conceptual Profile, 71, 75, 76, 100–101, 173
Structural/Conceptual/Social Profile, 55, 79

Structural/Social Profile, 71, 74, 91–93, 111, 147, 161, 173–74, 206–8, 211–12, 225
Structural Thinking, Structural thinkers, 3–6, 7–8, 31, 33–34, 37–42, 50, 63, 85, 99, 109, 112, 116, 153, 154, 187, 188, 202, 232, 283–99
Analytical Thinking vs. 111–12
challenge-solving, 223, 224
characteristics of, 7, 37, 38
in clearing the mist, 243–44
communication filter of, 178–84
as concrete thinking, 41, 71, 74, 79, 195
in conflict management, 206, 207–8
in corporate cultures, 273
creativity of, 246, 247
decision-making by, 240
direct reports and, 190
drawbacks of, 39, 40
examples of, 38, 39–41, 94–96
gender norms for, 105, 106, 107
ideal office for, 260
job changes of, 266–68
in job interviews, 270, 274, 275–76
journal-keeping of, 255
key question for, 37, 40
knowledge base of, 50
leading questions for, 158–61
learning approach of, 38–39, 40, 235
making presentations to, 196, 199
managerial strengths of, 167–68
money and, 203, 204
motivations of, 155, 156–57, 226
at perfect meeting, 229
performance evaluations and, 192–93
phrases for communicating with, 186
problem-solving of, 38
Profile changes and, 123, 124, 125, 126, 127, 128, 152
reasons for derailment of, 267
rewards preferred by, 227
strengths of, 38
21-Day Plan for increase in, 139–40
in WE*teams,* 215, 218, 223, 224
writing style of, 163, 164
submucosal plexus, 44